Landlord Power and Rural Indebtedness in Colonial Sind
1865–1901

Centre of South Asian Studies,
School of Oriental and African Studies,
University of London

LONDON STUDIES ON SOUTH ASIA

10. John Bullion's Empire
G. Balachandran

11. Landlord Power and Rural Indebtedness in Colonial Sind
David Cheesman

Landlord Power and Rural Indebtedness in Colonial Sind
1865–1901

David Cheesman

CURZON

First published in 1997
by Curzon Press
St John's Studios, Church Road, Richmond
Surrey, TW9 2QA

Typeset in Plantin by LaserScript, Mitcham, Surrey

Printed in Great Britain by
TJ Press (Padstow) Limited, Padstow, Cornwall

British Library Cataloguing in Publication Data
A catalogue record for this book is available from the British Library

Library of Congress in Publication Data
A catalogue record for this book has been requested

ISBN 0–7007–0470–1

To
Nazia

Contents

Tables

Figures

Acknowledgements

This book is based on my University of London PhD thesis. I should like to thank my Supervisor, Dr Z.H. Zaidi, for inspiring me to take up the topic in the first place, and then for encouraging me during the research; Professor Kenneth Ballhatchet, Dr Peter Hardy and John Harrison for the advice they have given me over the years; and to my examiners, Dr Percival Spear and Dr David Taylor, for encouraging me to publish the thesis. Much of my research was carried out at the India Office Library and Records (now the Oriental and India Office Collections of the British Library). It is a pleasure to pay tribute to the efficient and courteous service provided by the staff there and to the friendly atmosphere which has made the Library not merely a place of work, but almost a second home for many students of Indian history.

Innumerable Pakistanis showed me kindness and generosity during a year's study leave in Sind. I am particularly grateful for the hospitality extended to me by Behram Rustomji and his family, Ghulam Rabbani Aggro, Jam Sadiq Ali, Mir Mohammad Bux Khan Talpur and his sons, Mir Ahmed Khan Talpur and Mir Ali Ahmed Khan Talpur. I would also like to thank Dr M.H. Rizvi, Moinuddin Khan, Safdar Mehdi, Dr Hamida Khuhro, Sayad Pir Bakhsh, Rukundin, Dr G.A. Allana, Pyarali Allana, P.K. Shahani, Mustafa Hussain Lahori and all the staff at the Commissioner's Record Office, Karachi, especially Ghulam Hussain.

Finally, I should like to thank the Economic and Social Research Council, who financed my research. It would have been impossible to undertake the project without their backing.

Select Glossary

Afrinama	Letter of recommendation given by a government official in recognition of services rendered.
Akhund	Teacher.
Amil	Revenue officer; used in Sind to signify a non-*bania*, upper class Hindu.
Autaq	Guest house.
Bajri	Spiked millet.
Bania	Hindu trader.
Barani land	Land watered by rainfall.
Batai	Division of the crop at harvest time.
Bigah	A measure of land (2,500 square yards in Sind).
Bund	Earthen embankment or dyke.
Charkhi land	See 'lift' land.
Darbar	Public audience given by senior person to invited notables.
Deh	Village.
Faqir	Religious mendicant.
'Flow' land	Land watered by overflow from a canal.
Hakabo	Water rate.
Hari	Ploughman, landless labourer.
Hurlo	Area irrigated by a Persian wheel.
Izzat	Status, prestige.
Jagir	Land given free of government assessment.
Jirga	Council of elders of a Baluch or Pathan tribe.
Juari	Great millet.
Jungle	Scrub, wild plants.
Kacho land	Land newly created by the river, which is submerged at each inundation.
Kalar	Salt-impregnated land.

Karia	Water-course.
Kasa	One sixtieth of a *kharar*.
Kharar	Twenty-nine and a half bushels; equivalent to twenty *maunds* of paddy or twenty-four *maunds* of *juari*, *bajri* or husked rice.
Kharif	Hot-weather cultivating season (May or June to October).
Khaskheli	Hereditary servant.
Lakh	One hundred thousand.
Lapo	A zamindari fee.
'Lift' land	Land watered by means of a Persian wheel.
Lungi	Piece of decorated cloth, worn as a scarf in Sind.
Maund	Forty *sers* (eighty-two and two-seventh pounds).
Mir	High ranking Muslim chief.
Moki land	See 'flow' land.
Mukhtiarkar	Government official responsible for a *taluqa*.
Munshi	Subordinate officer of a *Mukhtiarkar*.
Murid	Disciple.
Nar	See Persian wheel.
Paddy	Unhusked rice.
Patel	Village headman (in the Deccan).
Persian wheel	Machine, worked by cattle or a camel, to raise water from a canal or a well.
Pir	Hereditary saint.
Rabi	Cold-weather cultivating season (September or October to March or April).
Raiyat	Peasant.
Raiyatwari settlement	System under which land revenue is collected from individual *raiyats*.
Raj	Community.
Sailabi land	Land watered by river floods.
Sanad	Title-deed.
Sardar	Chief of a tribe.
Saiyid	Descendant of the Prophet.
Ser	One-fortieth of a *maund* (approximately two pounds).
Seri grant	Small grant of rent-free land.
Shaikh	Recent convert to Islam.
Taluqa	Administrative unit.
Taqavi	Loan given for agricultural purposes at the beginning of the cultivating season.

Wadero	Title of respect given by the rural community to a powerful Muslim landholder.
Zamindar	Landholder.

Introduction

Other People's Countries

In 1843, an Arab accosted a British traveller in North Africa:

> 'Why do you go so far from home to take other people's countries from them?' he demanded.[1]

He wanted an explanation for Britain's conquest of Sind and his anger was a measure of the passion this had aroused around the world. Even Sind's conqueror, Sir Charles Napier, who was never one to accept criticism, conceded there might be a certain moral ambiguity about his achievement. 'We have no right to seize Sind,' he reflected as he laid his plans, 'yet we shall do, and a very advantageous, humane and useful piece of rascality it will be.'[2]

Napier's 'piece of rascality' dragged Sind into the international order which Britain, France, Russia and other European powers were imposing upon the world through the capture of vulnerable countries in Asia and Africa. There was no escape. This vast and formidable system enabled a small number of nations to dictate economic, political and military terms to the rest of the planet. Decolonization in the 1950s and 1960s, and the disintegration of the Soviet Union after 1992, have wiped the empires from the map, but their impetus remains. It continues, for good or ill, to shape the development of the modern world.

At the time of Sind's conquest, the imperial hegemony seemed permanent and invincible. Accordingly, the simplest answer to the Arab's question might have been that the British seized countries like Sind precisely because they were able to do so. There was no United Nations Charter to bind their hands and they were the greatest military power on earth, so who was to stop them? In one sense, that was justification enough. The instinctive assumption in nineteenth century Britain (which has not altogether disappeared at the end of the twentieth century) was that the rest of the world formed a colourful backdrop against which British soldiers, traders, administrators and adventurers could manifest their heroic qualities. Edward Said caught the essence of this proprietorial outlook on the global community in *Culture and Imperialism*, when he commented: "abroad" was felt . . . in some way or other "ours" to control, trade in "freely," or suppress.'[3]

If the earth, or at least that portion of it which we nowadays characterize as the Third World, was assumed passively to be awaiting the benefits of the Pax Britannica, that was in itself a powerful spur to conquest. While recognizing the economic and strategic imperatives which impelled European expansion, one should not underestimate the sheer exhilaration of power itself. Western adventurers, without the political or moral constraints of later generations, felt free to carry war into other people's homes for much the same reasons as other adventurers climbed mountains – because they were there.

Napier himself is a case in point. His career started on a peak with the Peninsular War but the defeat of Napoleon in 1815 frustrated his ambitions. By the time he reached Sind in 1842, he was sixty, and he had spent the previous twelve years on half-pay in Britain, a period of purgatory enlivened only by the suppression of Chartist protests in northern England in 1839–40. His horizons had closed in around him and at first he expected little from his appointment to the Indian staff. He reflected, 'I am too old for glory now . . . If a man cannot catch glory when his knees are supple, he had better not try when they grow stiff!'[4] However, once Napier reached India and sniffed the air heady with the perfume of British power, his mood changed. Anything seemed possible. As he sailed from Bombay to take up his command in Sind, he wrote:

> Charles! Charles Napier! Take heed of your ambition for military glory; you had scotched that snake, but this high command will, unless you are careful, give it all its vigour again. Get thee behind me Satan![5]

Many a pensioned warrior, before and since, has regaled the saloon bar with self-dramatizing braggadocio of this sort, but it usually goes not further than the last whisky-soda. What is alarming on this occasion is that the half-pay general really was given a second chance to relive the lost opportunities of his youth. He was set loose with an army, a budget and discretion to do more or less as he pleased. Again, Edward Said expresses the spirit of Napier and others like him when he contrasts the romance of the colonies with the restrictions of life at home:

> How very different this all is from the lustreless world of the European bourgeoisie, whose ambience . . . reconfirms the debasement of contemporary life, the extinction of all dreams of passion, success, and exotic adventure. . . . For what one cannot accomplish in one's own Western environment – where trying to live out the grand dream of a successful quest means coming up against one's own mediocrity and the world's corruption and degradation – one can do abroad. Isn't it possible in India to do everything. Be anything? Go anywhere with impunity?[6]

This could have been written especially for Napier as he emerged from retirement and prepared to play the Napoleon of the Indian frontier. Truly, in India, Napier could 'do everything, be anything.' His initial brief had been unpromising – dull, in fact: to secure one end of a line of communication between Sind and Afghanistan. He was far from the scene of the action in Kabul, where the Army of the Indus had restored Siraj-ud-Daula, the exiled Afghan king, to his throne. This was intended as the first step in an ambitious enterprise to carry British influence deep into Central Asia and block the expanding Russian empire. Sind's role in this great undertaking was mundane. It was a base camp. However, Britain's plans were shattered during the winter of 1841–42, when rebellion in Kabul wiped out the newly established government and destroyed the Army of the Indus itself. It was arguably the worst disaster in British military history until the fall of Singapore a hundred years later. It dealt a sickening blow to British morale and Britain's standing as a great power. It also put an end to her bid to expand westwards from India. Central Asia was surrendered to the Russians.

Napier was understandably frustrated. A catastrophe of historic proportions had taken place and he was left kicking his heels in a backwater. He was eager to play his part in salvaging his country's reputation. His chance came when he received allegations that the Talpur Mirs who ruled Sind were plotting against Britain. Napier lost no time in convincing himself of the truth of the rumours, and of the urgent need for retribution. The Mirs must be hit hard. They, and anyone else with similarly mischievous thoughts, must be taught that, whatever might have happened in Afghanistan, Britain was as dangerous as ever.

Napier's wish to pick a fight was reinforced by his assumption that a country like Sind was, as it were, at Britain's disposal. To recall Said's aphorism, it fell within that part of 'abroad' which was 'ours'.

Once he was satisfied that the Mirs had ruined Sind through misgovernment, Napier almost inevitably concluded that a spell of enlightened British administration would be the ideal way of putting the country to rights. This would restore its natural wealth, to the mutual benefit of the Sindhi farmer and the British exchequer. The only obstacle to this exercise in philanthropy was the legitimate government of Sind but, since the Mirs did not deserve to rule, that was a minor consideration. Once again, we hear the saloon-bar philosopher setting the world to rights with a whisky-soda and a few admiring cronies. In this case, what is more, a philosopher with no experience or understanding of India. Under other circumstances, it might have seemed an act of lunacy to turn his ill-informed grumbles into a policy but, in the context of nineteenth century India, it was the logical next step.

Napier therefore determined to occupy Sind. Rejecting all overtures for peace from the Mirs, he forced them into war and defeated them at the battle of Miani on 17 February 1843. Sind was added to the British empire and the half-pay general, like one of Bonaparte's Marshals installing himself on the throne of a conquered Italian principality, became Governor. The Mirs, Britain's erstwhile allies, were stripped of their rank and exiled to Calcutta. For no particular reason, and without much thought behind it, Britain had, yet again, taken over somebody else's country.

It is worth pausing a moment to reflect upon this piece of 'rascality,' as Napier so wittily put it: for it constituted an act of unprovoked aggression which, in modern times, would be almost literally unthinkable. If one compares Napier's 'rascality' with notable attempts to subjugate independent states in the twentieth century – the German invasions of Czechoslovakia and Poland, say, or the Iraqi occupation of Kuwait – his pretext was far more flimsy. Germany and Iraq had long-standing claims against their neighbours, whether justified or not. Britain, by contrast, had no claim, long-standing or recent, justified or unjustified, against Sind and indeed no discernible war aim beyond straightforward conquest. The Franco-British invasion of Egypt in 1956 has a similarly grubby air of fabricated provocation, but at least ownership of the Suez Canal was a genuine cause for dispute and Nasser had taken a calculated risk when he nationalized it. The Sindhi Mirs, by contrast, had walked on eggshells to avoid offending Britain. They had allowed their country to be commandeered by British military and diplomatic personnel. They were Britain's principal allies in the Afghan enterprise. Napier's action constituted aggression against a friendly state. In the twentieth century, it would have provoked a flurry of angry, if impotent, resolutions from the Security Council of the United Nations.

Conquest was however only the first step in any colonial enterprise. It was in some ways the easy part. With the legitimate government overthrown, the country had to be held. The initial glow of military triumph was followed by the long, laborious and often painful process of occupation. This is where the real interest of the European empires lies. Having stolen other people's countries, how did they manage to cling on to the loot for so long?

Sind's history is a classic manifestation of successful colonial consolidation. It is almost archetypal – a cycle of military suppression, some soul-searching in London, and finally legitimization of the fait accompli.

The first phase was military. The defeat of the Mirs triggered a guerrilla war. One of the former rulers, Mir Sher Muhammad Khan Talpur, refused to surrender. He waged a campaign against Napier until June 1843, when he retreated to the Punjab. This did not end the turmoil, and Napier had to put his province under martial law. Such turbulence did not enhance Britain's glory. Napier's gift of a new province was received less graciously than he had anticipated.

The problem was compounded by his poor timing. Britain had already managed to redeem its reputation in Afghanistan, without any help from Napier. Troops had fought their way back into Kabul in September 1842, massacred a substantial proportion of its citizens, blown up the town centre, and then returned in triumph to India before the Afghans had a chance to regroup. This satisfied national honour. The occupation of an obscure country hundreds of miles away a few months later seemed both irrelevant and unnecessarily vindictive. Napier found himself reviled from all sides. Sir Charles Metcalfe, one of India's elder statesmen, sneered that Napier had turned Sind into 'a sad scene of insolence and oppression. Coming after Afghanistan, it put one in mind of a bully who had been kicked in the streets and went home to beat his wife in revenge.'[7] James Outram, Napier's deputy, broke with the general over his treatment of the Mirs and they engaged in a long and acrimonious public squabble. A considerable body of opinion in Britain urged that Napier's actions be repudiated and Sind restored to its rightful rulers.

The restoration of conquered countries to their rightful rulers was not, though, a notable feature of Britain's imperial destiny. As time went by, and Napier succeeded in keeping the lid on Sindhi discontent, the consensus developed that what was done could not be undone. It was better to live with a bad conscience than lose face through a public admission of guilt. The official seal of approval was conferred on the conquest when Napier returned home in 1847 and, far from being given back to Mirs, Sind was incorporated into the Bombay Presidency.

The acquisition of Sind, then, like so many colonial adventures, was messy, controversial and bloody. It is tempting to suppose that only a policy of ruthless intimidation, enforced by British bayonets, could have kept the province under control, yet that was far from the case.

In 1857, only fourteen years after the occupation, when the Great Rebellion destroyed the British administration in Oudh, the Government of Sind felt so secure that it sent almost all British troops out of the province to join the siege of Delhi. Only 139 British soldiers were retained in Sind as protection.[8] What is even more extraordinary is that this confidence was justified by events. The people who had fought the British so bitterly in 1843 did not take advantage of the chaos in 1857–58 to overthrow the government which had been imposed on them by force of arms. Sind remained calm.

Nor was Sind an isolated case. One of the most striking features of the 1857 Rebellion was that it was confined to a relatively small area of northern India. The vast southern peninsula was virtually unaffected. Even the Punjab, seized only eight years previously after two wars, did not join the revolt on its doorstep. On the contrary, recently defeated Sikhs from the Punjab fought alongside the British at the siege of Delhi, seeing it as a chance to wreak revenge upon the Muslims.

The inaction of such large parts of India was as significant to the maintenance of imperial rule as 'the curious case of the dog in the night-time' which caught the attention of Sherlock Holmes during his investigation into the abduction of Silver Blaze, a racehorse. When it was pointed out that the dog had done nothing while the horse was stolen: "That was the curious incident," remarked Sherlock Holmes.'[9]

Just as one expects a guard-dog to raise the alarm when a thief enters the house, so one expects a soldier to take advantage of his enemy's weakness. The revolts which did not happen are as significant as those which did. The strength of the British empire is revealed not only by the military campaign of 1857–58, but also by the administrative system throughout India which was able, while all this was going on, to keep raising the revenue to finance the operations. It was precisely because the greater part of India remained calm that the British were able to spare the troops to suppress the Rebellion and reestablish their empire. If imperial rule had consisted entirely, or even mainly, of a cycle of rebellion and repression, then the European empires would not have survived for long. A small number of European administrators and soldiers could not have held vast territories for decades, or centuries in some cases, by force alone. They would have drowned in their own blood. Brutal campaigns such as the British reconquest of northern India in 1857–58 and the French occupation of Algeria after 1830 certainly devastated large tracts of land and terrorized whole populations. Charismatic leaders like Amir Abd al-Qadir in Algeria and Tantia Tope in India brought the imperial powers to the brink of defeat and provided inspiration for twentieth century nationalists, but life cannot persist at such an intense level of experience. Violent upheavals were only part of the story. The empires were not sustained by force alone. There was a grumbling discontent throughout the period of colonial rule, but uprisings were sporadic. For the most part, life simply went on. The empires were sustained by those provinces and territories which remained relatively tranquil, for that was how their governments were able to spare the resources to deal with the troublespots.

Having conquered a country, then, the priority for the occupying power was to develop a degree of equilibrium, so that the imperial status quo was generally accepted by the local population. With armies and administrators in limited supply, garrisoning entire countries was obviously not practical. This effectively left only two options.

The first was to eliminate the native population and replace it with European settlers who could hold the land by sheer weight of numbers, backed by the firepower of the metropolitan army. This solution was applied with genocidal success in the 'white' colonies – notably the Americas and Australia – but could only work in places where Europeans wished to put down permanent roots.

The second option was to rule at arm's length, through existing institutions, so that the conquered populations did not feel the weight of the empires upon them. That is to say, if the imperial government was not a significant factor in their day-to-day lives, they were less likely to respond to attempts by politicians to whip up opposition.

The experience of Algeria illustrates the two approaches, since it was a country where both were adopted. Algeria was invaded by France in 1830, and there followed a prolonged process of occupation. It was clear from the outset that the Tell, the Mediterranean northern region, whose climate is similar to southern Spain, France and Italy, was readily susceptible to European settlement and the Arabs were duly thrown off their land. An officer of the Arab Bureau summed up official thinking with remarkable candour for Alexis de Tocqueville in the 1840s: 'No colonization is possible, Sir, without land. We must therefore dispossess the tribes in order to put Europeans in their place.'[10] This policy was pursued with such vigour that by 1876, the Arab population had fallen from three million to two and a half million.[11] A French traveller who visited the country at this time was disappointed to find no traces of the romantic Orient he had been hoping for, only transplanted French villages.[12] By 1962, when Algeria won independence, nearly a million 'pied noir' settlers were living there, cultivating vineyards and living almost as they would have done in Europe.[13] Ninety per cent of the land in the Mediterranean littoral was owned by Europeans,[14] and its original Algerian identity had been so thoroughly submerged that it had been absorbed administratively and legally into France. Oran, Algiers and Bône (now Annaba) were the headquarters of three départements, returning deputies to the National Assembly and living under French civil law. They were in theory as French as Marseille or Calais. In 1938, a French minister felt free to claim that Arabic was 'a foreign language' in Algeria.[15]

When French politicians spoke of Algeria, however, they did not have in mind the southern desert hinterland, 'the Great South.' No fertile farms were waiting here for conversion to vineyards. Cultivation through irrigation in the oases was a specialized and ancient craft. Agricultural skills acquired in southern Europe were of little use, so few colonists were tempted to cultivate the desert. The territories of the South were not part of France. They were not départements. They did not return deputies and French civil law did not apply. The area was under military rule. It was virtually left to the Bedouin and Tuareg tribes who lived here, with a scattering of military and civil command posts to collect taxes, suppress revolts and generally keep the flag flying. The southern territories were once described as 'those still to be occupied,' in recognition of France's tenuous hold upon them.[16]

Northern Algeria shared the characteristics of the white settler colonies of the British empire – South Africa, Kenya, Australia, New Zealand, and in some respects the United States. These were countries where Europeans transported themselves en masse, displacing the indigenous inhabitants and imposing a new social and political order. This pattern considerably simplified the process of maintaining power, for the settler population formed natural allies who not only supported the colonial administration, but in turn looked to it for support. The situation was somewhat complicated in South Africa, where the Afrikaaners combined the role of settlers with (especially during the Boer War) that of a dispossessed indigenous population. In Algeria and Southern Rhodesia, though, the policy of white settlement was so successful as to be positively embarrassing. When France and Britain lost their stomach for the imperial struggle in the 1950s and 1960s, they found their erstwhile allies carrying on without them. As Sellar and Yeatman put it in the context of Ulster in an earlier period, the settlers waged 'loyal rebellion.'[17] They defied both the retreating metropolitan powers and the triumphant forces of Third World nationalism in a vain attempt to restore the values of the nineteenth century. They were more loyal to the empires than the imperial governments themselves.

Administration was more problematic in places like the southern territories of Algeria which European settlers were not willing to occupy. There was no choice here but to reach some compromise with the indigenous inhabitants. A district officer with his few subordinates physically could not exercise direct rule over an area which might be the size of a European state. He had to work through local institutions, making the best of whatever strengths and weaknesses they possessed. The more discretion given to local leaders – in other words, the less obtrusive the colonial regime itself – the easier it was to maintain order, and the less the administration had to rely on trouble-shooting by the military. The system adopted for the Algerian desert therefore represents the pattern applied throughout most of the European colonies in Asia and Africa.

Under this system, the imperial power superimposed itself on top of established social and political structures. It gained the support of local people of influence – tribal chiefs, village elders, landowners, caste leaders or whoever happened to be available – and left them to get on with their own business. In effect, it allowed the indigenous society to run itself. The European government remained a shadowy presence in the background so far as many of its subjects were concerned. The inhabitants of the more remote regions might scarcely be aware of its existence.

This approach, often known as 'indirect rule,' tends to be associated with Lord Lugard in Nigeria at the end of the nineteenth century. He entered into agreements with tribal chiefs, whereby they recognized the paramountcy of the British government, while being largely left to their own devices within their fiefdoms. But Lugard's system was not a new departure. He merely codified what his colleagues around the world had been doing instinctively for years.

The most elaborate system of indirect rule involved the Princely States of India. Nominally, they were independent countries, under the overall protection of the Raj. In practice, they had internal autonomy only so long as they did nothing to disturb the stability of equanimity of the surrounding British territories. Their freedom was rigorously policed by British political agents, civil servants appointed by the Government of India to enforce its own interests.

The philosophy of indirect rule was summed up by Lord Cromer during his lengthy tenure as British Ambassador in Cairo – effectively the political agent in a country which theoretically was not even part of the British empire, but was in practice treated as a protectorate. He remarked: 'We do not govern Egypt, we only govern the governors of Egypt.'[18]

This was a more subtle approach than large-scale European settlement. It was cheap and effective. The threat of force was certainly there in the background, but if the system ran properly it should not be needed for the local dignitaries had a vested interest in coming to terms with the colonial regime. Any prolonged agitation or rebellion was just as likely to threaten their own position as the government's. Like elites the world over, they regarded instability, whatever its origin, as a threat to their survival, and for the most part they were correct. The Indian princes survived the British Raj by only a few years. The Indian Republic stripped them of their powers and then their titles. Similarly, it is no coincidence that land reform has played such a large part in the post-colonial politics of so many newly independent countries. So long as the colonial government interfered as little as possible with their rights, privileges and powers, local magnates had little reason to spurn its assistance in preserving the status quo and keeping the lower orders in check.

Indirect rule, then, was an effective way of spreading limited administrative and military resources, but its foundations were shallow. The cost of failure could be disastrous, as the British discovered to their horror during the Indian Rebellion of 1857, when whole provinces blew up in their faces. The apparently solid edifice of their government across a vast tract of northern India was swept away in a few weeks of popular fury.

The 1857 Rebellion highlights the ultimate fragility of the European empires, which would destroy them a century later. Imperial proconsuls walked tall because they were resting on the shoulders of a host of collaborators. If the collaborators stumbled, or were no longer willing or able to co-operate, then the colonial authorities tumbled into the dust. So long as the upsets remained local, brute force could be applied to redress the position. Isolated rebellions were put down by troops brought in from elsewhere. But, if the discontent became sufficiently widespread, as happened in India in the 1940s and Algeria in the 1950s, then the imperial power's resources would be overstretched. No sooner had it put out the fire of revolt in one place than the flames flared up somewhere else. The days of any government are numbered when its legitimacy rests purely on the capacity of its soldiers to inspire dread among the civilian population. It may take many years and much bloodshed before it admits defeat, but defeat is the inevitable outcome. This was the pattern of decolonization during the latter part of the twentieth century. At different times and at different places, the bluff of the imperial powers was called: and the structure of indirect rule crumbled.

The speed with which this happened across the world was startling. For centuries, the European empires were the dominant fact of international relations. But, within a few decades of the Allied victory in 1945, they had disappeared so thoroughly that it is hard to believe they ever existed. As the twentieth century sinks into history, the idea of a British Viceroy in the President's House in New Delhi seems almost as remote as a Mughal Emperor in the Red Fort. A visitor to the oasis resort of Biskra in Algeria, only a dozen years after independence, found the traces of the French as eerily evocative as the Roman ruins at Timgad a few miles up the road – the gaudy advertisements for 'Thés dansantes' pained on the walls of the cafes, the empty balconies of the Ouled Naíl courtesans.[19] As Hugh Tinker commented in the context of India:

> In retrospect, the whole movement towards independence has an air of inevitability. To anyone under the age of fifty-five in 1980, what seems extraordinary is that a small nation on one side of the world should ever have presumed to control the destiny of an empire on the other side of the world. Yet, at the time, imperial rule did seem almost immutable.[20]

The fact was, imperial rule seemed immutable because passive acquiescence in it was confused with positive loyalty. A province like Sind was hailed as a model of loyalty, whereas its leaders had simply abstained from challenging the British government. They might not have helped the rebels in 1857, but they did not lift a finger to help the British. Over the next decades, local magnates throughout India were assiduously cultivated and wooed and bribed to support the colonial system. But when the crunch came in the 1930s and 1940s, once again they did nothing. Despite the benefits they had supposedly gained from the British, virtually none of the traditional leaders of Indian society made a stand against the tide of Indian nationalism, even if they were not particularly sympathetic towards it. The passive 'loyalty' which had permitted the British to reconquer India in 1858 stood revealed as sheer indifference when it permitted them to quit in 1947.

In a sense, therefore, the British empire was won and lost in the apparent backwaters like Sind, where the colonial regime seemed to have reached a successful accommodation with its subjects. These are the areas to which one should turn to understand the true anatomy of imperialism. Here one can see the reality of indirect rule. One can dissect the healthy carcass of a colonial system, and form hypotheses on how it survived for so long, and why it died. That is the objective of the following study.

Like Cromer in Egypt, the British did not so much govern Sind, as its governors. They had formed an alliance with the great Muslim landholders of the province. Known respectfully as Waderos, they held enormous estates which gave them wealth and almost unlimited local power. Their position as the virtual rulers of the Sindhi countryside was independent of government. The Waderos had been on the scene long before the British arrived, and they are still there today, after the British have quit. So long as their estates were left intact, the Waderos were prepared to live with the colonial government, just as they had lived with its predecessors and now live with its successors.

Indirect rule, then, flourished in Sind. However, it was axiomatic that indirect rule could only be as secure as the intermediaries chosen to support it. If one is governing the governors, one has to be confident that they themselves continue to govern, or the system will collapse. Egypt itself proved the point in 1952 when Colonel Nasser overthrew King Farouk and, by removing the governors cultivated so assiduously by Lord Cromer and his successors, swept aside British power almost as an afterthought. British colonial administrators were fully aware of their own vulnerability and their need for allies. As the nineteenth century progressed, many of those serving in Sind began to fear that their protégés were weakening. Agricultural indebtedness, the perennial evil of India, was sapping the strength of the Waderos. Land – and with it wealth and power – seemed to be slipping away from indebted Waderos to their creditors, who were Hindu money-lenders. The collapse of the Waderos and their replacement with Hindu traders would constitute a social revolution so profound that it could not pass peacefully. It would unleash turmoil in the Sindhi countryside and destroy the foundations of British rule in the process. There would be no governors to govern, because they would be too busy fighting the usurping Hindus. The edifice of the Raj would be submerged. It was a fearful prospect. The British government devoted itself to averting disaster by redressing the balance and preserving the status quo.

The main theme of this study, therefore, is power – the nature of power in rural Sind: how it was exercised and modified and how it related to the overall power of the colonial regime which Napier had imposed upon the country by force of arms. It focuses on one province, and on the individuals within that province. It tries to build up a picture of what indirect rule meant in day to day terms. In this way, it hopes to provide an insight into the techniques which enabled European administrators to remain as uninvited guests in other people's countries for so long: and into the reasons why, eventually, they were thrown out.

Chapter 1

The Scene of Romantic Achievements

I

Sind was an intriguing and idiosyncratic laboratory in which to conduct an experiment in direct rule. It was the first region of India to embrace Islam. Its conversion dated from 711, making it one of the earliest additions to the Muslim world. Classically educated British soldiers and administrators, however, were more fascinated by Alexander the Great's brief incursion into Sind in 327–325 BC. They saw themselves as his heirs in constructing a second European empire in the subcontinent. Alexander Burnes, one of the architects and principal victims of the disastrous Afghan policy which provided the pretext for Napier's aggression in 1843, proclaimed that his travels in the region had been inspired by:

> a desire that I had always felt to . . . visit the countries of Alexander. As the first European of modern times who had navigated the Indus, I now found myself stimulated to extend my journey beyond that river – the scene of romantic achievements which I had read of in early youth with the most intense interest.[1]

Burnes' books are full of references to his Greek hero. He uses the Greek names for the rivers of the Punjab, and is eager to link his experience with that of his namesake as he 'sailed on the stream which had wafted the fleet of Alexander.'[2]

The glamour of history, though, could not always compensate for the sheer physical rigour of life in Sind. Its climate was harsh and the countryside bleak. Malcolm Haig, who served there for nearly a quarter of a century between 1859–81, had to admit that the province was 'in its outward aspect one of the least lovely in India.'[3] A single visit was enough for Sir Richard Temple when he was Governor of

Bombay in the 1870s. 'Nevertheless,' he exclaimed in astonishment, 'the European officers who serve there love the province; nowhere in the Empire is local attachment more intense than in Sind.' The only explanation Temple could offer for their eccentricity was that there was something in the spectacle of the Indus river, descending from the Himalayas to irrigate the desert, which 'affects the imagination of educated men.'[4]

This was a polite way of saying they were mad, but he had caught something of the spirit of the place. Like Egypt, 'the river enters one's sensibilities, becomes the point of reference for all things, it is the yardstick of the country, its beginning and its end.'[5] Just as Egypt without the Nile would merely be an eastern extension of the Libyan Desert, so Sind without the Indus would have been a featureless tract in the western part of the Indian Desert. The river has moulded its landscape, shaped its history, determined the evolution of its social institutions and economy. Sind's very name comes from the river. The Sanskrit word, 'sindhu,' meaning 'ocean,' has since ancient times denoted both the river and the region, although the Persian word, 'darya,' meaning 'sea,' is generally used by modern Sindhis to distinguish the river. Indeed, the main legacy of Alexander's incursion is that, through the Indus, he gave Europeans the name they still apply to the entire Indian subcontinent.

As with Egypt, then, there can be no understanding of Sind without its river. It gives Sind its most visible physical characteristic – the stark contrast of blinding aridity and soft green fertility. Its physical geography is an annual drama of destruction and creation, the routine cycle of human existence based on confrontation with some of the most powerful forces of nature. This is the stuff of heady primal poetry. It is an environment to nurture poets and mystics: an environment to scare off governors and seduce British administrators into collective insanity.

II

Napier brought this exotic country into the Indian empire as its furthest outpost, an enclave of British territory on its north-west frontier (see Figure 1). It was cut off from the rest of British India by a clutch of quasi-independent states along its eastern border – Kachchh in the south-east, the Rajput states of Marwar and Jaisalmir due east and the Punjab state of Bahawalpur to the north-east. To the north and west was Baluchistan, which was beyond the sphere of British influence until 1876. Although Sind was administered as part

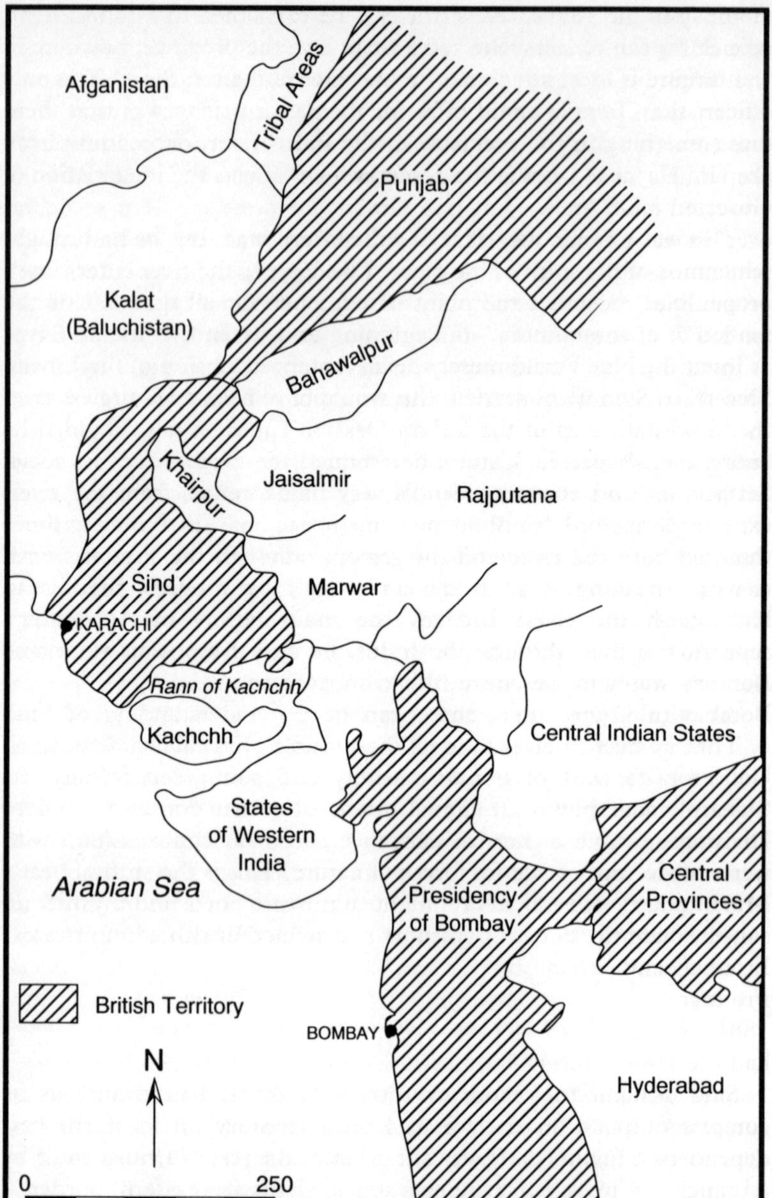

Figure 1 Position of Sind

of the Bombay Presidency, it was separated from the 'Presidency proper' by the Arabian Sea.

It accordingly enjoyed considerable internal autonomy. The senior officer, the Commissioner in Sind, wielded powers far greater than those exercised by Commissioners of Divisions in the Presidency proper. He could not initiate policies without the sanction of the Governor of Bombay, but had almost complete freedom of action over local administration. His discretion was enhanced by the reluctance of successive governors to visit. Officers in the Presidency proper loathed Sind, and it may be that a particular type of character tended to gravitate there – officers who were, in British Indian terms at least, misfits. This tendency was formalized until 1890 by giving Sind its own cadre of service. Most district officers were drawn from the 'Sind Commission' of military and civil officers who spent their entire careers there. While junior officers from the Bombay Civil Service did occasional tours of duty in Sind to broaden their experience and generally toughen them up, one has the impression that they received remissions for good behaviour, being pulled back to what was considered civilization if they showed signs of becoming high bureaucratic flyers. In many respects, then, Sind was treated as a separate province, subordinate to Bombay only in the same sense that Bombay was subordinate to the Government of India in Calcutta. Bombay ruled through remote control.

The capital was Karachi, and the province was divided into three Collectorates, with their headquarters at Karachi, Hyderabad and Shikarpur (see Figure 2). The Collectorates were broken into Sub-Divisions, presided over by Deputy Collectors. The Sub-Divisions were made up of 'taluqas,' which were put in the charge of a Mukhtiarkar, who was always a non-European. Taluqas were further sub-divided into 'dehs,' or villages. The border regions of Upper Sind Frontier and Thar and Parkar were administered under special Frontier Regulations by military Political Superintendents until 1881, when civilian Deputy Commissioners were appointed. They had the same internal administrative structure as the Collectorates.

Sind occupied an area of 53,000 square miles. British Sind comprised 47,000 square miles. The remainder formed the 'independent' state of Khairpur, which had been left in the possession of a branch of the Talpurs, the former ruling family of Sind.

Nearly half of the province was desert – Baluchistan in the east and the Great Indian Desert to the east (see Figure 3 for physiographic divisions of Sind). Much of the border with Baluchistan was marked by the Khirthar hills, running about 150 miles north-south. These

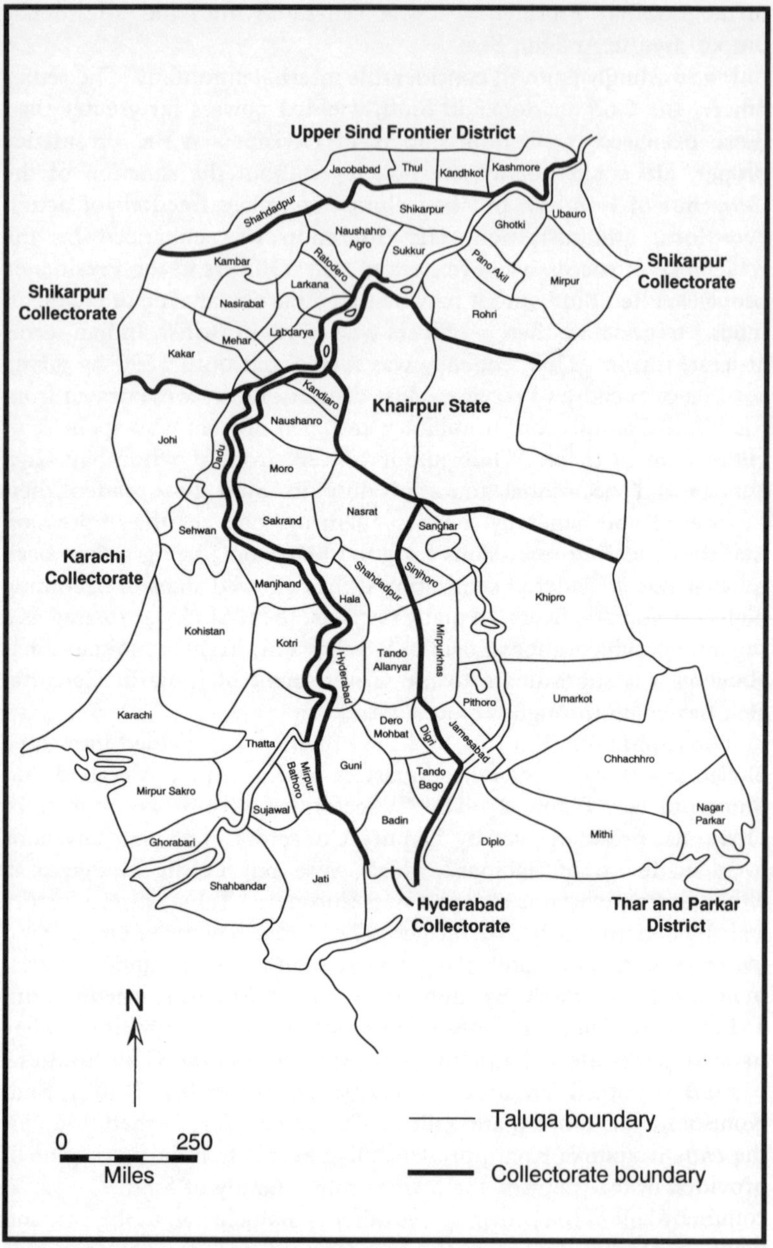

Figure 2 Administrative divisions of Sind

merged into a less elevated region known as the Sind Kohistan, a barren area of sand and scrub which covered about 8,500 square miles of south-western Sind. The Great Indian Desert covered 13,000 square miles in the east. It was divided into two parts – the Thar in the south and the Pat in the north. To the south, the desert disappeared into the salt marshes of the Rann of Kachchh. Here, the water-table was just a few feet below the surface: but further north it could be 300 feet down. Sandwiched between these desert regions was the productive portion of the province – the alluvial plain of the Indus and the Indus Delta. They accounted for about 31,000 square miles, rather more than half of Sind's total area.

There were three climatic regions. The Lar, or Lower Sind, comprised the Indus Delta and the country below Hyderabad. The Vicholo, or Middle Sind, extended about a hundred miles north of Hyderabad. The last division was the Siro, or Upper Sind. The climate of Upper Sind was especially harsh. It was crossed by the thermal equator, making it one of the hottest places on earth, and the temperature rarely fell below 100°F between May and July. On the other hand, the winter could be cold, with even the occasional frost. Conditions in Lower Sind were milder, benefiting from the moderating effect of the sea. The temperature at Karachi rarely went above 90°F in summer, although it could be chilly in winter.

The rainfall throughout Sind was scanty and unpredictable. It was unusual for any part of the province to receive more than ten inches of rain per year, while in 1899 not a single inch was recorded. The monsoon had little effect except in the Thar, which caught its last drops. Somewhat perversely, Nagar Parkar, in the heart of the desert, averaged the highest rainfall in Sind, with a mean of 13.7 inches, although that masked a range of 0.7 inches in 1899 to 38.5 inches in 1915. Kohistan also enjoyed relatively high rainfall, at around 8.5 inches on average, thanks to the orographic influence of the Khirthar mountains – though, again, the quantity was negligible in some years.

Even in good years, therefore, the rainfall in Sind was insufficient to support substantial agricultural activities. '*Barani*' cultivation, based on direct rainfall, was regularly practised only in the Thar and Kohistan. The Thar was surprisingly fertile. After the rains, many of the *bhits* (sandhills) were covered with low shrub and cactus which provided excellent fodder for cattle. It was, as an observer commented in 1870, 'one large grazing ground.'[6] The monsoon also made cultivation possible on a limited scale in *talis*, level areas between sandhills where water collected. In Kohistan, *barani* cultivation took place at the foot of the Khirthar hills. Low *bunds*

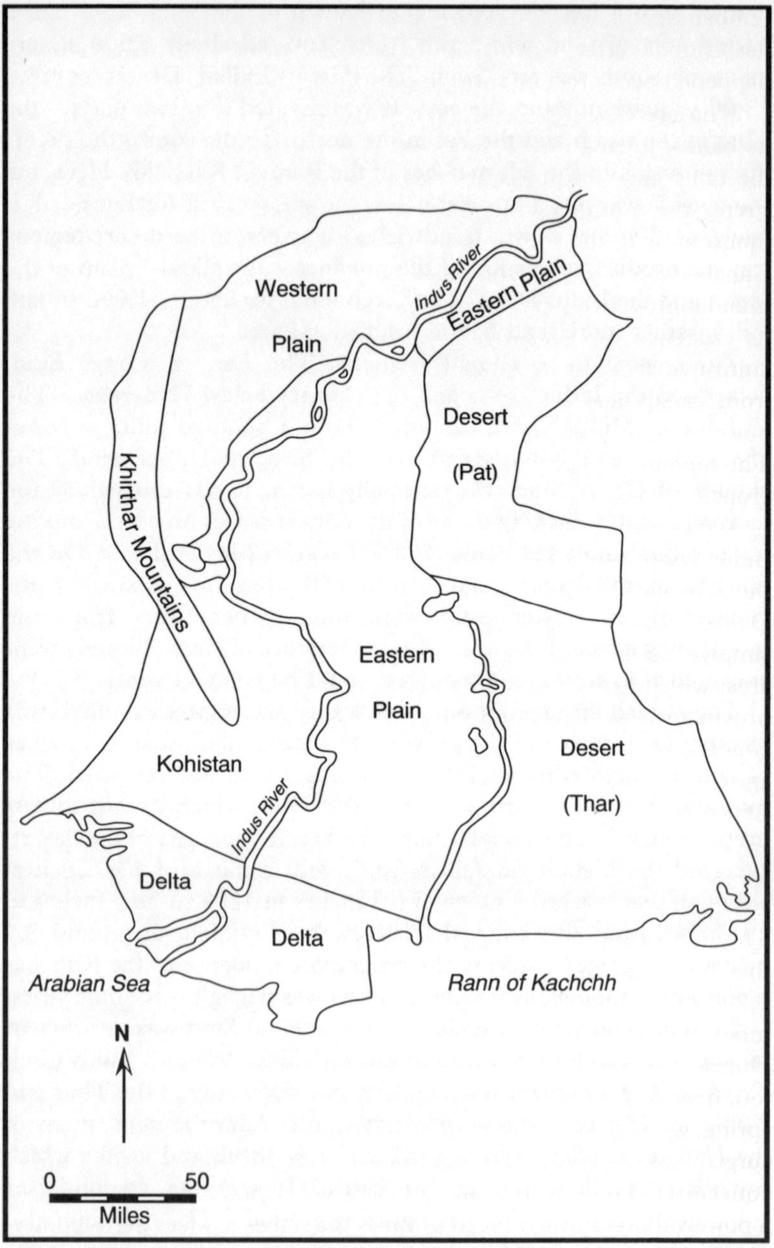

Figure 3 Physiographic divisions of Sind

(embankments) were built at strategic locations to trap water from flash-floods after storms. When there was insufficient rain, as happened every two or three years, the fields lay barren.

What gave Sind life was the river Indus. Every year, it overflowed its banks, freeing the surrounding countryside from dependence on the rains and making large-scale cultivation possible. As Sir Bartle Frere, the Commissioner in Sind, explained in 1854, 'What the monsoon is to the rest of India, the inundation of the Indus and the Canals which distribute its waters are to Sindh.'[7] It was the inundation which gave Sind its magic, and irrigation was the key to its existence. In 1904–05, no less than ninety-one per cent of the cultivated area was irrigated from the Indus system – 2,802,962 acres from canals and 253,457 acres directly from the river. This was however only a fifth of the potentially irrigable area of the province. The remainder lay waste, lacking the irrigational facilities to support crops.[8]

Kohistan and most of the desert were beyond the range of the Indus floodwaters. The area affected by the inundation consisted of the alluvial plain of the Indus, the western fringe of the Pat and the Delta. This was 'Sind proper,' the region Sindhis still refer to as, simply, 'Sind,' to distinguish it from the Thar, Kohistan and other areas which happen to fall within the administrative boundaries of the province. It is the region where the majority of the population is concentrated. The irrigational system determines the pattern of their agriculture and the rhythms of their lives – even, perhaps, their social structure.

II

The Indus rose in a remote area of Tibet, within a hundred miles of the sources of the Sutlej and the Brahmaputra. It flowed for some 1,200 miles before reaching Sind, where it completed the final 590 miles of its course. Its catchment area was 373,000 square miles.[9] During the cold season it was an unspectacular stream, less than a foot deep in some places and not much over six feet at its deepest. In spring, when the ice melted in the Himalayan mountains, hill torrents surged into the Indus and its tributaries. All five rivers of the Punjab concentrated their waters into it before it reached Sind, swelling it to a powerful flood which raced towards the sea at ten feet per second – nearly seven miles per hour.[10] Rainfall over the catchment area above Sind in July and August added to the torrent. The river reached its peak in August, when it was seventeen or eighteen feet deep in places.

The water carried an enormous amount of silt. Himalayan rock was soft, and the soil was parched when the floodwaters ripped through it in the spring, with no grass to bind it until after the rains in July and August. The river carried on average 8,299 million cubic feet of silt every year, enough to cover an area of 9,100 square miles – nearly a tenth of the province – with one foot of silt.[11] The heavier particles sank to the bottom of the stream, while the finer ones were spread over the countryside by floodwater. In this way, the river built up the alluvial flood plain, raising it by about seven inches each century, so that by now it is some 2,000 feet deep. Since the river silt constantly renewed the topsoil, this made the land extremely fertile.[12]

At the same time, sedimentary deposits choked the river, forming mud-banks and sand-flats. Since the gradient was slight, descending no more than three inches per mile, the Indus developed a tortuous route. As one channel silted up, the river would cut a new course through the loose sedimentary soils surrounding it. This gave the river an alarming propensity to change direction, compounded by a tendency to move westward. The river-profile in Figure 4 illustrates the point. The channel was deeper on the right bank (west), where the maximum erosion took place. Meanwhile, as the river abandoned the left bank, it left behind a tract of *kacho* lands (newly formed by sedimentary deposits) to the east. Westward erosion reduced the area of taluqa Larkana, on the right bank, by nearly fifty square miles over the twenty years before 1881. The river took a gigantic step to the west in 1758, when the city of Hyderabad found itself transferred from the right bank to the left.[13]

The westward movement of the river might be connected with the rotation of the earth, but no explanation has yet received general acceptance. Moreover, the Indus was not so consistent as to shift in one direction only. When Alexander Burnes visited Sehwan in 1831, he reported that the river, which used to flow close to the town, had moved east, leaving a two-mile stretch of swamp between it and the town. By 1858, it had switched back. It ran next to the city walls and river steamers used to lie alongside the bank, opposite the government offices. By 1883, the river was again three miles east of the town.[14] It has been argued, especially by Lambrick, that a more catastrophic eastward shift in the direction of the Indus annihilated the Indus Valley civilization some 4,000 years ago. Lambrick's hypothesis is that the main towns were left, literally, high and dry. Their water supplies dried up, the farms surrounding them turned to desert, and it became impossible to support large urban populations.[15]

Life in Sind depended on controlling this capricious river and its

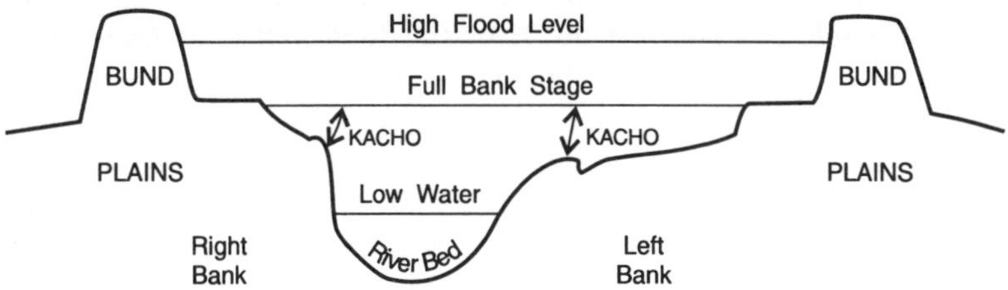

Figure 4 Profile of Indus river

As a result of the westward trend of the river, *kacho* land is more extensive on the left bank (east) than on the right bank. *Kacho* land is normally flooded during the inundation, and is exposed after the inundation subsides.

Source: Govt. of Sind, Public Works Dept., *Bund Manual* (Karachi, 1954), Fig. 1.

annual inundations. Since the heavy silting had raised its bed, the country on either side sloped away in a series of terraces marking abandoned beds.[16] Left to itself, the overflow would have swamped the alluvial plain. Nineteenth century Sindhis had a frightening glimpse of the prehistoric inundation after the river changed course near Kashmore in the mid-1860s. Much of the water was diverted into the Sind Dhoro, an old river bed, from which it spilled onto the plain, devastating the country from Kashmore to the Manchar Lake. The floodwaters destroyed people's homes and halted cultivation over an enormous area. They were exceptionally destructive in 1874, sweeping away eighty towns and villages. The Sind government took action to protect the region. The Kashmore Bund, reinforcing seventy-three miles of the Indus bank, was completed in 1878–79.[17] The effect both of the floods and the bund can be illustrated through taluqa Shikarpur. Its cultivated area fell from 57,000 acres in 1861–62 to 16,481 acres in 1877–78, but by 1896–97, cultivation had surpassed the former level, reaching 64,632 acres.[18]

In ancient Sind, uncontrolled floods like these must have been the main source of cultivation, and a very precarious one. Even in the nineteenth century, *sailabi* cultivation, from natural overflow, was fairly common, especially along the river banks on the newly formed *kacho* lands. This was cheap and, if all went well, easy. The flood churned up the land, in effect ploughing it, while the silt fertilized it. The cultivators just had to wait for the waters to subside and sow their seeds. *Sailabi* lands produced *rabi* (cold season) crops such as rice, oil seeds, pulses and wheat. Cultivation in some taluqas – notably Ghotki,

Kambar and Rohri – was almost entirely dependent on river floods, and they could give good results. Even the floods from the Sind Dhoro had their positive side. While causing massive destruction in Naushahro Abro, for example, they gave the taluqa some fine *sailabi* cultivation as a by-product: the acreage under rice increased nearly three-fold during the 1860s. In the end, though, the floodwaters deposited so much silt that the land became choked with tough grasses before the waters subsided, making it impossible for seed to be sown in time.[19] This was a common side effect of heavy flooding.

An additional hazard, in Sind as in all irrigated countries, was waterlogging. This prevented natural salts from leaching away, creating tracts of *kalar* (salt-impregnated soil) which was unfit for cultivation. Uncontrolled flooding increased the risk.

The other danger of *sailabi* cultivation was that the waters might not recede in time for crops to be sown. This ruined the lands around Lake Manchar, the largest region of *sailabi* activity, in the 1860s. The lake was fed by two rivers, the Western Nara from the north and the Aral from the east. As the river rose, water escaped down these channels into the Manchar, whose area was increased from fifteen square miles in the cold season to as much as 200 square miles at the height of the inundation. When the flood retreated, water drained out of the Manchar, back along the Aral into the river, exposing thousands of acres of fertile land.[20] When, as was mentioned earlier, the Indus moved away from the nearby town of Sehwan, it left in its old bed a bank of silt several miles wide through which the Aral had to pass. This blocked the Aral's twin functions of filling and draining the Manchar. Some lands were no longer submerged at all; others emerged too late to be sown. Up to 15,000 acres of cultivable land were lost.[21] The same problem attended the cultivation of *kacho* land along the river bank elsewhere in Sind. Provided the waters fell in time, farmers could make a good living but, as Figure 4 makes clear, *kacho* lands were liable to remain under water for a long time if the flood was high.

Since natural flooding was risky, most cultivation was based on waters distributed by canals. This was more reliable. The pattern of irrigation in Sind has been transformed in the twentieth century by the construction of barrages across the Indus. The Sukkur Barrage, opened in 1932, irrigates over half of the cultivable area of the province, while the Kotri and Gudu Barrages, opened in 1955 and 1962 respectively, cover the remainder of the alluvial plain. The barrages block the river at critical points, controlling the flow of water and putting irrigation on a more scientific basis. The water is distributed through a network of canals, largely freeing agriculturists from dependence on the luck of the inundation. The barrages have given agriculture a security it never previously enjoyed in Sind.[22]

Before the barrages were built, irrigation was provided through 'inundation' canals. These were fed by overspill from the Indus during the inundation and were dry for the rest of the year. A typical inundation canal system consisted of a main canal, known as a 'feeder,' which 'took off' (ie received water directly from) the river, then distributed its waters into a number of branch canals known as 'distributaries.' These in turn might act as feeders for other distributaries. The point at which a canal took off its feeder was referred to as its 'head,' the other end as its 'tail.' Water was brought from the branches to the fields by *'karias'* (water courses).

Most main feeders were owned and maintained by the government. Branch canals were more often privately owned, and had generally been cut according to the needs of their owners rather than a strategic assessment of the overall requirements of the surrounding areas. It was not uncommon to find two or three branch canals running parallel to each other where one would have been enough.[23] Since private enterprise along these lines wasted water, the government attempted during the nineteenth century to regulate the process by taking over branch canals where possible. *Karias* were invariably cut and maintained by the agriculturists themselves.

There were two methods of cultivating from canals: *moki* or 'flow' cultivation, through natural overflow from a karia, and *charkhi* ('lift') cultivation, where water physically had to be lifted into the field by means of a Persian wheel drawn by a camel or bullocks.

'Lift' cultivation was expensive and troublesome, but more common. It was practised where the water lay too low in its channel or the land was too high above the banks. Water was raised twelve to fourteen feet on average, though farmers sometimes had to lift it as much as forty-five feet.[24] 'Lift' lands were generally near the tails of canals, where the water supply petered out. The whole of taluqa Mirpurkhas, for instance, suffered from scanty and unreliable water supplies because it was at the tails of several canals, a long way from the Indus. 'Flow' cultivation was almost unknown there.[25]

In fact, few parts of Sind had a guaranteed capacity for 'flow' cultivation. If the inundation was exceptionally low, or if there were problems with the feeder canals, or if the inundation suddenly fell early one season, lands which were normally irrigated by 'flow' might have to be converted to 'lift,' farmers being obliged to set up Persian wheels before they could water their fields. If this happened, lands towards the tail of the canal system, already dependent on 'lift,' would suffer even more. For example, river erosion at the head of the Ghar Canal reduced its efficiency and hence its water supply in the late 1870s, converting a great deal of 'flow' land to 'lift.' An engineer commented that anyone walking along the banks of the Ghar could see at a glance 'that the difference of a few inches in the level of the land has made all the difference between a very good crop and a few withered stems of grass.'[26]

Alternatively, a high inundation might drown 'flow' lands. Cultivators had to keep watch over the canal banks and protective bunds and be ready to turn out *en masse* to reinforce any weak spots. If the worst happened and the lands were flooded, the crops would be destroyed but the agriculturists might be able to recoup their losses by sowing *rabi* (cold weather) crops in the fields – now converted to *sailabi* lands – after the water drained away. On the other hand, as with any *sailabi* land, the flood might not subside in time: in which case the farmers lost everything. This happened with infuriating frequency in taluqa Kakar during the 1860s, when the Western Nara developed the habit of submerging the crops just as they were ripening, turning the farms into a huge swamp. The area remained waterlogged too long for *rabi* crops to be sown later. Many of the frustrated farmers gave up cultivation altogether and turned to raising and stealing cattle instead.[27]

Meanwhile, if the 'flow' lands were under water, the farmers on the 'lift' lands at the canal tails were probably enjoying a welcome opportunity for 'flow' cultivation, leaving their Persian wheels idle for the season.

Since the pattern of the inundation was so erratic, few areas in practice depended wholly either on 'flow' or 'lift' cultivation. Most farmers used both methods, often within the same season. They might start cultivation under 'lift' but, as the inundation reached its peak in July and August, give up Persian wheels and rely on natural overflow.

Everything therefore depended on the working of the canals. Several factors could affect their performance. The positioning of the heads of main canals was critical. They needed to be in places where the river bank was permanent and the canal mouths were neither blocked with silt because the stream was sluggish nor eroded because it was too swift. Such conditions were not easy to fulfil, and problems could arise if there was a change in the 'set' of the river (alignment of its current). In the late 1880s, a change in the set of the Indus silted up the head of the Begari Canal, while over the same period the entire canal system of taluqa Dadu suffered from the erosion of its canal heads (see Figure 5

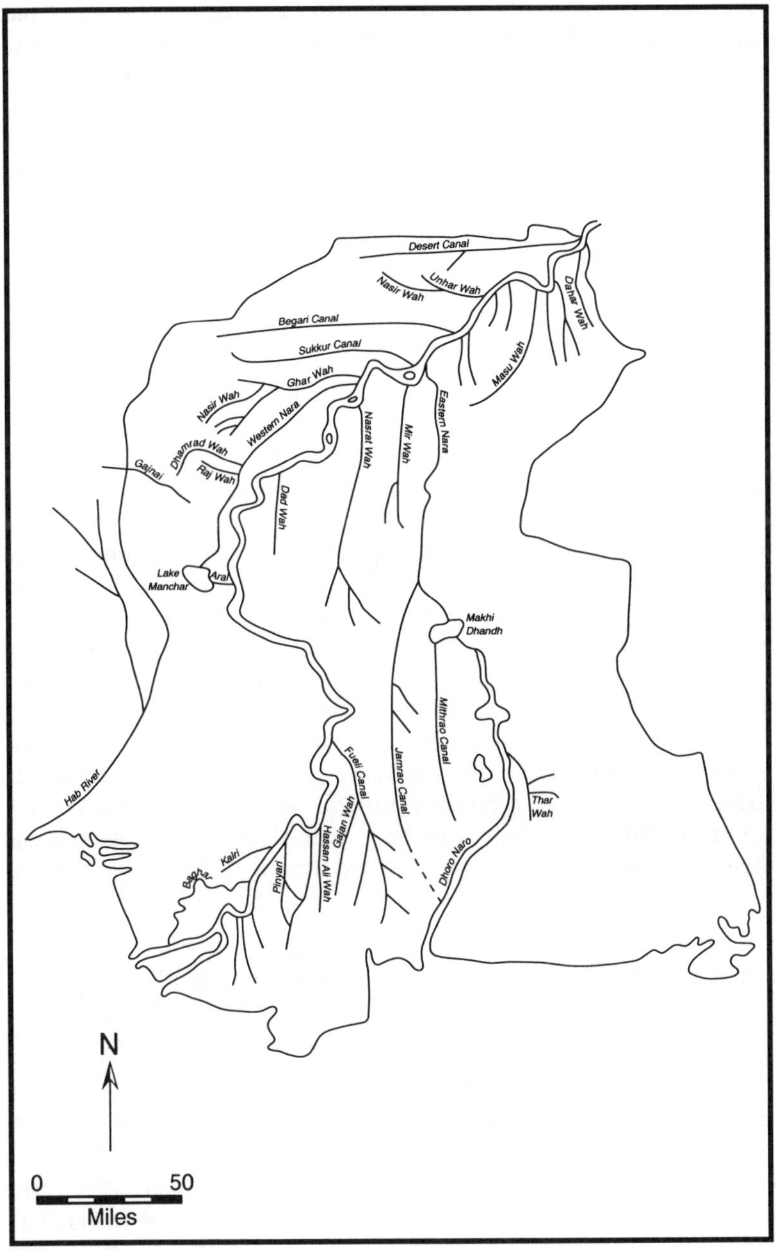

Figure 5 Principal canals in Sind, 1907

for principal canals in Sind). By contrast, a change in the set of the river in the 1870s improved the Western Nara by scouring away deposits of silt which had been choking it: but the same change so eroded the mouth of the Ghar Canal that its very existence was threatened.[28] Many canals also performed badly because, instead of being purpose-built, they followed abandoned river beds. Their tortuous courses reduced their rates of flow, preventing water from reaching the tails in time for crops to be sown. The Fuleli, the Ghar and the Western Nara were all former river beds.[29]

The heavy silt content of Indus water created particular problems. By the end of the inundation, the canals were choked and massive efforts had to be made to clear them so that the water would be distributed properly during the following inundation. The responsibility for clearing the main feeder canals, on which all the branch canals depended, fell to government. The consequences of neglect could be catastrophic. During the confusion of the war in Afghanistan and Napier's military campaign, the Talpur government had been unable to fulfil its obligations. By the time the first British engineers examined the irrigational system in the 1840s, they found that many of 'the fairest streams in Scinde' were 'totally ruined' for want of clearance. Cultivation had virtually been confined to the area around their headwaters.[30] Mismanagement of the canal system by the Collector of Hyderabad produced the same result in the Hyderabad Collectorate during the 1840s and 1850s.[31] This annual obligation was onerous and expensive. Over the decade 1860–70, sixteen per cent of the revenue earned each year from cultivation based on Sind's canals had to be ploughed back into maintaining them.[32] This expenditure was an investment without which there would have been no return. As an officer explained in 1863:

> Persons at a distance not practically acquainted with Sind, are apt to forget that the cost of canal clearances in Sind is, in fact, the price paid for the land revenue, and that unless it were paid, the Government would generally get no land revenue at all.[33]

As for the government, so for the agriculturists. Unless they cleared and maintained their water courses, they could not cultivate: they would have no income. This made agriculture expensive.

It also meant that the preconditions for successful agriculture owed as much to human energy as to nature – which is to say that individual agriculturists might have to rely, not only on their own hard work, but on the energy and dedication of their neighbours. The enthusiasm, or lack of it, with which farmers towards the heads of canals cleared their own channels could determine the quality of next year's crops for the farmers at the tails.

While individuals might be pressured or cajoled by their neighbours, government was almost immovable, and the consequences of government policy could be devastating. A slight change of emphasis in the targeting of resources could make or break the fortunes of thousands of agriculturists.

Nothing illustrates more dramatically the helplessness of Sindhi farmers in the face of changes in irrigational policy than the twentieth century history of taluqa Umarkot. Throughout the nineteenth century, the eastern part of the taluqa was irrigated by the Dhoro Naro, the western part depending on the Thar Wah. After 1900, the water supply to the Dhoro Naro was reduced to maintain supplies to the newly opened Jamrao Canal, a project into which the government had sunk a large amount of money and about whose success it was understandably anxious. The Jamrao was given priority and by 1915 cultivation from the Dhoro Naro was all but impossible. The Dhoro Naro tract, which used to be well irrigated and fertile, had become 'a barren and desolate country. The zamindars [landholders], who were prosperous fifteen years ago, have been reduced to the verge of poverty.'[34] Meanwhile, the Thar Wah was working extremely well, helped to some extent by the shutting off of the Dhoro Naro water. The cultivated area had increased and the zamindars prospered.[35]

The opening of the Sukkur Barrage in 1932 restored the fortunes of the Dhoro Naro farmers but the Thar Wah silted up. By 1977, the area which used to be watered from it and which forty years previously had been described as rich rice land abounding in water fowl, was completely uninhabited. The land had turned to 'paki' – soil which, after being irrigated, has been exposed to continuous drought and is baked rock hard. Not a single plant could fight through it. The Thar Wah tract presented a scene of utter desolation, stretching flat and bleak to the horizon like the cracked concrete of a derelict car park. The adjacent Dhoro Naro tract was a fertile expanse of shady mango groves and green crops. They were like different worlds, but they were separated only by a ruined *bund*.[36]

Such contrasts were painful, but were inevitable by-products of changes in the irrigational infrastructure which turned tracts of desert into lush farmlands. A line had to be drawn somewhere between cultivation and desolation and overall the farmers themselves undoubtedly benefited. In Sind, human intervention could transform the environment. This made it an ideal laboratory for optimistic Victorians to live out their dream of setting the world to rights through perseverance, science and public works. No farmers were in such hopeless desperation that they could not be rescued by a competent military engineer. When engineers surveyed the Fuleli Canal in the 1840s, they found it choked with sediment and drifting sands. Cultivation was confined to the fringes of the large ponds in which the water was trapped, while the rest of the plain lay parched. The engineers, however, looked beyond the desolation. They recognized that the Fuleli could become one of the most important canals in Sind, with the potential to maintain a perennial water supply – that is, a constant supply throughout the year, regardless of the annual inundation. A relatively simple irrigational project, they declared, would convert hundreds of square miles of land 'from a howling waste of babool brushwood and fire plants into a fertile and populous tract of country.'[37]

They were correct. They had located the canal system's weakness at its head, which had been damaged by changes in the course of the river. In 1858, a five-mile supply channel was cut from Jamshoro, eighteen miles downstream of the old head, where the Indus seemed more stable. This small operation resolved the problem. By the end of the century, over 300,000 acres were irrigated from the Fuleli Canal system each year.[38]

Similar action revitalized the Eastern Nara. This, like the Fuleli, was an ancient water course, but it had never been used for large-scale irrigation. For 120 miles, the dry bed of the Nara passed through the sandy deserts of Khairpur State until it reached a lake, the Makhi Dhandh. From here, it wound along the foot of the sandhills, with the alluvial plain to the west, to the Rann of Kachchh. During the inundation, floods swept down from the Indus. Some of the water, trapped in the *dhandhs* (hollows) between sandhills, provided small-scale *rabi* (cold weather) cultivation.

In 1852, Bartle Frere, the Commissioner in Sind, ordered a survey of the Nara valley. This revealed that more water flooded into it from the Indus than had been suspected, but most was wasted in the porous sands and deep *dhandhs*. A series of *bunds* was accordingly constructed across the channels feeding the largest *dhandhs*, to direct the water into the main Nara channel and bring it to the fertile plain to the south. After that, a thirteen mile supply channel was cut from the Indus at Rohri to improve the head of the Nara and guarantee a perennial water supply however low the river fell. These two operations virtually created a new canal system for the barren taluqas of Sanghar, Khipro and Umarkot. Not only were about 40,000 acres of desert brought under cultivation, but two-thirds of the area was irrigated by 'flow,' a remarkable bonus for the cultivators. Unfortunately, the excellent water supply did have an unforeseen side effect. The still waters of the Nara valley became infested with mosquitoes and it grew to be dreaded as a malarial swamp.[39]

Cutting the Eastern Nara Supply Channel was only the beginning of a vast project for bringing perennial cultivation to the eastern desert so far as Lieutenant Fife, the officer in charge, was concerned. He prepared a blueprint for the whole area, although the slow grinding of the bureaucratic machine delayed realization of his vision until the turn of the century.

The next step was not taken until 1879, twenty years after his report, when the Mithrao Canal was opened. This took off from the Makhi Dhandh and 'commanded' (ie brought irrigation to) one and a half *lakhs* of acres.[40]

The culmination of Fife's design took yet another twenty years. This was the development of the Jamrao Canal system, opened in 1899–1900. It was the greatest irrigational work undertaken in Sind before the construction of the Sukkur Barrage in 1932. It was an extension to, and immense improvement on, the Eastern Nara system. It took off the Nara in the north-eastern corner of taluqa Sanghar, upstream of the Makhi Dhandh, and tailed into it again in the extreme south of taluqa Samaro. The Jamrao Tract had a total length of 130 miles, with an average breadth of ten miles. The canal commanded 934,300 acres, about a third of which was cultivated each year. It provided perennial irrigation, but the water was severely rationed. Supplies to most government canals in Sind were scientifically controlled through 'regulators' – mini-barrages which, built along the canals, could reduce the flow of water or cut it off altogether. This allowed water to be switched from one canal to another for a fixed period, such as a fortnight. That is to say, it was 'rotated' between the two canals so that they shared their supply, the same amount of water irrigating two areas of cultivation. This technique was practised on a grand scale in the Jamrao Tract. Water was provided to villages in strict rotation to spread it as wide as possible, while the cultivation of rice was restricted because it demanded more water than the system could sustain.[41]

The Jamrao Canal system differed from previous irrigational works in Sind in that it was more ambitious in its scope and more methodical in its implementation. Before the project started, Evan James, the Commissioner in Sind, visited the 'canal colonies' which had been established on irrigated lands in the Punjab. He was impressed by their efficiency and, on his recommendation, administration of the newly created villages in the Jamrao Tract was based on the Punjab model. Every village had its own water course, to make rotation easier. The land was broken into sixteen-acre squares, each consisting of one-acre plots. Water courses ran around the edge of the plots, making boundary marks unnecessary, while roads and paths ran alongside the distributaries and water courses to save space. At the same time, the landholdings were consolidated. All new holdings were parcelled out in uniform blocks. Zamindars already holding land in the Jamrao Tract were obliged to trade in their estates for squared holdings which were equal in area but bundled into a continuous tract instead of scattered in fragments as was the traditional pattern of holdings.[42] Anticipating these regulations, James explained enthusiastically: 'There will be the same difference between the Jamrao area and an area watered by the old Indus canals as between an American town built in regular blocks, and the native Town of Karachi.'[43] It was a perceptive remark, for the Jamrao did indeed herald the dawn of a new era in Sind. It marked a great step forward, away from the jumbled array of haphazard fields of the nineteenth century, towards the planned efficiency of twentieth century agriculture.

Unfortunately, the Jamrao never fully lived up to the expectations held of it – another feature it shares with much twentieth century progress. It damaged the working of the other canals of the Nara valley, taking water away from the Mithrao and the Nara itself. A system of rotation had to be adopted between the Jamrao and the Nara for the *rabi* season when the Indus was low, and occasionally for the *kharif* (hot weather) season as well. Cultivation from both systems was declining by the time the Sukkur Barrage came to their rescue in 1932.[44] However, the setbacks should not detract from the overall achievement. Whatever the disappointments, the entire region had been pure desert before the canal system was completed.

Other major irrigational schemes of the nineteenth century included the reclamation of the wastes of Upper Sind Frontier through the Begari and Desert Canals, the construction of the Fordwah, and the extension of the Dad and Nasrat Canals.

This brief sketch of Sind's irrigational system illustrates three fundamental features of Sindhi agrarian life. The first was that no matter how forlorn any part of the province might look, it only needed water to bring it to life. The soil was fertile once it was given a chance. As Table 3 shows, the nineteenth century irrigational projects doubled Sind's cultivated area from two million acres in 1871/72 to four million in 1900/01.

The second point might appear to be a truism, but it is so obvious that its significance can easily be overlooked: these were all major projects. They required substantial resources and extensive planning. The Jamrao scheme took forty years to reach full implementation, and the principle held true right down the line. Once the government canals were built, the smaller private distributaries or *karias* had to be constructed, and this was not a task to be undertaken lightly. These 'water courses' were daunting engineering work in themselves, several feet wide and hundreds of yards long. Sindhi canals were broader than most rivers in Britain, while karias were like short stretches of the English canal system. Great physical labour was required to dig and maintain these channels. Sind was no place for individual pioneers. A collective effort was essential to create the conditions for agriculture to commence.

The third point is that few of the canals lived up to the hopes of the engineers who designed and cut them. Silting, erosion or floods weakened their performance eventually. Once a canal system had been created, there followed a struggle to maintain it. It was a problem faced by government on a large scale, and by individual farmers on a small scale. Constant vigilance and hard work were required to preserve the water courses: for without them, even the most productive fields would, like the Thar Wah, degenerate into a wasteland.

It was this eternal competition between water and wilderness which fascinated so many officers serving in Sind, explaining the mystery which had puzzled Sir Richard Temple after his visit. Few sights are so striking as a tree-lined canal cutting its way through a dusty Sindhi plain, a gash of exuberant greenery across the drab desert. It is a vivid manifestation of the balance between life and death.

III

The power of the Indus was thrown into dramatic relief in the final years of the nineteenth century, when Sind escaped the famine that devastated the rest of Bombay and Rajasthan after the monsoon failed in 1896 and several succeeding years. Sindhis never endured the horrors of famine. The inundation of the Indus might be erratic and even destructive, but it never failed altogether. It always returned, year after year. Only Thar and Parkar, reliant on rainfall, suffered from the famine. During this period, starving refugees poured into the province in search of food and employment.[45]

When they reached Sind, they escaped starvation, but they had not come to a land of plenty. Sindhis lived frugally. Their staple food was rice, or bread made from *juari* (great millet) or *bajri* (spiked millet), supplemented by whey or lentils. Meat and fish were luxuries. Fish was readily available only during the inundation. Meat was even more scarce. Milk was indispensable to the diet of the poorer Sindhis who usually kept cattle as their main means of support. They sold butter and *ghee* (clarified butter), keeping the buttermilk for themselves.[46] All this adds up to a diet which would have been healthy if it had been adequate. However, figures presented in 1904 indicated that, if the entire population was living around subsistence level, then the outturn of food crops would fall some 50,000 tons short of the province's requirements.[47] A large number of Sindhis must have been living well below subsistence level.

They were, nevertheless, living. The province sustained a population which leapt by fifty-nine per cent between 1872 and 1911, from 2.2 million to 3.5 million. This still left it thinly habited. While there were forty-one people per square mile in 1872, there were only sixty-six in 1911.[48] This was the attraction of Sind for refugees and others. With such a low population, there was always a demand for labour, even in the worst years. In fact, the shortage of labour sometimes prevented the province from taking full advantage of the irrigational improvements.

Accordingly, Sind was traditionally a country of immigration. Lying between two tracts of inhospitable desert, its fertility had always acted as a magnet. It had attracted so many different peoples that the 1907 *Gazetteer of Sind* suggested that no other part of India had so mixed a population.[49]

The earliest known inhabitants of Sind were the people of the Indus Valley Civilization. They flourished around 2500 BC to 1700 BC and constituted, in Jawarharlal Nehru's words, the 'dawn of India's story.'[50] The archaeological evidence about their society comes from eighty sites. The most famous, at Mohenjo Daro in taluqa Larkana, was a sophisticated and well-planned city. Streets of brick houses were laid out in the rectangular grid-iron pattern of a modern American or Australian town rather than the twisting alleyways of Europe and Asia. There were granaries, with air vents to reduce mildew. Finally, most extraordinary of all, there were covered drains, a feature which did not become commonplace in the wider world for several millennia.

All this implied a strong social organization and well developed scientific knowledge. Sir John Marshall, the first excavator of

Mohenjo Daro, concluded that Sind and the Punjab 'must henceforth be recognized, along with Persia, Mesopotamia and Egypt, as one of the most important areas where the civilizing processes were initiated and developed.'[51]

This civilization ended about the middle of the second millennium BC, for reasons which are still disputed. The cities and their hinterlands may have fallen victim to flooding or a dramatic shift in the course of the Indus, or the inhabitants may have been slaughtered by the Aryan tribes who were beginning their invasion of the sub-continent and who wrote the early verses of the Rig Veda in the Indus valley. Or it may have been a combination of all these factors. What is certain is that the cities were abandoned and the Aryans established themselves in Sind on their way to the greater expanse of the Indian interior.

The next major recorded event in Sind's history was in 711 AD, the same year that Tariq ibn Zaiyad landed at Gibraltar to bring Islam to Spain. An Arab army led by Muhammad bin Qasim entered Sind, defeated its Hindu king, Rajah Dahar, and established Muslim rule. Whatever resonance the incursion by Alexander the Great a thousand years previously may have had for British administrators, it left no lasting impression on Sind and the arrival of Muhammad bin Qasim was, surely, the single most important moment in its modern history. From that time forward, Sind has been part of the Muslim world. Until Mahmud of Ghazni annexed the Punjab nearly three hundred years later, it was the sole enclave of Islam in the sub-continent. By the nineteenth century, three-quarters of Sind's population were Muslims.

As Table 2 shows, the Muslim population fell into three broad categories – Sindhis, Saiyids and Baluchis. There were also small communities of Memons, Khojahs and, in the Shikarpur region, Pathans.

The Sindhis were, as far as one can tell, descendants of the Hindu Rajputs who had been living in the country at the time of the Muslim

Table 1 Population of Sind 1872–1911

	Hindus %	*Muslims* %	*Others* %	*Total (millions)*
1872	18	78	4	2.19
1881	13	78	9	2.41
1891	20	77	3	2.87
1901	23	76	0	3.21
1911	24	75	1	3.51

Source: *Census Reports*, 1872–1911

Table 2 Muslim communities in Sind 1881–1911

	1881 %	*1911* %
Baluchi	22	22
Brahui	N/A	2
Sindhi	67	57
Saiyid	2	N/A
Pathan	1	1
Others	8	18
TOTAL	100	100
TOTAL (m)	1.89	2.64

Source: *Census Reports*, 1881–1911

conquest. The main tribes were Sammos, Sumros, Unars, Abros, Dahars, Mahars, Jokhios, Numrios, Jats and Mohanos. Most had long been settled as agriculturists on the alluvial plain. Their tribal differences were nominal. The tribal institutions had withered away, their chiefs had become figureheads and the members of the tribes were scattered. All that remained by the nineteenth century was a vestigial sentimental attachment to the tribal name, somewhat similar to a modern Highlander's association with a Scottish clan. Sindhi society was not organized around tribal *sardars* (chiefs), but around *Waderos* (large landholders), who seldom had tribal connections with the cultivators who owed them allegiance. The exceptions were the Jokhios and the Numrios, who lived nomadic, pastoral lives in the uplands of Kohistan, sometimes supplementing their fortunes by plundering caravans. They formed tightly knit communities who were, one might say, properly 'tribal' in character, dominated by patriarchal chiefs.[52]

The Jats and the Mohanos may have arrived after the Muslim conquest. The Jats may have been of Scythian origin. Their chief lived in taluqa Jati, although his tribe was dispersed throughout the province. In Baluchistan, a 'jat' signified a camel-handler and this seems to have been the original occupation of the Sindhi Jats, but many were also farm labourers.[53]

The Mohanos were an intriguing tribe who specialized in boating. They were concentrated along the Indus and around Lake Manchar, many living in their boats. They called themselves 'Mir Bahar,' or 'Lords of the Sea,' and could almost be described as an aquatic race. They came into their element – literally – during the inundation, when their boats were in demand as ferries and they could catch fish over the flooded fields. Mohanos practised a remarkable level of sexual equality. The women had no qualms about appearing unveiled in public, often taking command of the boats and manoeuvring the tiller while the men swam in search of fish.[54]

As indicated above, Sind's social organization revolved around powerful landholders known as Waderos, rather than tribal chiefs. The role of the Wadero is discussed fully in Chapter 3. For the moment, it is worth noting only that his position was very similar to that of a chief. Waderos' importance may have developed in the past partly because tribal people were accustomed to strong leadership and also because of the need to allocate responsibility for monitoring the water-courses and turning out labour in large numbers to maintain and repair them. Cultivators and smallholders had to belong to the 'raj' (community) of one of their local Waderos. Inevitably, allegiances tended to run in families but there were none of the formal blood-ties of a tribe and it was possible to switch loyalties – provided the new Wadero was willing and able to protect the defector against the displeasure of the old one. Members of the raj looked to their Wadero for leadership, adjudication in their disputes and representation of their interests to government. For his part, the Wadero expected the members of his raj to reaffirm their loyalty periodically by paying him tribute – sometimes through gifts, but more especially by turning out when required to repair canals or to hunt down bandits or cattle thieves.

And, finally, the use of the masculine gender is significant. A Wadero was a man then, and still is. Benazir Bhutto was able to take over from her father as Wadero in the 1980s,[55] but she occupies a unique position in Sindhi history, comparable only with the daughters of Rajah Dahar who avenged the murder of their father by hounding Muhammad bin Qasim to a shameful death. In the nineteenth century, a female Wadero would have been a contradiction in terms.

If the Wadero was the pillar of secular society, spiritual support was provided by religious figures known as Pirs and Saiyids. Their critical significance in Sindhi life has been explored in depth by Sarah Ansari[56] so only the briefest sketch of their social role is required here. Islam in Sind was strongly influenced by Persian Sufism, a mystical path to devotion through poetry and music. The most inspired lyricists were venerated as saints long after their deaths and the cultural heart of Sind was at Bhitshah near Hala, where Shah Abdul Latif, the country's greatest Sufi poet, had spent the last years of his life. His tomb had become a place of pilgrimage and he had acquired a powerful influence throughout Sind. Sindhis of all classes had some knowledge of his poetry and could recite from his poems even if they could not read.

Shah Abdul Latif was the greatest of Sind's poets, but the Sufi traditions which nourished him and sustained his reputation attracted teachers and faqirs (religious mendicants) from all over Central Asia and India. Honoured with the title of pir (saint), many were profound mystics. After they died, their graves became shrines, watched over by their descendants, upon whom the mantle of sanctity was deemed to have fallen. Their *mazars* (tombs) were scattered throughout the province. As one devotee exclaimed, 'There is not a sub-division of a district, but it is blessed with a place of pilgrimage.'[57] The guardians of the *mazars* inherited the title of pir, and were often themselves distinguished with a reputation for godliness and learning. The Pirs of Lohari, for example, lived as hermits, praying over the *mazar* and emerging from their retreats only to visit Mecca. Their *murids* (disciples) were as far away as Bombay, Calcutta, Arabia, Zanzibar and South Africa.[58] Other important places of pilgrimage included the shrine of Zinda Pir on an island in the Indus opposite Rohri, the shrine of Shaikh Tahir at Uderolal, and the shrine of Mangho Pir near Karachi. The best known *mazar* after Bhitshah was the shrine of Qalandar Lal Shahbaz in Sehwan. Shahbaz Qalandar exerted a particular fascination. So many pirs had made the journey to his *mazar* over the centuries, to preach in its shadow and eventually to die and be buried close by, that the town itself was known throughout Sind – indeed, throughout India and central Asia – as 'Sehwan Sharif' – 'Holy Sehwan.' It was known as the town of hundreds of saints, living and dead.

The importance of pirs in Sind cannot be overstated. Every Sindhi venerated a particular pir, to whose *mazar* a regular donation would be made at harvest-time. The living pirs were a source of spiritual guidance and inspiration, and gave practical advice on disputes. In this way, pirs complemented the Waderos as adjudicators and general practitioners of common sense. Indeed, a Wadero would frequently consult his pir before exercising his authority in difficult or complex cases, while a cultivator who had lost his Wadero's good will, or who wanted a favour, might approach the great man through his pir. The pir and the Wadero shared the leadership of Sindhi society.

The importance of pirs helps to explain the uniquely powerful position of Saiyids in Sind. Saiyids were of Arab ancestry and claimed descent from the Prophet Muhammad through his daughter, Fatima. Membership of the direct family of the Prophet naturally invested them with the aura of the holiest of pirs. It was said that a Saiyid 'may commit any crime with impunity.'[59] Dr James Burnes, who visited Sind in 1831, was shocked to see that 'the meanest wretch, who can boast his origin from the holy stock,' enjoyed greater respect than worldly rank could bestow.[60] As well as their inherited sanctity, many Saiyids were also Waderos, a formidable combination of roles. This had been the source of strength of the Kalhoros, the dynasty who ruled Sind before the Talpurs. They claimed *Hazrat* Abbas, the Prophet's uncle, as their ancestor and had used their aura of holiness to augment their authority.[61]

The Kalhoros were responsible for bringing into Sind the Baluchis, the third of the three main Muslim groupings in the province. Baluchis formed about a fifth of the Muslim population. They first entered the country in large numbers in the eighteenth century, as soldiers of the Kalhoro princes. Among the tribes who responded to the invitation were the Talpurs. Members of this tribe seized power from the Kalhoros in 1783 and maintained their rule until the British conquest of Sind in 1843. Naturally, the Talpurs relied on their fellow-Baluchis for support. Their army was almost entirely composed of Baluchis and since military wages were normally paid in land, many of the most important landholders in Sind were Baluchi warlords. Consequently, Baluchis had an importance in Sind, even into the British period and beyond, which was out of proportion to their numbers.

Those Baluchis who settled on the alluvial plain devoted themselves to agriculture. In the process, as had happened to the Sindhi tribes before them, their tribal structure withered away and they lost much of the culture which marked them off as Baluchis, including their language. Only their tribal names distinguished them from the Sindhis among whom they lived and, like their Sindhi neighbours, they looked to local Waderos for leadership and advice rather than the tribal patriarchs. A description by a British official in 1904 of Dost Muhammad, a leading figure of the Jatoi tribe, illustrates the integration of Baluchi agriculturists into Sindhi society:

> in manner, dress, language and in every other respect he is as perfect a Sindhi as anyone can be – I think the mere fact that he belongs to a tribe which is a subdivision of the Baluch tribe does not make him a Baluch like the Chandias or other real Baluchis of Upper Sind. There are any number of Jatois, Lasharis, Kerais, Chandias, Jamalis &c scattered all over the Karachi, Hyd: & other Districts of the Province – No one would think of

> saying that these men – although belonging to Baluch tribes – are Baluchis in the same way that the Frontier Baluchis are – They have no more of that sensitiveness about honor &c which characterizes the Frontier Baluch, than any ordinary Sindhi.[62]

These remarks could be applied with equal justice to the Talpurs and other 'Sindhi' Baluchis.

The 'real' Baluchis were concentrated in the north and west of Sind where, in the early days of British rule, they were regarded as a threat to the stability of the province. This was because they enjoyed a staunchly individualistic social order with, as it were, a privatized system of justice in which every man had an obligation to take the law into his own hands. Baluchis relied on a sense of individual male honour to enforce the rule of law, with the tribe – in the form of a *jirga* or council of elders – intervening only as a last resort. This sense of honour should not be confused with personal pride. It was a social duty, and powerful pressure was put on anyone who did not conform. In 1902, two Brahui brothers killed a man from the Mochi tribe who had cut off a plait of their niece's hair. Insults connected with the hair were considered particularly gross and a jirga convened to consider the matter concluded that the brothers had no choice but to avenge the insult unless they wanted to be 'held up to universal scorn and execration by all their fellow tribes men.'[63] In another case, Dhani Bakhsh Dombki tried to resist peer group pressure to kill his wife, Bhaiti, because, although she had been unfaithful, he still loved her: but he was driven to it by the taunts of his neighbours and relations.[64]

The Baluch code, then, laid upon the individual a sometimes terrifying responsibility to enforce the law. The British judicial code, by contrast, transferred such responsibility to the state. Justice was interpreted and executed through an edifice of laws and formal legal procedures, sustained by a bureaucracy of law enforcers and administrators. Taken together, these constituted the state itself, an entity outside and above the individual. The Baluch code was not simply different: it was actually incompatible with a properly constituted judicial system. Merely by living according to their own customs, Baluchis defied the state. This was why, at the time of the British conquest, the Baluchi tribes in northern Sind recognized the authority of none of the states surrounding them, including the Talpur government which Napier had overthrown. To do so would have meant recognizing their legal systems and giving up their own. As the usurpers of a power which the Baluchis despised in any case, this left the British with no status in a large part of their territory.

It might have been possible to ignore them and leave them to their own devices but, apart from the fact that such tolerance was not in the nature of an aggressive imperial power, the Baluchis did not always keep to themselves. An individualistic approach to justice can be idiosyncratic. One man's interpretation of his honour might not be another's. Blood feuds were inevitable and if they were not checked they could escalate into threats to the general peace. In 1883 a Banglani man accidentally killed a Rind passer-by while carrying out a murder in pursuit of a blood feud. He was hanged, but the relations of the dead Rind argued that, while this atoned for the intended victim, it did not cover the unintended killing. Another death was required to close the account and meet the Baluch principle of 'a life for a life.' They therefore killed a Banglani to even the score. Unfortunately, the Banglanis did not accept this interpretation of Baluch custom. Regarding the Banglani death as one life too many, they sent an armed party into Rind territory and succeeded in killing two Rinds for the loss of one of their own men. Relations between the two tribes became so bad that there was a risk of full scale tribal war and a jirga had to intervene to arrange a compromise.[65]

Furthermore, the Baluchi tribes did not dissipate all their energies on each other. Living in hilly regions with little scope for cultivation, they had a somewhat cavalier attitude towards the more peaceable inhabitants of the fertile plains. Relying 'upon plunder as their legitimate profession,' they made continual cattle raids throughout Sind, carrying off cattle, women and anything else of value. The area around Shikarpur was especially badly affected because it was crossed by caravans from Central Asia which provided tempting targets for freebooters. At the time of the British conquest, its citizens could not venture outside the city walls in broad daylight without running the risk of a mugging.[66]

Interference with trade and agriculture struck at the revenues upon which the state treasury depended. The British could not tolerate it. As soon as Napier established his administration, he set about extending the writ of British law into the Baluchi tribal lands. He led an expedition against the Bugtis in 1845, but his most significant long-term initiative was to appoint Captain John Jacob as Superintendent of the Upper Sind Frontier. Jacob was a charismatic character whose memory is honoured by the Baluchis of Upper Sind to the present day. A Pakistani Deputy Commissioner complained in the mid-1970s that the local inhabitants still compared his own decisions, unfavourably, with those they believed Jacob, in his greater wisdom, would have adopted. The town of Khangarh, where he established his headquarters, is still known as Jacobabad, while Upper Sind Frontier has been renamed Jacobabad District. And, in a remarkable gesture to Baluch nationalism, the Pakistani government restored Jacob's grave in an attempt to win over tribal opinion during the Baluch separatist movement of the early 1970s. The new monument, resplendent in marble, has the look of a Muslim shrine, and it stands out from the rest of the graves in the British cemetery at Jacobabad. This effectively marks Jacob's posthumous naturalization as a Pakistani citizen, a fitting tribute to a man who left Britain at the age of sixteen and is remembered in his home country only by a handful of specialists.

Jacob's reputation in Pakistan derives from the eleven years he spent in Upper Sind, from 1847 until his death in 1858. He was in charge of an area which, though administratively part of Sind, was really a buffer zone between Shikarpur Collectorate and the tribal lands of Kalat State. He patrolled the Upper Sind Frontier with detachments of the Scinde Irregular Horse and used draconian measures to instil into the tribespeople 'a wholesome dread of the gallows.'[67]

However, Jacob's memory would not have survived for long, or with any respect, if his notion of order had gone no further than a rope's end. His objective was not to subdue the tribes, but to convert them into voluntarily law-abiding citizens. Agriculture was his policy instrument. Jacob recognized the stability that the discipline of cultivation imposed. Though ruthless in stamping out blood feuds and suppressing plundering expeditions, he established a policy of settling the tribespeople on the land. He did this by involving them in a collective effort to improve agricultural conditions. After restoring and extending the badly silted Begari Canal, he announced the construction of a new Desert Canal. The land irrigated from it, he declared, would be reserved for members of Baluch tribes and given to them on especially favourable terms – on condition that they first helped to dig it. The tribespeople responded enthusiastically, and Jacob was able to declare that 'Not a hand save those of the reformed Belooche Robbers has been put to the work which presents an example alike encouraging to us and them.'[68] When the lands were given out, the settlers not only had a stake in the land, but a pride in the irrigation system which they had made with their own hands. The Desert Canal also performed a strategic function. It ran close to the border and much of the land was given to people whose permanent homes were in the hills of Kalat State, on the reasonable assumption that they would not plunder their own property. Jacob's policy met with considerable success. By 1887, one of his successors considered that the settlers 'have permanently abandoned the sword for the plough share.'[69]

Nevertheless, old habits died hard, and till the end of the century the government retained the fear that the Baluchis might revert to their former lawless ways. Instability in Kalat intensified the risk. The ruler, the Khan of Kalat, was unable to impose his authority over the tribal *sardars* and from 1857 to 1876 he was engaged in a series of squabbles with them, tantamount to intermittent civil war. During this period, border raids from Baluchistan were a regular feature of Sindhi life. The perpetrators were seldom punished. One Zarur Brohi, a Kalati subject, entered British territory in 1874 and kidnapped a woman and four children. When he heard that a constable from the British police had been sent after him, he threatened to kill him and scoffed at the authority of the *Sarkar* (British government):

> What can the Surkar do? Last year the Luss Beyla wallah [a neighbouring chief] went into the Surkars territory and brought off loot by force having killed two men. What have they suffered? Nothing. And in like manner it will be with me, so I care not and have no fear.[70]

He was right. The British might appeal to the Khan of Kalat to return men like Zarur Brohi who were wanted by the police, but the Khan could not exercise power he did not have. If the police took the initiative of pursuing such people across the border, they ended up miles from base, foraging for supplies in hostile territory where they had no legal status and no more fire power than their intended prisoners. They were held in open contempt by the Kalatis, who frequently outgunned them and chased them off their land.[71] Unless they were prepared to mount full scale punitive expeditions, and risk triggering a war, the British authorities were as powerless as the Khan.

This had alarming implications for the preservation of order in Sind. The Baluchis in British territory would remain peaceful only while they were convinced that justice could be left to the government, rather than following the Baluchi way of judicial self-help. If Kalatis could rob and attack British subjects with impunity, the time would eventually come for revenge and the border would revert to anarchy. By the 1870s, there was discontent on the British side of the border. Bahawal Khan, a Baluchi living near Sehwan, where border raids were commonplace, spoke for many of his fellow Baluchis when he complained:

> times are not good when these people oppress my tribe like this. Formerly if they took a tooth from one of my people we took five teeth in return, but now under Sirkar rule we get no redress and we are not allowed to help ourselves. If we rob them and they complain they have every assistance from the Sirkar, but if they take our property nothing is done and we have to keep quiet.[72]

The problem was resolved in 1876, when Major Robert Sandeman, an officer from the Punjab, achieved the impossible. He negotiated a compromise between the Khan of Kalat and the tribal *Sardars*. They signed a treaty which made the Imperial Government the final arbiter in any future disputes. British troops were permanently quartered in Kalat to enforce the decisions and Sandeman was appointed Resident, in charge of a newly created Baluchistan Agency. In other words, although Baluchistan remained nominally independent, supreme control of its internal affairs had passed to the British government.[73]

These events had far-reaching implications for Sind. It ceased to be a frontier province, for the country over the border was practically under British administration. Offenders from Kalat could be hunted down by British officers, with British troops in reserve if necessary. Raiders into Sind were no longer certain of escaping punishment. The temptation for British subjects to make retaliatory raids diminished. The danger of border tension receded. The Sind government was able to relax its hold on the border, and in 1881 Upper Sind Frontier was put under civilian rule.[74]

Naturally, the difficulties did not disappear altogether. Jacob had allocated lands in Upper Sind Frontier on concessionary terms, as has been mentioned above, to encourage the Baluchis to settle down. In 1883, the Deputy Commissioner of Upper Sind Frontier advised that plans to bring their conditions into line with rest of Sind should be postponed. If land was seized for failure to pay land revenue, as prescribed in the Bombay Code, the tribespeople might give up their agricultural careers in disgust and revert to their more congenial plundering traditions.[75] Ten years later, the Baluchi farmers were reported still to be 'hankering after their former freedom,' complaining that 'restraint is irksome, and that the trouble and uncertainties of agriculture, as a livelihood, are distasteful.'[76] As late as 1902, fifty sabres of the Scinde Horse were needed to disarm a *lashkar* (raiding party) of Bugtis who had invaded British territory and seized lands belonging to some Jakhranis.[77] This and similar episodes confirm that the warlike instincts of the hill tribes were not far beneath the surface, and that even at the end of the nineteenth century, disturbances could flare up.

Sind's eastern border was also inhabited by independent tribes, mainly Hindu Rajputs. The chiefs of the Sodho tribe of Umarkot had enjoyed considerable autonomy under the Talpurs. They had been granted rent-free lands and had the special privilege of levying a cess on Hindu marriages. This they prized, not as a source of income, but as a symbol of their authority. The Talpurs had made these concessions because the Sodhos' desert strongholds were beyond their military reach. They had made similar concessions to Baluchi chiefs for the same reasons. After the conquest, Napier cancelled all these privileges. The Sodhos did not take this blow lying down and in 1846 the most influential chiefs, led by Rattan Sodho, rebelled. The uprising prompted a rapid British climb-down. To save Napier's face, Rattan Sodho gave himself up in 1847, but was promptly released and the chiefs had all their privileges restored.[78]

The Hindu Rajputs played no further significant role in the history of nineteenth century Sind. This was because they were isolated socially as well as geographically. The largest group of Hindus in the Sindhi desert were outcaste tribes – Bhils and Kolis – who formed a nomadic population of labourers on the cultivated lands which skirted the desert. They had no tribal or caste affinities with – and hence no loyalty towards – the Rajput Sodhos.

As to Sind 'proper,' there were no Hindu Rajputs living there in whose breasts the deeds of the Sodhos might strike a responsive chord. The Hindus of the cultivated plains had little in common with the Hindus of the desert. This made Thar and Parkar less sensitive politically than Upper Sind Frontier. Events on the Baluchi frontier could have repercussions in Sind itself. Baluchis throughout the province might feel tempted to throw off the restraints of British rule if chaos returned to the borderlands. The eastern marches were self-contained. Accordingly, when military rule was lifted from Upper Sind Frontier in 1881, it was removed from Thar and Parkar at the same time, even though nothing had happened to change the local situation.

The majority of Hindus in Sind were not Rajputs. They were Lohanos who had emigrated from the Punjab in the distant past. They may have been descended from the people also known as Lohanos who fled from Sind after the Arab conquest of 711. They were generally reckoned to belong to the Vaishya (trader) caste, although they often claimed Kshatriya (warrior) status for themselves by descent from Lar, the son of Sri Ram Chandar, the hero of the Ramayan.[79]

Whatever their caste may have been, they were heterodox in their beliefs and practices. Most were followers of Guru Nanak, and there was some doubt as to whether they should properly call themselves Hindus or Sikhs – which caused much confusion among Census enumerators.[80] They also revered many of the same shrines as the Muslims. Qalandar Lal Shahbaz was Raja Bharat-Hari to the Hindus, Shaikh Tahir was Uderolal and Zinda Pir was the river god, the focus of the Indus cult which was the most popular form of worship among them.[81] They wore the thread of the twice-born, but Brahmins were few, the *shastras* (scriptures) almost unknown, and the Lohanos had few taboos about mixing with other castes or non-Hindus, or travelling by sea. They ate meat, except for beef, and had no objections to alcohol. Their most common beast of burden was the donkey, which was regarded as unclean in Hindustan.[82] As one British visitor to Sind exclaimed, the Lohanos' neglect of caste and religion would have horrified Hindus elsewhere in India.[83]

Lohanos were divided into two groups, the *Amils* (revenue officers) and the traders, generally referred to as *banias*. 'Amil' is actually the designation of a profession but, from the mid-eighteenth century onwards, Lohano Amils had held the highest administrative offices under their Muslim rulers, and they came to form the elite of the Hindu community. In time, the professional title was used proudly to identify the upper class of Hindus. Their pre-British careers gave Amils a thick veneer of Muslim culture. They often grew beards and wore Muslim dress, although their shirts opened on the left breast, the Muslims' shirts opening on the right; and they kept the *tilak* (caste mark) on their foreheads. Amils were fluent in Persian, a language they needed for their administrative duties under the Kalhoros and Talpurs, but which many also admired for its literature since they were usually educated by Muslim teachers.[84] After the British conquest, Amils switched from Persian to English education and continued to provide most of the locally recruited government servants.

Banias were less integrated with Muslims than the Amils. They preserved their Hindu dress, most visibly the *dhoti* (loin cloth), and they were seldom familiar with Persian.[85] While Amils traditionally dominated the civil service, the banias virtually monopolized trade. They also achieved prominence – and often notoriety – as money-lenders.

Sind's trade had long been in the hands of Hindu banias. Sindhi traders were famous throughout Asia, both for the vastness of their commercial network and for the honesty of their dealings. Thomas Postans, who visited Sind before the British conquest, declared:

> It is proverbial and a great proof of the honour of the Sindhian Soucars [merchants] that their bills are always considered as cash in every part of the vast countries to the north-west and are recognized as such all over India.[86]

Charles Masson obtained an insight into their reputation for integrity when he travelled through Sind in the 1830s. He told the story of Khalik Dad, a companion of his, who sold some raisins to a bania who lived near Sehwan, accepting in payment a draft on another town. The draft, however, turned out to be worthless. After a few days, the bania arrived with the cash, apologizing and explaining that he had given a false draft because he did not have access to money at the time and he was afraid Khalik Dad would not have gone ahead with the transaction without it. At no stage had Khalik Dad been concerned since he was confident that no Sindhi bania would ever dishonour a draft.[87] No doubt this reputation for honest dealing was a key factor in the Sindhi banias' commercial success.

Shikarpur was the centre of their trade. Postans compared it to the Great Bazar at Cairo because of the variety of goods on sale and the diversity of people thronging its streets.[88] Prosperous merchants from Shikarpur were scattered all over Asia. One of the gates of Kabul was named after it. Alexander Burnes saw Shikarpuri merchants in all the towns through which he passed on his way to Bukhara in the early 1830s. The Government of India had given him a letter of credit for Rs 5,000, payable on the public treasuries of Ludhiana or Delhi. He found ten Shikarpuri houses of agency in Kabul, each willing to cash his letter for gold on the spot, or provide bills payable on places as diverse as Nijney Novgorod, Astrakhan and Bukhara. Burnes estimated that there were some 300 Hindus in Bukhara itself, mostly from Shikarpur. They were trading in English fabrics as well as such Indian goods as Dhaka muslin, Varanasi brocade and shawls.[89]

Until 1824, Shikarpur had been under Afghan rule and its prosperity had risen with the Durrani monarchy in Afghanistan. Its merchants were said to have financed the Durrani invasions of India but its fortune declined with those of the Durrani kings and the process accelerated under British rule.[90] In 1839, a British cantonment was established in the derelict town of Sukkur, and gradually Sukkur replaced Shikarpur as the economic focus of Upper Sind. The conquest of the Punjab in 1849 altered the pattern of Sind's trade by throwing open the province's markets and granaries to Sindhi

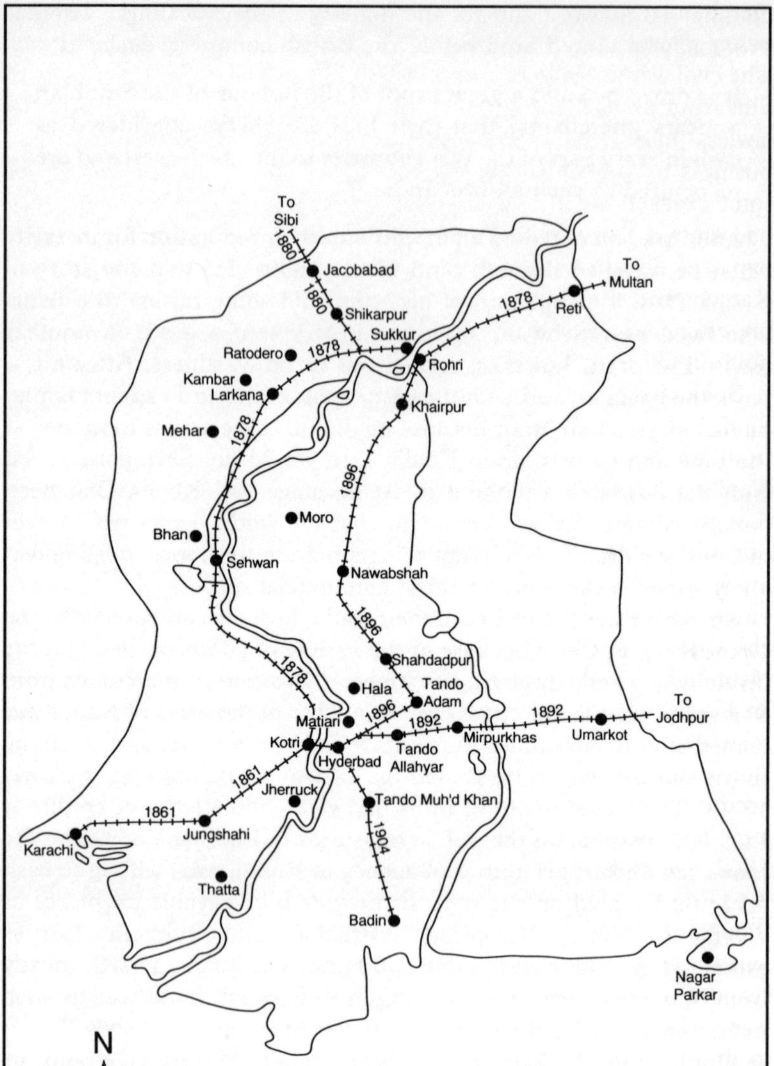

Figure 6 Principal towns in Sind, and railways, 1876

merchants. Sukkur, situated at a crossing point on the Indus, was better placed than Shikarpur to take advantage of the Punjab trade. The civil war in Kalat between 1857 and 1876 dealt a further blow to Shikarpur as its Central Asian caravans fell victim to bandits in the lawless hills. Many Shikarpuri trading houses transferred their business to Sukkur and as early as 1862, George Bease wrote with some exaggeration in *The Sind Directory* that all the trade of Shikarpur had shifted there.[91] The Indus State Railway, completed in 1878, bypassed Shikarpur altogether, making Sukkur the main link between Karachi and the Punjab (see Figure 6). This further enhanced the pre-eminence of Sukkur, although Shikarpur continued to keep its hold on the trade in silks and precious stones.

Sukkur replaced Shikarpur as the chief trading mart of Upper Sind, but the real boost to the trade of the region as a whole came from the phenomenal development of the port of Karachi. When Napier occupied Sind in 1843, it had been of little importance – though not quite as insignificant as later observers sometimes made out in the interest of telling a good story. Even at that time, it had international connections. The firm of Seth Naomal Hotchand, based in Karachi, had agents in Bombay, Kachchh, Calcutta and elsewhere before the British conquest. In 1832, the manager of Naomal's Calcutta branch bought a European ship and put it under an English master, on a salary of Rs 400 per month, and an English mate on Rs 250. The ship plied between China and Java, as well as Bombay and other parts of the Malabar coast.[92] There was accordingly a tradition of commercial enterprise in Karachi, but on a modest scale. George Bease hailed it as 'the gate of Central Asia' in 1862, declaring that it was 'likely to become to India what Liverpool is to England.'[93] These grand expectations were never quite fulfilled, though in 1878–79, Karachi did overtake Calcutta as India's premier wheat exporter and by the end of the century, it was India's fourth seaport, its volume of trade nearly equal to that of Madras. Karachi's trade figures, during a non-inflationary period, give a vivid picture of its dramatic growth. Its external trade was valued at Rs 1.2 million in 1843; by 1858 it amounted to Rs 14.2 million; and by 1901 it had reached the total of Rs 135.8 million.[94]

Karachi was essentially a clearing house for foreign trade. Its development did not reflect the economic advance of Sind itself. Industrial activity in the province was negligible. In 1907, there were only thirty-nine factories with more than fifty employees in the whole province. Thirty of these were cotton ginning, cleaning and processing plants, of which twenty-three were in the Hyderabad

Collectorate, six in Karachi and one in Thar and Parkar. The remaining factories comprised railway workshops in Karachi and Sukkur and, concentrated in Karachi, two bone-crushing mills, two metal foundries, one tin works, the government arsenal and the government printing press. There were also various small flour mills, rice-husking mills and soda water plants, all with less than fifty staff. For the rest, there were merely artisans' shops scattered over the country, providing services to their local communities – blacksmiths, carpenters, potters, jewellers and the rest.[95] What little industry existed in Sind, therefore, was largely engaged in processing agricultural products or serving the agrarian population.

The economy of Sind rested wholly on agriculture, but most of its exports were from outside the province. In 1862, wool was the chief export, to the value of nearly Rs 330,000, but the best supplies came from Afghanistan and Baluchistan, not Sind. Cotton, the second most valuable product, came mostly from the Punjab since the Sindhi variety was considered inferior.[96] By the turn of the century, wheat had replaced wool as Sind's main export, followed by cotton and oilseeds. Wool was now fourth, with hides and skins fifth. Two-thirds of the wheat and half the cotton were produced in the Punjab and the United Provinces, but Sindhi produce was starting to figure more prominently. Almost all the oilseeds were grown in the province, while most of the hides and skins were also of Sindhi origin.[97]

Between a fifth and a quarter of Sind's cultivated area was given over to wheat and oilseeds, both grown almost exclusively for export. The acreage under oilseeds increased sharply towards the end of the century (see Table 3). The cultivation of cotton and other cash crops, though, never made much headway in nineteenth century Sind. Most of the cultivated area remained under food crops to feed the people of the province. Two-thirds to three-quarters of Sind's cultivation was devoted to juari, bajri, rice and pulses, the mainstays of the Sindhi diet.

Nine-tenths of the population lived in the countryside and most did not participate in the expansion of Sind's external trade. They were only concerned with the extension of the cultivable area and the state of the internal grain market. The growth of trade, however, did have an indirect effect on the agrarian population. As merchants' profits increased, more of their capital became available for investment. Many took the opportunity to broaden their business interests by investing in land. They found an additional outlet for their resources in moneylending. The mechanical problems of bringing water to crops ensured that Sindhi agriculture required a

Table 3 Crop production in Sind 1871/72–1900/01

	1871/72		*1900/01*	
	acres	*%*	*acres*	*%*
Food crops				
Rice	529,239	26	927,002	23
Juari	509,287	25	805,634	20
Bajri	444,039	22	896,529	22
Wheat	210,605	10	451,789	11
Pulses	42,909	2	297,702	7
Total food crops	*1,736,079*	*86*	*3,378,656*	*84*
Cash crops				
Oil-seeds	120,816	6	451,789	11
Cotton	53,875	3	83,561	2
Tobacco	7,641	0	8,464	0
Sugar-cane	2,777	0	2,337	0
Total cash crops	*185,109*	*9*	*546,151*	*14*
Miscellaneous	106,192	*5*	*96,059*	2
TOTAL	**2,027,380**	**100**	**4,020,866**	**100**

Source: Reports on the Administration of the Bombay Presidency

high level of capital investment. A large number of businessmen financed the farmers who wished to bring newly available land under the plough, advancing them capital at high rates of interest. Accordingly, the expansion of agriculture was accompanied by the growth of indebtedness among agriculturists.

Some of the poorer members of the community took advantage of new land and easy credit to establish themselves as smallholders, but they found it difficult to sustain their initiatives without running further into debt. Lieutenant Fife, the architect of Sind's nineteenth century irrigation system, once compared cultivation from the inundation to 'a species of lottery.' The cultivators, he wrote:

> are successful one season and bankrupt the next. No one who sows can tell what he will reap. Too little or too much water, the supply coming too early or too late, and the blight arising from sowing at the wrong time, combine to render speculation on the result of the cultivation a riddle which none can solve.[98]

Only the wealthy could afford to play these stakes regularly and prosper. It was the Hindu banias and the Muslim Waderos who competed to take advantage of the opportunities created by the irrigational improvements of the Victorian engineers.

Within a couple of decades of the British conquest, a number of officers serving in Sind began to suspect that the Waderos were getting the worst of the competition. They were floundering in a mesh of debt and usurious interest payments. Their estates were breaking up and passing to their Hindu creditors. The Wadero was evolving off the face of the province and would soon become extinct. In a word, the traditional power structure of rural Sind was disintegrating.

The prospect of social revolution on such a scale was appalling. If the rural power structure disintegrated, it would take the colonial regime with it. The Waderos were, as Lord Cromer might have put it, the governors through whom the British governed Sind. Without them, little would remain of the local administration. The threat was, potentially, as devastating as the more straightforward challenge of overt rebellion and in some ways, with no identifiable enemy, more difficult to confront. Alarmed officials urged action to preserve the status quo. For the rest of the century, their priority was to devise a means to check the insidious decay of the institution upon which their government depended.

The next step in the investigation of the exercise of indirect rule in Sind is therefore to examine the role of the Waderos – the basis of their power, the ways in which they wielded it, and the nature of their relationship with the colonial administration. The study will then consider how realistic the fears of the British officials were, and assess the impact of the various expedients they adopted to bolster the Waderos' power.

Chapter 2

The Serfs of the Soil[1]

I

Power in the rural areas of Sind was exercised by Muslim jagirdars and big zamindars, and by Hindu banias. Between them, they shared the profits of agriculture and dominated social and economic life.

Jagirdars and zamindars were often the same people. A zamindar was a landholder. Large landholders, distinguished by the honorary title of *Wadero*, were effectively the rulers of rural Sind. Their position was founded on wealth from their estates, but there was more to it than that. First of all, it was a pre-requisite that a Wadero should be a man, not a woman. He earned his initial status through the traditional authority his family had built up over the generations, and maintained respect through his personal reputation. His power over the landless *haris* (cultivators) who worked his lands and the petty zamindars who were his neighbours was visible and immediate: a word from him would turn out a whole village to repair a *bund* (embankment) or to pursue *dacoits* (bandits).

Jagirdars had higher status than zamindars. Government had granted them a share of the land revenue, so that zamindars holding land within the area of a jagir paid tax to the jagirdar instead of the government. This could be an important source of income, but the honour was usually more significant. Many jagirdars were also zamindars, though not necessarily within their own jagirs, and in some cases the jagir was a relatively small part of their portfolio.

Banias were traders. Though many were wealthy, they were unable, as Hindus, to command the respect of the mass of the Muslim population. Their influence was less apparent than that of Waderos; they had to operate in the background. They lent money to agriculturists, receiving a share of the produce as interest. As the nineteenth century progressed, many of the great estates were mortgaged, and some sold up, to banias. Accordingly, banias competed with Waderos for the produce of the estates and, in the process, threatened the economic foundation of their power. They lent money to pettyholders as well, and even to haris. But since these people did not 'count' socially, their indebtedness did not have such critical political implications.

The great estates, then, were the pillars of the rural power structure. Jagirdars, big zamindars and banias all depended on them. Before one looks at the way in which power was exercised, and the rivalry between Waderos and banias, one should look at the origins of their wealth – the great estates, the haris and the division of the agricultural produce.

II

All landholders in Sind were known as zamindars. They held their land directly from government or a jagirdar and paid land revenue on it, without any intermediaries. The word 'zamindar' literally means 'landholder,' but it was applied in nineteenth century India to petty chiefs and superior holders rather than mere peasants or smallholders. The latter were more commonly known as *raiyats* (peasants).[2] Under this definition, only Waderos would have qualified as zamindars in Sind. This can create confusion because the term 'raiyat' was unknown in Sind and Victorian writers used 'zamindar' to cover both cases. An author who refers to 'zamindars' will always have largeholders in mind, but it may not be clear from the context whether smallholders are also covered. As Evan James, Commissioner in Sind, commented in 1896:

> The word "zamindar" . . . in Sind, when used by authors or European officers, is generally applied to the Musulman landed gentry, or holders of large estates, one or more of whom are to be found in every village . . . though it also applies nowadays to peasant proprietors who have occupancy rights side by side with them.[3]

In the present study, 'zamindar' will be used as an all-embracing term, with peasants, smallholders and largeholders specified as necessary.

The terms large and smallholders are naturally relative. In Kotri, for instance, holdings were small by Sindhi standards and 598 acres entitled Abdul Rahman Thebo to be considered the leading zamindar in the 1870s. In Larkana, by contrast, holdings were larger and the leading zamindar, Tharo Khan Lahori, had 2,210 acres in 1881. In Upper Sind Frontier, nobody with less than a thousand acres had any significance. The largest holder was Dodo Khan Bhutto in Jacobabad, who held 10,714 acres in 1885/86 and 18,102 acres by 1893/94.[4] Allowing for local variations, a reasonable general rule for Sind is to take 500 acres as the dividing line between large and smallholders. Certainly, those with under a hundred acres were very small fry. Evan James reckoned that anyone paying less than Rs 300 per year as land revenue (i.e., holding 300 acres) 'is considered a small and insignificant person,' while the Collector of Larkana believed that no-one with less than 300 acres could hope to remain solvent.[5]

Whatever their size, these estates were unwieldy and fragmented. They were not usually held by individuals, but were divided among four or five cosharers. The division was often arranged by attributing to the estate a nominal value of one rupee and dividing it into sixteen anna shares. It was a simple way of representing the different partners' interests. A partnership in Sehwan will illustrate the system. Tubjaram and Jashanmal held shares of six annas each, while Jan Muhammad held four annas, making sixteen annas or one rupee. In 1892, Khemchand bought into the partnership, by purchasing two of Jashanmal's shares. Jashanmal's commitment was reduced to four shares, while the total investment remained at sixteen shares.[6] Cosharers could not simply withdraw their money, since that would harm their partners. They had to sell or transfer their shares to someone else. The produce, profits and expenses were divided according to the interest held by each shareholder, and the estate was worked with a common stock of cattle and tools. One commentator compared the arrangement with an English joint-stock company.[7]

Sometimes all the cosharers were entered together in the Land Register as joint holders, but more commonly only one person would be recorded as the *khatedar* (registered occupant) for each Survey Number (field) and made responsible for paying land revenue on behalf of the cosharers. A khatedar was not the zamindar as such, but a partner. He or she became khatedar for convenience, to pay the land revenue. Usually, cosharers made their own arrangements for dividing their liabilities, but the Land Revenue Code did contain provisions enabling government to collect revenue directly from them if the khatedar had any difficulty.[8]

Cosharing enabled agriculturists to pool their resources. It also helped to preserve estates from breaking up through inheritance. Each heir was entitled to a portion of the property. Joint holders could all receive their rightful shares, without subdividing the property. When one speaks of 'the' zamindar, one may not mean an individual, but an undivided zamindari family.

Equally, 'an' estate, was not normally a continuous tract. Most were parcels of scattered land. As with cosharing, this was common throughout India, largely as a result of subdivision through inheritance. In Sind, where irrigation was so erratic, there may also have been a determination by those who could afford it to hedge their bets against bad inundations by spreading their holdings.

The estates of large zamindars were remarkably far-flung. Dodo Khan Bhutto and his two sons held upwards of 30,000 acres in Upper Sind in the 1880s. Their home village was in Ratodero, where they held 6,709 acres in 1882/83. In addition, they counted as great zamindars in Jacobabad, some thirty miles away, where they held 21,026 acres in 1885/86, and in Naushahro Abro, adjoining Ratodero, where they held 2,749 acres in 1894/95. During the 1870s, they bought into Larkana, where Khuda Bakhsh held 919 acres in 1881/82, a modest holding by their standards.[9] Similarly, Saiyid Ghulam Rasul Shah, one of the leading zamindars of Sehwan, held 1,714 acres in Mehar, about fifty miles away, in 1892/93, while Shah Ali Khan Dombki held 15,785 acres in Kashmore in 1894/95 and 6,957 acres in Kandhkot. Rahim Khan Khoso held only 441 acres in Sukkur in 1889/90 but 5,082 acres in Jacobabad.[10]

Even within a single taluqa, estates tended to be scattered. This is revealed by those few Settlement Reports which recorded in which *dehs* (villages) largeholders held their land. The map of taluqa Nasirabad reproduced in Figure 7 illustrates the point. There were seventeen largeholders in 1895/96 but only one, with 588 acres, held all his land in a single deh. Deh Bisharat Khuhawar contained lands belonging to four zamindars, while Gaji Khuhawar, Ahun, Jalbani, Jogi, Mangio, Phekratho and Lakho each contained the lands of three big zamindars. In six of the dehs, it was the same three zamindars, from the same tribe, who shared the land: Pahilwan Khan Khuhawar, Faiz Muhammad Khuhawar and Fateh Khan Khuhawar. Ten years earlier, Pahilwan Khan's land was confined to Jogi and Ahun, where the land was not good. He had subsequently inherited from his father, as well as taking land up on his own account. Much of his new property was on the Wicholo Canal, where the irrigation was better. Some was up to ten miles from his original holdings in Ahun and Jogi – a fair distance on poor roads. Faiz Muhammad held 1,162 acres spread over eleven dehs, in addition to 428 acres in Labdarya, a long way from the main body of his estate. His purchases included valuable land on the newly constructed Gajrot Canal in deh Kothiro.

The estate of Ali Muhammad Lakho is especially interesting. It was spread among three dehs. Potho and Khandu were adjacent and, since other Lakhos held land there, they probably contained his home estate. They were among the poorest dehs in the taluqa. The rest of his holding was in Yaru Dero, twelve miles away, which was one of the best dehs in Nasirabad.[11]

The day-to-day administration of such portfolios of land could not be carried out from the zamindars' base villages. Largeholders used to appoint *kamdars* (overseers) to the different villages to act as their representatives. Kamdars supervised the cultivation, keeping the cultivators at their work and making sure that they did not pilfer the crop. They were not zamindars' tenants or lessees, but their paid officials. In 1900, Gianchand Chandumal paid his kamdars one *kasa* per *kharar* of the total crop – one kharar was 60 kasas, a bundle equivalent to nearly 38 cubic feet in volume. This was worth Rs 123 that year. G.M. Bhurgri, twenty years later, paid his kamdars 180 to 240 rupees each per year.[12]

Most kamdars were promoted from the ranks of the cultivators, but the more prominent Waderos employed *khaskhelis* (hereditary servants). After generations in the family's service, their loyalty was guaranteed. Rukundin, khaskheli of Saiyid Pir Bakhsh Shah of Sehwan, was proud to declare in 1976 that his ancestors had migrated with the Saiyid's from Bukhara several centuries ago, and had served them faithfully ever since.[13]

Whether they were khaskhelis or promotees, few kamdars reported directly to their Waderos on the management of their farms. Waderos from good families tended to feel such practical details were beneath them. They preferred more gentlemanly pursuits like hunting and cock-fighting. Several contemporary observers alleged that their holdings were inefficiently administered and they themselves defrauded. It was sometimes claimed that such nonchalance was speeding many Waderos along the primrose path to debt and dissolution. In 1892, the Commissioner in Sind emphasized that the prosperity of the Waderos in Larkana was attributable specifically to the fact that they were beginning to manage their estates themselves instead of relying on agents. Their business-like approach made them more competitive than the other Waderos, and he felt this was sufficiently unusual to be worth mentioning in a letter to the Governor of Bombay.[14]

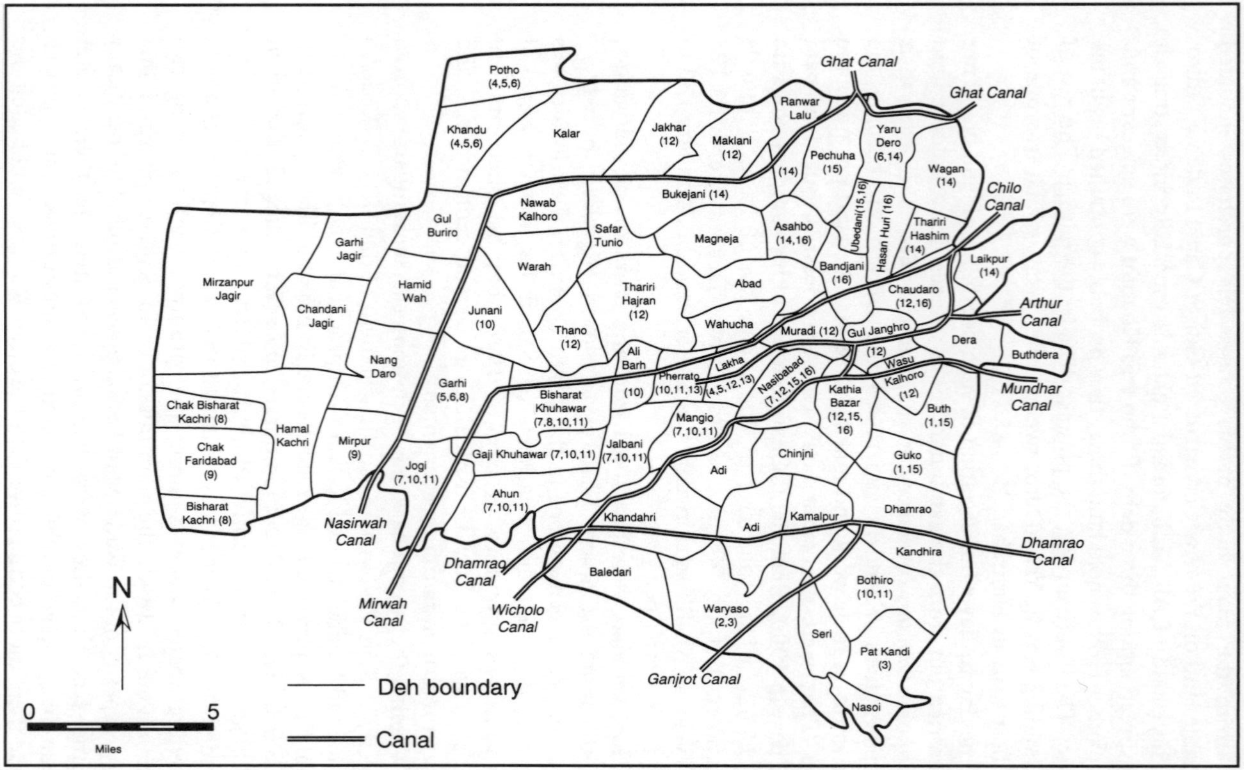

Figure 7 Largeholders in taluqa Nasirabad

Numbers on map indicate in which *dehs* their lands were situated in 1895–1896.

1. *Fateh Mohammad Junejo*
   1882–1883: 478 acres
   1895–1896: 539 acres – took up new land
2. *Allah Bakhsh Unar*
   1882–1883: Nil
   1895–1896: 588 acres – took up new land
3. *Nahi Bakhsh Suhol*
   1883–1884: 424 acres
   1895–1896: 651 acres – inherited from father and new land
4. *Abdul Baki Lakho*
   1883–1884: 367 acres
   1895–1896: 540 acres – inherited from father and new land
5. *Illahi Bakhsh Lakho*
   1883–1884: 103 acres
   1895–1896: 540 acres – took up new land
6. *Ali Mohammad Lakho*
   1883–1884: 557 acres
   1895–1896: 1,540 acres – took up new land
7. *Pahilwan Khan Khuhawar*
   1883–1884: 280 acres
   1895–1896: 1,381 acres – inherited from father and new land
8. *Pir Mohammad Khuhawar*
   1883–1884: 950 acres
   1895–1896: 1,026 acres – took up new land
9. *Gahi Khan Chandio*
   1883–1884: 896 acres
   1895–1896: 618 acres – relinquished fallow land
10. *Faiz Mohammad Khuhawar*
    1883–1884: 505 acres
    1895–1896: 1,162 acres – took up new land
11. *Fateh Ali Khuhawar*
    1883–1884: 175 acres
    1895–1896: 700 acres – inherited and took up new land
12. *Udernomal*
    1883–1884: 1,194 acres
    1895–1896: 813 acres – estate divided on father's death
13. *Sayed Khan Phulpoto*
    1887–1888: 518 acres
    1895–1896: 597 acres – inherited from father and new land
14. *Mahhub Khan Wagan*
    1887–1888: 676 acres
    1895–1896: 758 acres – took up new land
15. *Namomal*
    1887–1888: 972 acres
    1895–1896: 773 acres – estate divided on original owner's death
16. *Narumal*
    1887–1888: 402 acres
    1895–1896: 637 acres – inherited from father and new land

Source: W.S. Cole, Actg. Sup., Land Records and Agri., Sind, to Commr., Sind, 7 Aug. 1897, App. XXI (*B.N.S.* no. CCCXVIII, *Nasirabad S.R.*, 71).

Whether zamindars were looking after the properties themselves, or whether the books were being kept, or cooked, by agents, the emotional centre of an estate lay in the Wadero himself, at his home village. Kamdars and agents were nothing without his backing, and it was to his *autaq* (guest house) that cultivators and kamdars alike came for help, rewards and reprimands. No respectable Sindhi zamindar would receive non-family members into his private residence, so he entertained guests and held audience in his autaq. The size of an autaq depended on the wealth or pretensions of the Wadero. Some were fortresses which dominated the countryside, some were mansions, while others were little more than mud huts. The autaq of a particularly great man might actually cover a larger area than the village itself, the cultivators' huts huddling outside the walls like a cluster of beehives.

III

In other parts of India, great estates of this sort were rented out to tenants. In Bengal, there could be a long chain of sub-lessees between the cultivator and the zamindar. That was not the pattern in Sind. The cultivators, known as haris, held their land directly from the zamindar, and they could be thrown off it at any time. They are usually described as 'tenants-at-will,' but the literal translation of 'hari' is 'ploughman' and that gives a better idea of their status: they were more like landless labourers than tenants. They were hired by the season and did not necessarily work for the same zamindar in consecutive seasons. Though some worked the same plots for generations, others moved on as soon as the harvest was over.

The haris presented themselves for work at the beginning of each season. They were allocated fields of eight to twenty acres. They frequently took the responsibility as families rather than as individuals, pooling their labour. Usually, they had to bear all the costs of cultivation themselves. Apart from physical exertion, this meant finding the seed, manure, tools, cattle, etc. Since few haris had the money to buy these essentials, they sought help from the zamindar. He might lend them the capital himself, or arrange credit facilities for them with the local bania; or else he might give them the materials and equipment and recover the value later. Many zamindars gave their haris *taqavi* (agricultural) loans, which the haris had to pay back over a set period, or when they left the zamindar's service. The value of *taqavi* loans varied. Generally they ranged between ten to forty rupees, but loans as high as eighty to a hundred rupees were reported in Jati in 1899.[15] A hari family's first step on gaining employment was to take out a loan so that they could actually pursue their livelihood as cultivators. They then had to think about their rent.

Rent was paid at harvest time. Haris paid it in kind (the *batai* system) or in cash (the *danai*) system. The batai system, under which produce was divided between the hari and the zamindar in fixed proportions, was more common.

The batai (division of the crops) began after the haris had piled their produce into separate *kharos* where they threshed and cleaned it. A kharo was a heap of grain, protected by a thorn fence to keep out thieves. The batai was made according to rates agreed between the hari and the zamindar. If the field was irrigated by 'lift' (requiring a Persian wheel to lift the water from the canal to the land), then a good deal of labour and maintenance was necessary, as well as a team of cattle to work the wheel. The zamindar therefore took only two-fifths to a third of the produce, leaving the rest to the hari. In some places, the 'lift' rates were calculated by dividing the crop into three equal portions. The hari and the zamindar took one share each and the last went to whoever provided the cattle: it was invariably the haris, so this gave them their two-thirds share.[16] 'Flow' lands (watered by natural overflow from a canal) were less expensive to cultivate, so their crops were generally divided equally. The zamindar was always responsible for paying the government assessment.

There was a carnival atmosphere at batai because many members of the local community had an interest in the produce. In addition to the main division of the crops, a small proportion – a twelfth or a thirteenth – was set aside for the other people who had helped to make cultivation possible, such as the carpenter and blacksmith who had manufactured and repaired the implements, the *kuhungai* who scared away birds, the *surtan* who kept off swine, and the *lahayars* or reapers. The lahayars were usually the haris themselves, and many of the other odd jobs were also done by members of their families. At the same time, local pirs and any faqirs in the neighbourhood would come to the kharo for a share in return for services rendered over the year. The main batai, between the zamindar and the haris, took place after these different claims had been met.[17]

Table 4 contains some examples of nineteenth century crop division. The figures do not reveal the individual circumstances of the hari families involved, but they give an indication of the quantities of grain haris could hope to take home. Estates 1 and 2 were in the Delta region, while Estates 3 and 4 were in Sukkur. It will be noticed that the Delta zamindars took two-thirds of the crop, whereas their counterparts in Sukkur took only half. It was customary for zamindars in the Delta to retain two-thirds of the produce on 'flow' lands which elsewhere were divided equally. One explanation offered at the time was that the extra share was for the assessment.[18] If that was correct, the zamindars on these particular estates had the better side of the bargain. In both cases, the assessment on ten acres was thirty rupees: but the difference in value between the zamindar's share and the hari's was over eighty rupees.

These examples illustrate how widely haris' portions at batai could vary. Everything depended on the quality of the land and the agreements they had made with their zamindars. The land on Estate 3 was excellent and the outturn of twenty-seven maunds per acre was exceptionally high (a maund was slightly over 82 pounds). Contemporary crop experiments put the average outturn of rice per acre in Sukkur at only thirteen to seventeen maunds.[19] For every ten acres worked, a hari on this estate could expect to keep 126 maunds. The outturn on the other Sukkur farm, Estate 4, was less remarkable at eighteen maunds per acre, and the haris would only have received eighty-nine maunds. The Delta haris were the poorest. The outturns on both estates were average – seventeen maunds per acre on Estate 1, thirteen on Estate 2 – but, as a result of the unfavourable division of crops, a cultivator's share on ten acres would have amounted to forty-two maunds on Estate 1 and to a mere thirty-two and a half maunds on Estate 2. To put these figures in context, a report in 1873 stated that a family of peasants in Sukkur, consisting of ten people (two men, two women and six children) consumed sixty maunds of cereal per year – which is roughly the amount the Indian Famine Commission estimated to be necessary for a family of this size at the end of the century.[20] On this basis, the Delta families could scarcely subsist, but the Sukkur families would have had a surplus which they could feed to their animals, keep for seed or sell; the families on the wealthy Estate 3, indeed, should have had a large surplus.

However, the basic rates were not the full story. In none of these examples was any account taken of the haris' costs or expenses. Moreover, in practice, the hari seldom received the whole of his theoretical share at batai. It was cut down by debts and various deductions made by the zamindar.

One of the most important deductions was *deh kharch*, a contribution to a fund kept to meet the expenses incurred by the zamindar on village business – for example, his travelling expenses and the cost of entertaining and bribing junior government officials

Table 4 Examples of crop division in Sind

Estate No. 1: 1 acre of middle class rice land in the Indus Delta (1874)

The produce was divided into 12 shares	– Zamindar	8
	– Hari	3
	– Artisans	1

If the hari had cultivated 10 acres altogether, then:–	**Outturn Maunds**	**Value @ Rs 1-3-3 per Maund Rs**
Total outturn	**166.7**	**200-1-0**
Zamindar's shares	111	133-4-10
Hari's shares	41.6	49-15-4
Artisan's share	14	16-13-0

		Rs
Zamindar's expenses:–	Canal clearance	15-6-6
	Seed	15-6-6
	Taqavi owed to government	12-8,0
	Assessemnt	30-0-0
	Miscellaneous	5-0-0
	TOTAL	*78-4-12*
Therefore net value of zamindar's shares		*54-15-12*

Estate No. 2: 264 acres in taluqa Jati, Indus Delta (1900)

The produce was divided on the same terms as Estate No. 1

If the hari had cultivated 10 acres altogehter, then:–	**Outturn Maunds**	**Value @ Rs 2-2-3 per Maund Rs**
Total outturn	**130**	**277-15-12**
Zamindar's shares	86.7	185-6-5
Hari's shares	32.5	69-8-0
Artisans' share	10.8	23-1-7

		Rs
Zamindar's expenses:–	Canal clearance	6-2-1
	Seed	28-6-8
	Assessment	30-1-2
	TOTAL	*64-9-11*

Therefore net value of zamindar's shares 110-6-8

Estate No. 3: 10 acres of first class rice land in taluqa Sukkur (1874)

The produce was divided equally after 1 share had been deducted for the artisans:

		Outturn Maunds	Value @ 14 annas per Maund Rs
Total outturn		**266.7**	**233-5-4**
Zamindar's shares		125.8	110-1-2
Hari's shares		125.8	110-1-2
Artisan's share		15	13-3-0
			Rs
Zamindar's expenses:–	Canal clearance		5-0-0
	Taqavi owed to government		6-0-0
	Ploughing		25-0-0
	Assessment		26-9-0
	TOTAL		*57-9-0*
Therefore net value of zamindar's shares			*52-8-2*

Estate No. 4: 5.4 acres of second class rice land in in taluqa Sukkur (1874)

The produce was divided on the same terms as Estate No. 3

If the hari had cultivated 10 acres altogehter, then:–		Outturn Maunds	Value @ 14 annas per Maund Rs
Total outturn		**185**	**138-12**
Zamindar's shares		89	66-12-0
Hari's shares		89	66-12-0
Artisans' share		7	5-4-0
			Rs
Zamindar's expenses:–	Canal clearance		3-11-4
	Taqavi owed to government		4-6-5
	Plouging		12-11-10
	Assessment		27-1-5
	TOTAL		*47-13-10*
Therefore net value of zamindar's share			*18-14-4*

Sources: 1 Estates 1, 2, 4 – Settlt. Offr., 17 MAch 1874, *Papers Relating to the Revenue Survey in Sind* (Bombay, 1875), 519–21.

2 Estate 4 – Manager, Encd. Estates, Sind, 27 March 1900 (P.G.B., R.D.L., 1900 (July–Dec.), 1235).

and policemen.[21] Some zamindars also charged small zamindari fees and levied charges for the wages of their servants and kamdars. One British official condemned this as 'fleecing the haris under the excuse of "incidental expenses."'[22] Another alleged that zamindars recovered a great deal more than the expenses incurred. The average zamindar, he maintained, did not levy any fixed amount but 'takes according to the practice of his ancestors or the extent to which he thinks he can squeeze his tenants.'[23]

In addition to the formal division of produce at the harvest, demands were made on the haris throughout the year. The straw which remained after threshing, for example, was valuable fodder and haris were entitled to keep it, apart from a couple cartloads as a zamindari fee at batai: but many zamindars felt free to demand it, and also butter and milk, without payment, whenever they or their guests needed it.[24]

The hari's share was further reduced by debt. It has already been mentioned that zamindars often gave haris *taqavi* loans. These seldom covered all ongoing expenses, and so the haris required further loans throughout the season, obtaining them from the zamindar or a bania or both. The dues had to be paid at batai. According to Captain Preedy, the Collector of Karachi, in 1847, haris' debts, along with the other deductions made by the zamindar, were more than enough to swallow up their share of the grain. Consequently, part of the share was returned to the hari for subsistence and its value added to the 'already overwhelming accumulation of the debt against the unhappy wretch.' Preedy concluded that zamindars:

> under various pretences appropriate the greater part if not the whole of the produce to their own use. On the above system it is evident that the Ryot [cultivator] can never free himself from debt. The zamindar for his own interest affords him a scanty supply of food and clothing and he is nominally his tenant, but in reality the great majority of Sind Ryots are nothing more or less than serfs of the soil.[25]

Arthur Young, a Deputy Collector who conducted an investigation into the batai system a few years later, reached the same conclusion. 'The bulk of cultivators,' who had no capital 'but the labour of their hands,' were so deeply in debt to banias or their zamindars that 'their share of grain is insufficient to pay off their debts.'[26] Young revealed that several Muslim zamindars had devised an ingenious expedient for avoiding the odium of charging interest on loans given to haris.

The levy of interest was, of course, strictly prohibited by their religion. When they advanced seed to their haris, they used a 'fictitious price' to make a profit out of the deal. Young claimed that if, for example, the selling price of juari in the open market was four kasas per rupee, the zamindar supplied it at three kasas. Prices fell at harvest-time, so the hari repaid the loan at the current market rate, which might be five kasas of grain to the rupee. In this way, for every three kasas of seed which the haris borrowed they paid back five – but the value of seed repaid was the same, in rupees, as that borrowed. And so the zamindars' consciences remained untroubled.[27]

Since haris' shares at batai were insufficient to pay their debts, they required further credit to settle the current year's accounts and feed their families. This pushed the arrears of debt up still further, so the haris applied to their zamindars for extra work, such as clearing canals, carting produce, acting as beaters for *shikar* (hunting) and being supplied to the government as labour for the construction of roads, canals or bunds. Zamindars also lent haris to each other for similar tasks – the practice of pooling haris' services was known as 'wangar.'[28] Nominally, the haris worked for wages but in practice they received subsistence only, the rest being credited to their current accounts against their debts.[29]

Such forced labour, known as *begar*, was officially abolished in 1846, but the practice persisted. As late as 1918, Abdullah Umar Khan, a great zamindar, confirmed to the *Rasai* Committee that haris were still employed as begaris: 'When they have cultivated the lands and got into debt they cannot leave the lands and consequently do all sorts of jobs on which the zamindars put them. They receive no payment from the zamindars.'[30] Another Wadero informed the Committee: 'Mostly haris are servants.'[31] Muhammad Khan Pathan, also a big zamindar, explained that if a hari refused to do jobs, the zamindar was likely to take an extra share at batai, or else publicly humiliate or beat him.[32] In 1949, M. Masud, a senior government officer, wrote in a Note of Dissent to the Hari Committee Report: 'The produce of the land being insufficient to sustain him, the hari has to borrow and to labour from year to year to pay off the inextinguishable debts. Generations die in pursuit of the mirage of solvency.'[33]

Masud was writing as a Pakistani just after the end of British rule. He was clearly describing the same society which Preedy and Young had condemned a hundred years earlier and which the British administration had inherited from the previous government. The inference, confirmed by the evidence to the Rasai Committee, must be that the intervening century of foreign domination had made little difference, for good or ill, to the hari.

A trifling sum could entangle a hari in debt. That is why many zamindars preferred not to collect their *taqavi* loans until the haris left their service. The amounts might be small by the zamindars' standards but for the haris they were vast debts which put them under permanent obligation. One can appreciate this more clearly if one takes another look at the accounts in Table 4. No details are known of the agreements between zamindars and haris on Estates 1, 3 and 4, but it was recorded that the haris of Estate 2 received an initial *taqavi* loan of twenty to fifty rupees as 'a means of binding them to the estate.' It was to be repaid when they left or were dismissed.[34] It is hard to imagine haris on this estate repaying such sums. It will be recalled that, even if they managed to keep their whole share at batai to themselves, it would not have been enough to survive on and they would had to borrow in order to live: and no allowance was made in these figures for their expenses, debts or any other deductions made from their shares. If the family had renounced food and sold all their grain, the total value of their share on ten acres would have been Rs 69–10–8. A debt of twenty rupees would therefore represent more than a quarter of their total income, while fifty rupees would virtually account for an entire season's work – and, of course, this assumes they could do without food for a year. In practice, the haris on this estate would have been struggling to keep themselves alive and could hardly have considered such academic matters as the repayment of *taqavi* loans. They would have been more concerned with further borrowing to buy food. Even the relatively prosperous haris on Estate 3 would have found it difficult to repay loans on this scale. The total value of their produce was Rs 110–12–0. Assuming, which is unlikely, that they had no other debts and that the zamindar made no deductions from their share, then they might have been able to repay a taqavi loan of twenty rupees, but fifty would have hit them hard.

Leaving their zamindar and seeking employment with another was therefore an expensive business, however dissatisfied haris might be with their conditions. With impossible *taqavi* loans hanging over their heads, the threat of dismissal must have conjured up frightening visions of insolvency: if they were sacked, haris had to pay back all the outstanding debts. It is small wonder that some haris went to great lengths to prove their loyalty. It was alleged in 1896 that a hari was pressured into committing murder on behalf of his zamindar because he owed twenty rupees to the zamindar's father.[35]

It was cattle which saved haris from complete dependence on the grain allowed to them at batai. They owned their own cattle, and this enabled them to earn some money by selling milk and butter. The butter-milk they kept for themselves and this, with bread made from juari, formed their staple diet.[36] Masud went so far as to say that it was only their cattle which rescued haris from destitution.[37] Certainly, cattle products helped to keep haris above subsistence level and under the right circumstances could earn them a small degree of independence – provided they were not already indebted to the zamindar on account of money borrowed to buy the animals in the first place. The haris in Guni were reported to be particularly independent and relatively prosperous as a result of cattle breeding. A British officer claimed in 1883 that:

> probably in the whole of Sind there is no class of cultivators in such good circumstances. All own cattle – generally buffaloes, from which they gain their chief support; this makes them independent of the Zamindars, and upon the least provocation they threaten to leave and cultivate the lands of others.[38]

A few years later, the Commissioner in Sind remarked, with more than a hint of sarcasm, that the zamindars of Guni were complaining that their haris 'are a miserable lazy lot compared with those further north, and are apt to desert their employer if he presses them to work.'[39] In 1908, the haris of Guni were still said to be 'generally comfortably off according to their standard,' although the author cautioned that their standard 'is a low one.'[40] The haris of Guni were by all accounts exceptional but they confirm how important cattle could be in winning haris a degree of freedom. Freedom, though, can be two edged. Some modern zamindars refuse to take on haris if they have their own cattle because they are more likely to move on after a season or two. Instead, they insist on haris using cattle from the zamindar's own herd to work the land.[41] There is no record of this solution being adopted in the nineteenth century, but it is reasonable to suppose that, given the choice, Victorian zamindars would, like their twentieth century descendants, have preferred haris with no means of their own, rather than those who threatened to be too independent.

Moreover, it is not quite true that haris could keep all the benefit of their dairy cattle. It has been mentioned that zamindars sometimes demanded milk and butter from them. In addition, they often used the allocation of grazing rights on their land to increase their authority over their workforce.[42] Some haris, feeling that cattle breeding alone was insufficient to compensate for the privations of their lives, turned to crime. Most of the country's thriving population of cattle thieves were haris who, according to the 1926 Cattle Theft Committee, 'find a life of crime easier and more profitable than the cultivation of land in which they have no proprietary right or security of tenure.'[43] But they might not even be able to keep the fruits of crime to themselves for the Committee also established that many of their patrons were big zamindars who, besides taking a cut of the profits, employed the thieves as strong-arm men to bully the other haris.[44]

If zamindars made extortionate demands upon their haris, haris in turn regularly defrauded the zamindars by pilfering produce at batai. This was particularly prevalent on the largest estates, where the zamindar was remote and the kamdars could be bribed to turn a blind eye.[45]

Many zamindars tried to avoid the pilfering which was endemic under the batai system by adopting the danai system, whereby they gave out their lands for cash rents. They invariably favoured this system when growing valuable cash crops like oilseeds, cotton or vegetables, where the misappropriation of relatively small quantities of the harvest could prove expensive.[46] The danai system had another advantage, which led to it being applied to lands where the water supply was especially precarious: by taking a cash rent in advance, the zamindar could insure against loss if the crop failed. However bad the crop might be, the zamindar was always certain of paying the government assessment.[47]

At first sight, the zamindar appears to have had the better side of the bargain, but actually the danai system was popular with haris. When zamindars in Upper Sind Frontier wished to raise rents on lands given out under danai, they just had to threaten to revert to the batai system. This would provoke an outcry from the haris who eventually considered it a fair compromise to continue with higher rents instead.[48] Such evidence gives the lie to the assertion that the pilfering of produce by haris at the batai seriously eroded zamindars' profits. Similar claims are commonly made today and yet the batai system remains widespread in Sind even though the money economy is now universal, which was hardly the case in the nineteenth century. If it really damaged their interests, zamindars would have abolished the batai years ago.

The value of the danai system to haris was that, however high the rent might be, it was fixed, so they could calculate their profits. It saved them from 'all the petty exactions which a mean and oppressive zamindar is apt to make at the time of division.'[49] It also meant that if the outturn was high, the haris did not have to share it but could keep the benefit for themselves. In 1918, for example, the cotton crop was remarkably good in Sakrand and prices also reached record levels. The local zamindars had to endure the galling sight of their haris waxing rich while they themselves had to rest content with their usual twelve rupees per acre.[50] This is an excellent illustration of how haris, under the danai system, could make profits which, under batai, were absorbed by their zamindars. Moreover, they had nothing to lose if the crop failed since, under either system, they simply resorted to further debt for subsistence.

That is not to say that, for the hari, danai was wholly satisfactory – only that it was more satisfactory than the batai. Even under danai the zamindar claimed his perquisites. Malcolm Haig, an experienced revenue officer, quoted an example of cash rent in Kotri in 1873. Land was given out per *hurlo* (the area irrigated by a Persian wheel – usually nine acres). A typical rent, he said, was twenty-four rupees per hurlo. This amounted to about Rs 2–10–0 per acre which, since the assessment was one rupee, gave the zamindar a modest profit of Rs 1–10–0 per acre. But that was not the whole story. The zamindar also demanded three maunds of grain as *lapo* (a zamindari fee), as well as forty bundles of straw. Haig estimated the value of the grain and the straw together at eight rupees, so that the real rent per hurlo was thirty-two rupees, or about three and a half rupees per acre. In reality, then, the zamindar's profit per acre was two and a half rupees and the hari's income was reduced in proportion. Haig also quoted a zamindar with 'magnificent' lands on which he was able to charge rent of four rupees per acre. According to Haig, his share of straw alone was worth twelve rupees per acre.[51] Several decades later, in 1918, rents in Kotri were said to vary from eight to eighteen rupees per acre, plus two and a half maunds of grain as lapo and fifty bundles of straw per hurlo.[52] Zamindari fees along these lines were standard features of cash rent agreements in Sind. Additional items were sometimes inserted which sound suspiciously like the 'incidental expenses' of the batai system. Zamindars in Hala, for instance, charged an extra anna in the rupee on their rent, on the ground that they needed it to cover the Local Cess Fund levied by government. In fact, the average cess was only three annas per acre so, since rents ranged from five to fourteen rupees per acre, they were making a further two to eleven annas on every acre they let out.[53]

The danai system, then, was marginally more advantageous to haris than the batai system but, through various pretexts, the amount of produce which haris could call their own was whittled down as surely under the former as the latter. Besides, paying cash did not change their basic situation. They still needed *taqavi* loans for the seed and they had to feed and clothe their families. They could not avoid contracting the same debts as the haris who made batai. Much of their surplus crop, after paying the rent, was taken by the zamindar or a bania in satisfaction of those debts. What was more, haris did not carry cash around with them and so they had to run up an account with a bania to pay the zamindar in the first place. Sometimes they arranged to repay the bania's loan by making batai with him on much the same terms as they would have done with the zamindar.[54] Under these circumstances, the danai system hardly differed from batai, so far as the hari was concerned.

Whether they rented their lands under the batai or the danai systems, therefore, haris saw their profits syphoned off through *taqavi* loans, subsistence allowances and claims for incidental expenses. Unable to sustain themselves through the produce, they had to borrow to live. The harvest was merely the time when their accounts were updated. They were tied into a cycle of debt: they borrowed to cultivate, they borrowed to survive while they were cultivating and then, at the harvest, they borrowed again to make up the difference between their accumulated arrears and the value of the crop. At each harvest, their debt to their zamindar mounted. And, as their indebtedness increased, the haris were tied more deeply into the zamindar's service. In this way, over the generations, many haris had become, to all intents and purposes, the servants of their zamindars.

Haris had no choice but to do their zamindars' bidding, for they had no rights in the land other than those the zamindars chose to grant them. These were generally reduced to a seasonal right to retain for themselves a certain amount of the produce which they had cultivated – but, as has been seen, even this minimal concession was often modified out of existence in practice, the hari managing to retain little of his crop.

It is important to appreciate that haris' rights, such as they were, extended no further than the produce. This contrasts with tenure systems elsewhere in India, where tenants leased the property and that was the end of the matter. The landlords did not care what they did with it so long as they received their dues. That was not the position in Sind. Haris could not make use of the land in which their crops grew without the zamindar's express permission. Indeed, they could not even choose what crops to grow in it: they followed the zamindar's instructions. Arthur Young stated bluntly in 1855: 'There is no trace of anything like right of cultivation by the cultivators, or of any right except that of the zamindar.'[55] It may even be misleading to think of haris as tenants of the zamindars, although they were, and still are, officially regarded as such. Thomas Hart-Davies, Manager of Encumbered Estates in Sind, insisted in 1882 that haris 'are purely day labourers, getting a share of the produce as their pay.'[56] His opinion was echoed in 1928 by the non-official members of the Fallow Rules Committee, who were all big zamindars. They asserted that, since the earliest days of British rule in Sind, haris had been 'labourers, who were brought to work on the land by the zamindars' and who 'received, as their wages, a share of the produce from the zamindars.'[57] The implication is clear. Like the land, the crop belonged not to the haris but to the zamindar. At batai, the haris were not sharing their harvest with the zamindars to pay rent; they were receiving part of the crop by the zamindars in payment for their labour.

The best-defined tenancy rights can be overruled by powerful landlords, but the question did not arise in Sind since tenancy rights scarcely existed. Haris were 'subject to be ousted at any time, according to the caprice of the Zamindars.'[58] Sometimes they were dismissed in mid-season. One officer illustrated the tenuousness of haris' connection with the land they cultivated by remarking that zamindars engaged haris in exactly the same way as canal contractors engaged coolies. That is to say, they could be hired and fired as the zamindars pleased. He added that zamindars had no interest in the welfare of their haris unless they happened to be linked by tribal or family bonds.[59] Even if haris did work for the same zamindar over a period of years, they could not rely on being allocated the same piece of land since zamindars often rotated haris around their estates. The custom probably originated out of the practical difficulties of coping with the vagaries of the inundation, haris being sent wherever water was available, but the 1945 Tenancy Legislation Committee concluded that it had developed beyond that into a deliberate policy, to forestall any claims which might arise for rights in particular plots of land.[60] The conclusion which Masud drew in his Note of Dissent in 1949 applied to the whole of the preceding century:

> The *hari*, who has cultivated a piece of land for several generations, does not know how long he will be allowed to stay on it. Fear reigns supreme in the life of the *hari* . . . *The Zamindar might, at any time, get annoyed with him and oust him.*[61]

Naturally, there was more to it than that. The threat of expulsion hanging over the haris was useful to enforce obedience, but cultivation would have been impossible if zamindars had exercised their powers indiscriminately – in fact, civilized life itself would have become difficult. Colonel Haig in 1876 gave a more judicious account of how the system operated in practice:

> though many of them pass their lives on the same estates yet [they] possess no right of occupancy and are subject to such conditions as the landholder may from time to time find himself able to impose on them. A prudent landholder however, knows it to be for his interest to keep on good terms with his tenants, and understands the benefit of maintaining in his service a body of cultivators who have grown up on his property: hence most of these tenants-at-will have almost as secure a footing on the land they cultivate as if they enjoyed a right of occupancy.[62]

Haris could therefore hope for continuity of tenure as a concession from their zamindars, based upon the zamindars' perception of their self-interest. It was convenient and prudent to have a workforce which was ready to hand and familiar. But, at best, such a vague and one-sided arrangement cannot be dignified by the term 'tenancy right.' At worst, a hari had no protection against a capricious and imprudent zamindar who did not have an enlightened perception of his own best interests.

When one considers the inequitable division of crops at harvest-time and the insecurity of the hari's occupancy, it is not surprising that there was sometimes little love lost between haris and their zamindars. An officer confessed in 1904 that, 'as far as I can see there are no sentimental ties between the land-owners and their tenants.'[63] Another asserted that, 'the hari who serves the zamindar out of sheer necessity seldom entertains any kindly feelings for his master who tyrannizes over him in various ways.'[64] This may have been more true of the widely scattered great estates, where there was little scope for haris to acquire loyalty towards a remote zamindar whom they might never have seen. Matters may have been different on the smaller estates whose zamindars were in a position to achieve more personal working relationships. Small zamindars were said to take 'a keen interest in their holdings, and [to be] infinitely preferable to large zamindars, who are much alike, whether Muhammadan or Hindu, in their indifference to the interests of their tenants.'[65]

This state of affairs had serious economic consequences for the great estates: they were notoriously inefficient. The very power of the great zamindars retarded the development of agriculture in Sind. Not knowing how much of the crop they would be permitted to keep, haris had no incentive to swell the profits of their zamindars. They were often irresponsible and careless cultivators. In 1893, an officer attributed the 'slovenly cultivation' in Kashmore to the fact that over a third of the cultivable area had fallen into the hands of fifteen individuals. The dispossessed farmers, reduced to being haris on their lands, were not prepared to exert themselves.[66] The attitude of some haris in Kandiaro in 1909 was typical. They explained that they never bothered to put down manure because they did not know if they would be allowed to cultivate the same piece of land next year: 'Why should I put manure in another man's land?' they demanded.[67]

Insecurity of tenure, therefore, cut both ways. Haris could be ejected, but equally they could run away. Because of the low population in Sind, there was always a shortage of labour and haris could hope to find employment with someone else if they did not like their current zamindar. If they were caught, the zamindar might sue them for recovery of unpaid *taqavi* loans but many took the risk, knowing that it would be difficult to trace them once they had moved on. The Manager of Encumbered Estates, who administered the property of indebted zamindars, commented ruefully in 1882 that haris 'exhibit as I know to my cost a remarkable readiness to change masters if not treated as they think they should be.'[68] Another officer made the same point twenty years later:

> A zamindar must keep his cultivators in a good humour, or they will leave him .... These men are generally careless cultivators, and unless allowed to go their own way, they will leave their landlord, possibly without repaying his advances. The unfortunate zamindar is often fined for breach of irrigation rules by cultivators upon whom he dare not put pressure, lest they throw up their cultivation. For the same reason, he is obliged to put up with a great deal of bad cultivation of which he does not approve.[69]

This was a zamindar's eye view of the problem, and the officer came to the odd conclusion that, 'the zamindar is entirely in the hands of his *haris*.' He did not concern himself with the reasons why haris might throw up their cultivation and damage their own livelihoods. He seemed to regard it as wilful perversity. Neither did he reflect that poor cultivation was bound to hit the haris' own stomachs if they were given their rightful share of the produce. The point was, it made no difference how well the haris cultivated: they would still receive no more than their subsistence after batai.

Admittedly, some haris were nomads by choice. In the north and west, Baluch tribespeople came into Sind for the *kharif* season, returning to their villages for the cold weather; and in the east, pastoralists from the desert did some cultivation as a sideline while following their herds. Elsewhere in Sind, however, haris formed a settled population who did not uproot themselves and their families unnecessarily. They would not leave their employment of their own accord unless there was a sound reason for it. For example, they might move on to high quality lands where they could get a better reward for their labour – which did not always mean more favourable rents. In 1905, 'the somewhat cut-throat competition of the haris' for some rich sailabi lands in Hala forced up the danai rates in one deh.[70] Similarly, Bahadur Khan Khoso of Kandhkot was able to charge high batai rates (two-thirds for 'flow' and half for 'lift' lands), because he spent a great deal on improving his estates. His outturn was correspondingly high and the haris kept more produce than would have been possible on poorly maintained fields which were given out at nominally better rates.[71]

Bahadur Khan's good husbandry drew haris away from his neighbours. He had his pick of the best cultivators. Similar situations occurred on a large scale when irrigational improvements were carried out. They acted as magnets for labour, attracting haris away from less fortunate areas. When the Desert Canal was opened in 1872/73, hundreds of haris left Sukkur and Rohri where the water-supply was undependable.[72] The Desert Canal supply was so abundant that haris could pick and choose where they would work. Predictably, they went wherever they could hope for the greatest outturn from the least effort. They did not develop the region. After a few years they had overwatered and exhausted the soil and they moved on elsewhere. The same mentality was at work as those haris who did not wish to put manure into other men's land. If the land was ruined, it was the zamindar's problem, not theirs, and they could go on to pastures new. Their lack of concern laid waste formerly productive fields. Whole villages were deserted. Worst hit were Thul and Kashmore which, irrigated from the main canal, had received a particularly good water-supply. The cultivated area was reduced from 62,445 acres in 1881/82 to 37,000 acres by 1885/86.[73] By this time, new canals had been opened further north and the haris moved on, to Bahawalpur State in particular. A few years later, as the Desert Canal lands recovered, they began to make their way back again, leaving desolation behind them.[74]

A similar problem arose when the Jamrao Canal was opened in 1901. Most cultivation in Sind was conducted by 'lift,' in the kharif season only. It was laborious, costly and insecure. The greater part of the Jamrao lands, by contrast, were irrigated by direct overflow and the supply was guaranteed throughout the year. It was an enticing prospect, especially for the hari who actually had to do the work. When Evan James, the Commissioner in Sind, reported on the future colonization of the Jamrao Tract, he foresaw the danger that haris might desert the old lands and migrate to the Jamrao. He recommended that land grants and cultivation within the Tract should be strictly controlled. Eighty-five per cent of the available land was given to zamindars whose estates were in or adjacent to the Tract. Twelve of the remaining fifteen per cent was given to settlers from outside Sind, mainly peasants from the overcrowded regions of the Punjab. These were accustomed to cultivating their own land and, as Punjabis, were considered by the British authorities to be sturdy yeomen of the sort who would spurn assistance from haris. They received small, readily manageable, plots of sixteen to thirty-two acres. Only two per cent of the cultivable area was given to zamindars from other parts of Sind. They were carefully selected as reliable people who would run their farms efficiently. They had to settle in the Tract itself and they were not permitted to bring with them any haris who were already cultivating from government canals. They had to recruit their labour locally, or else bring in non-Sindhis. The remaining one per cent of the land was given on the same terms to military pensioners, capitalists and to a few men of political significance. The main political grantees included Muhammad Yakub, a Deputy Collector, and Nawab Shahbaz Khan, chief of the Bugti tribe, who had both helped to put down the Hur Rebellion of 1896, and the 'Junior' (non-royal family) Talpurs. By 1903/04, a total of 578,395 acres had been given out in the Jamrao Tract:

Table 5 Landholdings in the Jamrao Tract 1903–1904

	acres
Local landholders	482,253
Sindhi zamindars from outside the Tract	11,038
Punjabi colonists	51,992
Non-Punjabi colonists	17,353
Junior Talpurs	9,731
Military Pensioners	4,860
Others	1,168
TOTAL	**578,395**

Source: *Commr., Sind, to Govr., Bombay, 11 Dec. 1899 (P.G.B., R.D.L., 1900 (Jan.–June), 217–22, 229–33); Coln. Offr., Jamrao Canal, to Commr., 23 Aug. 1901, App. I (ibid., 1904 (July–Dec.), 2488.*

The grant rules had been framed to prevent the Jamrao from prospering at the expense of the rest of Sind. Any Jamrao zamindar found to have imported haris from elsewhere might forfeit his grant if he did not send them back. The Jamrao Colonization Officer admitted in 1901 that those haris who formed a floating population, drifting from zamindar to zamindar, could not be kept out, but he was sure the precautions taken by government would ensure that haris in adjoining areas did not desert their zamindars.[75] He was proved wrong. It was impossible to exclude Sindhi haris. From the outset, haris left the nearby Mithrao Tract, where irrigation was poor, and ran away to the Jamrao.[76] Even the Punjabi peasants succumbed to temptation when they found so many haris offering their services, and action had to be taken to stop them from taking haris on.[77]

The Jamrao Tract lured haris from all over Sind. The Indus Delta region was especially badly hit. It was, at the best of times, a poor area and Mirpur Sakro was reported in 1904 to have been reduced to 'a more wretched condition than any non-desert taluka in Sind' as a result of the malfunctioning of the Baghiar Canal. The haris, 'finding cultivation in this taluka did not afford them even a moderate livelihood, have fled across the river to Shahbandar, or gone to seek their fortunes on the banks of the Jamrao.'[78]

The emigration of haris from Mirpur Sakro was a long-standing problem which the opening of the Jamrao in 1900 exacerbated but did not create. Between 1891–1901, the population of the taluqa had increased by only six per cent (from 26,064 in 1891 to 27,600 in 1901), compared with twenty per cent over the previous decade (the population had been 21,711 in 1881). There would probably have been an actual decrease had it not been for an influx of famine-stricken refugees from Kachchh. As the labour force diminished, agriculture suffered. During the 1890s, the average cultivated area declined from 27,610 acres to 23,605 acres.[79] In the nearby taluqa of Thatta, the cultivated area was reduced from an average of 28,957 acres during 1894/1899 to 23,207 acres in 1899/1903. This, too, was said to be a result of the shortage of haris.[80]

The response of the Delta zamindars to their difficulties was instructive. Ghorabari, one of the Delta taluqas, was suffering an acute shortage of labour. Haris were leaving at such a rate that the population was actually declining. The population decreased from 34,360 in 1881 to 30,518 in 1891. By 1901, it had recovered to its level of twenty years previously, at 34,736, but this was still not enough to make up the shortfall in the workforce. Consequently, the zamindars were unable to take advantage of the good inundation which took place in 1904: they could not find the extra haris to extend cultivation. Under the circumstances, one might have expected them to attract labour by offering attractive batai rates. But they did not. The rates quoted in Ghorabari for that year were at the traditional meagre level of the Delta region – the haris kept only one quarter of the produce on 'flow' lands and half on 'lift,' with the zamindar lending seed and seeking reimbursement at batai. Instead of using the prospect of a better living to entice haris to stay, the Ghorabari zamindars resorted to punitive measures. They started to give huge *taqavi* loans, as high as a hundred rupees, to be repaid when the hari left their service. The intention was to tie the haris down with overwhelming debts. Unfortunately for the zamindars, the plan often misfired because, knowing repayment was impossible, many haris gave up hope, becoming lazy and indifferent, or else they simply took the risk and absconded. Either way, it was the zamindars who suffered in the long run, their estates losing profitability.[81]

Even when there was a chronic shortage of labour, then, market forces did not operate in favour of workpeople. This was because the law of the zamindar made short work of the law of supply and demand. The fact that the zamindars' policy was markedly unsuccessful only emphasizes the point: their power enabled them to perpetuate customs which, by discouraging their labourers, actually worked against their own best interests.

The cumulative impression of this evidence is that haris were feckless and disinterested in cultivation. Knowing that they would not get a fair share of the crop, but that the zamindars were bound to keep them alive if they were to harvest anything at all, they put the minimum effort into their work. For their part, the zamindars tried to bully haris into obedience through *taqavi* loans (which were also, in a sense, bribes) and by occasionally throwing them off the land. Only when conditions become intolerable, as in the Delta at the turn of the century, did haris try to remedy the situation – and their response was to go away and be haris elsewhere. In this way, Sind's labour shortage, rather than strengthening the position of working people, may actually have helped to weaken it by keeping alive the hope of escape. Instead of standing up to the zamindar, as they might have been obliged to do in a more crowded province, the haris could simply run away from their problem.

IV

Haris might have become more conscientious agriculturists if they had been given security of tenure, but nothing of the sort was discussed in nineteenth century Sind. For much of the century, British thinking was informed by laissez-faire principles. Administrators believed that contracts, freely entered into, were the best guarantee of justice and prosperity. The Irish Land Act of 1860 had overridden tenancy rights in Ireland by providing that relations between landlord and tenant should be governed by contract only, and there was no reason why rights denied to the Irish should be granted to Indians. Moreover, the Great Revolt of 1857 was believed to have taught the lesson that there should be no interference with the status quo.[82] This was an added incentive to leave well alone.

Towards the end of the nineteenth century, the conventional wisdom in India grew less rigid. The Famine Commission of 1880 recommended that tenants-at-will should be given greater protection, and some steps were taken in this direction in Oudh in 1886, when tenants-at-will were given a measure of security. After 1921, they were given life tenure.[83]

No similar measures were contemplated in Sind. The 1901 Famine Commission suggested that tenancy legislation would improve the condition of peasants throughout the Bombay Presidency but, after canvassing its officials, the Government of Bombay decided that no legislation was needed after all. Officials in Sind emphatically endorsed this conclusion. The consensus of opinion was that haris were already extremely well off. The Commissioner in Sind considered it would be positively harmful to interfere between zamindars and haris.[84] The Collector of Larkana expressed the classic view that the law of contract was more than adequate protection, if only the haris would take advantage of it. Because of the labour shortage:

> the tenant is generally in a better position than the landlord, and needs no protection whatever; and as a matter of fact he could make far more advantageous terms for himself than he does at present were it not for the extreme conservatism of the Mahomedan population in Sind, which induces the tenant quietly to accept the terms imposed by custom and tradition.[85]

This analysis was fine in theory, but it did not take account of the realities of the situation. If the zamindar was unwilling to alter 'the terms imposed by custom and tradition,' he could rely on rather more than the 'extreme conservatism' of the haris to maintain his position. He had the whole of the Bombay Land Revenue Code at his back. As a 'superior holder' under the Code, the zamindar was entitled to take the haris to court and force them to pay their customary rent. If a superior holder applied to a Collector for help in recovering his dues from a tenant, the Collector had to base his decision on 'the rent payable by the usage of the locality.' He had no discretion to withhold assistance for the recovery of rent which was lawfully due. Either party could appeal to a civil court against the Collector's decision but, in view of the costs involved, this was hardly an option open to the average hari. Besides, the court would have to base its verdict on the Land Revenue Code and be guided by 'the usage of the locality.'[86] The 'terms imposed by custom and tradition,' therefore, had the full weight of the British legal system behind them.

No legislation was introduced to protect haris until long after the creation of Pakistan. During the British period, only the Deccan Agriculturists Relief Act, extended to Sind in 1901, made a slight modification to the system by exempting haris from prosecution if they failed to repay their *taqavi* loans.[87] This made it less risky for haris to run away but, as the experience of the Delta shows, the risks had not deterred them in the past. In 1945, a Tenancy Legislation Committee recommended that some haris should be given limited protection: they should be granted tenancy rights if they had personally cultivated four acres of land annually for the same zamindar for ten years. There was nothing to prevent haris being evicted before they became eligible, except that the zamindar was supposed to give one year's notice (two if the hari had worked for him for six years or more). 'Protected' haris who had been given rights still would not have had full security, however. The Committee suggested that they could be evicted if, for example, the zamindar considered them to be 'inefficient' cultivators or if they did some cultivation for other zamindars.[88] Even these minimal concessions proved too much for the Sind Provincial Assembly to stomach and the Committee's proposals were never put into effect.

British administrators were remarkably averse to disturbing the relations between zamindars and haris. Though some expressed sympathy for haris, the majority viewed rural society through the Waderos' eyes. They had a degree of prejudice against the aspirations of haris. Successive generations of administrators convinced themselves that haris were prospering at zamindars' expense. The earliest reference in this vein came in a memorandum by Evan James in 1873. Haris, he said, were becoming too powerful. They were absconding from their estates and ruining their masters.[89] Thirty years later, an officer reported that the zamindar had recovered his strength, but that a few years previously, 'the zamindar was more or less at the mercy of the hari.'[90] One of his contemporaries, however, thought the danger was not yet past for he insisted that 'the party in power here is the cultivator. The zamindar is here on sufferance.'[91] A zamindar member of the 1945 Tenancy Committee complained: 'Haris today have usually the upper hand. It is rather zamindar who needs protection . . . against the haris.'[92] A Deputy Commissioner stationed in Sind said much the same thing in 1976: although zamindars had been powerful in the past, successive land reforms had eroded their position and within a few years the haris would be the power in the land.[93] This brings the wheel full circle, back to James' memorandum a century before.

There is a sameness about these comments. The hari is strong, so the zamindari system is about to collapse: but it never does. It is extraordinary that the hari, weighed down with debts, living at subsistence level, and in constant danger of dismissal, could ever be regarded as a rival to the zamindar. It is worth noting the impressions of Sir Lancelot Graham, who was appointed Governor of Sind in 1936. He confessed to the Viceroy that he could not appreciate the prevailing view of Sind officials that haris 'do not require to have any rights.' He himself believed that some form of tenancy legislation was vital, to improve haris' conditions and forestall an eventual agrarian revolt.[94]

Neither the reforms nor the revolt materialized, for Graham had underestimated the power of the Wadero. Haris had no option but to submit to the terms imposed by zamindars. That, of course, is the explanation of the partiality shown by British officers towards big zamindars. Since the local administration depended on the collaboration of Waderos, it was essential that the rural power-structure should be preserved, with them firmly at the top. These were the governors, through whom the British governed Sind. It was inevitable that administrators' sympathy should lie with them, leaving the haris in their traditional, lowly place.

Chapter 3

The Backbone of the Country[1]

I

The labours of the haris sustained the wealth, power and status of the great landed magnates of Sind, the Muslim jagirdars and big zamindars. These were the real governors of the country. In effect, they constituted the local administration. All village affairs were left to them. R.K. Pringle, the first Commissioner in Sind, commented in 1847:

> The population is not, as in India, divided into village communities each having its hereditary establishment for the management of its affairs; nor are there any hereditary district establishments; the heads of tribes and castes exercise an undefined influence among their members, and this may in some degree, though I apprehend very imperfectly, supply the want of those useful institutions which contribute so much to facilitate our revenue and police arrangements in India.[2]

The situation remained unchanged throughout the nineteenth century. In 1882, a report on *Land Tenures in Sind* emphasized that, if a village system had ever flourished in Sind, it no longer did so: 'all trace of an organization for administrative purposes, all traces of hereditary village-officers with assigned duties and remuneration, has long since passed away.'[3] These words were echoed by a Sind Commissioner in 1904:

> there is in Sind no village system . . . There are indeed few villages proper. The Deh of Sind is a revenue unit consisting generally of a cluster of hamlets rather than villages . . . There are no hereditary village officers or village servants.[4]

It was the great zamindars and jagirdars who looked after local affairs and represented local interests. Government and people relied on them to administer the countryside. Their influence was fully recognized by the British. The Government of Bombay declared in 1893 that they were 'the medium through which the administration of the province is mainly carried on outside the large towns. They are the interpreters between Government and the general body of the population.'[5] They were, in a word, the rock upon which British rule in Sind was founded.

II

Jagirdars were the senior partners. Before the British conquest, they had exercised virtually paramount power within their jagirs. Some were Baluch Sardars (chiefs) whose jagirs had been granted to buy their allegiance or, at least, discourage their enmity. Others were soldiers who had received jagirs in return for raising army units. Captain Preedy, who had been Political Agent at Karachi before the British conquest, described them as 'a fierce and turbulent body, like the Mamelukes of Egypt, formidable alike to princes and people,' who had pushed the Mirs into war with the British in 1843.[6]

Napier, the conqueror of Sind, had no intention of allowing jagirdars to retain their constitutional position. He deprived them of their legal functions, setting up a regular police force and giving magisterial powers to his own subordinates. However, he did not wish to humiliate them and risk driving them into rebellion. He regarded them as the aristocracy of Sind. He hoped that, overcoming initial resentment of their new rulers, they would in time use their influence, as country gentlemen, in favour of the British. One of his first acts as Governor of Sind was to confirm in perpetuity the jagirs of everyone who came to Karachi before 24 May 1844 to 'salaam' him as a gesture of submission.[7] It was a rash move, which he soon came to regret. As well as the great and the good whom Napier wished to encourage, the list of jagirdars included a host of officials from the defunct regime, who had been awarded jagirs in lieu of salaries. As the Collector of Hyderabad remarked, Napier had 'guaranteed to continue *pro tempore* more than half of the civil and military and some of the personal establishment of the ex-Amirs.'[8] He had confirmed, without any preliminary enquiry, no less than 1,993 *sanads* (title-deeds).[9] In the Hyderabad Collectorate alone, 170,000 acres had been alienated in jagir.[10]

The subsequent history of British jagir policy in Sind was a retreat from Napier's generous gesture. Traditionally, Indian jagirs were held at the pleasure of the ruler. When he died, all jagirs granted by him lapsed unless they were reconfirmed by his successor. By introducing the hereditary principle, Napier had transformed jagirdars into an aristocracy on the English pattern – an ornamental elite with an assured source of income and no public responsibilities unless they chose to take them up. The priority for Napier's successors was to weed out functionaries of the old regime, while making sure that people of no political value did not suffer.

Napier himself started the retreat almost as soon as he had created the problem. In 1845, he decreed that jagirs granted as remuneration for offices which no longer existed should lapse to government on the deaths of the incumbents, and that no jagir should pass to the heir without government approval.[11] Unfortunately, he neglected to lay down guidelines for deciding on jagir successions and no systematic record was kept of the terms on which sanads had been regranted.[12]

This confusion was unacceptable. When Bartle Frere became Commissioner in Sind in 1852, he decided to settle the jagir question once and for all. He appointed his deputy, Barrow Ellis, as Special Commissioner for Jagirs in 1853, with instructions to establish a permanent policy. The details of the jagir enquiry have been fully discussed by Hamida Khuhro,[13] so a summary of the outcome is sufficient in the present context.

Ellis did not complete his exhaustive investigations until 1858.[14] He established four classes of jagirs, based on the antiquity of the sanads. First-class jagirs predated the Talpur accession of 1783. Ellis reckoned that anyone whose jagir had survived so long must be sufficiently important to merit special consideration. First-class jagirs were held in perpetuity. The full area of the jagir was confirmed, and no land revenue was paid. 238,000 acres were 'alienated' under first-class jagir – that is to say, the government renounced its revenue rights on the land. This was no great sacrifice, since much of it was barren and uncultivable.[15] Fourteen first-class jagirs were confirmed, but six of them held eighty-five per cent of the area – Maliks Sardar Khan and Jehana Khan Numrio, Jam Mehr Ali Jokhio, Wadero Ghaibi Khan Chandio and Wadero Karim Dad Marri. These were tribal chiefs who held their jagirs on behalf of their tribes rather than as personal possessions. Ghaibi Khan Chandio's jagir was almost equivalent to a semi-autonomous state: he held 148,024 acres, over half the total under Class 1, all on Chandio tribal territory.[16]

Second-class jagirs were confirmed to members of the four great Talpur families (Shahdadani, Shahwani, Manikani and Khanani) and to the 'Sind Sardars,' whose sanads had been awarded between 1783 and 1810. As the former rulers, the Talpurs were a special case.

Napier had promised them greater privileges than the other jagirdars and good faith demanded that government honour his promise, although it was not clear what he had in mind. Napier had ruled that all jagirdars must 'resign' (i.e. give up) their wastelands and pay government a quarter of their revenue from jagir land as *chowth*. Ellis selected thirty-six individuals as eligible for preferential treatment. He 'resumed' (i.e. took back) their wastelands, reducing their holdings from 800,000 acres to 500,000 acres, but exempted them from payment of chowth. Their jagirs were confirmed in perpetuity to the lineal male heirs.[17]

The seventy-four Sind Sardars were a mixed bunch, of various ranks. They included fourteen less senior Talpurs, along with forty-nine Baluch notables and eleven assorted Sindhis and Saiyids.[18] In 1858, they held about 300,000 acres, but Ellis ordered each to resign all but 2,500 acres of their jagir land, reducing the total alienation to some 50,000 acres. However, Ellis did not apply the rule on chowth rigidly. This would have been an affront to the senior Sardars, but over-indulgent towards those of inferior status. He decided each case on merit.[19] Forty-five Sardars were excused payment of chowth altogether, seventeen paid at the standard rate of a quarter of the jagir revenue, two paid part of the government's normal land revenue demand and the ten least influential Sardars paid the full land revenue assessment.[20]

Ellis regarded jagirs created after 1810 as of little consequence. In that year, Sind had been divided between two Mirs, each issuing many sanads. The number multiplied after 1833, when the country was split into four, the rival Mirs bidding against each other for the loyalty of Baluch soldiers. People whose sanads dated from the first period, between 1810–1833, were third-class jagirdars. The grants were continued to the incumbents at the time of the British conquest without payment of chowth. When the incumbent died, his heir paid chowth and, on his death, the jagir lapsed back to government.[21] The conquest was dated from Napier's victory at the Battle of Miani on 17 February 1843. Those who died in the battle were regarded as the incumbents.

Finally, fourth-class jagirs had been granted between 1833 and the conquest, during the time of the four Mirs. Ellis made these into life-grants which reverted to government on the deaths of the incumbents.[22]

Ellis did not apply his rules strictly. The jagir enquiry was an exercise in politics, not equity, and the overriding concern was to protect the interests of influential families. Ellis would not deny them their privileges on technicalities. If a man's rank was sufficiently high, Ellis would upgrade his sanad even when it ought, strictly, to have been time-barred.[23] Wadero Ghaibi Khan Chandio's jagir had been granted in 1818 so he should only have been entitled to a third-class jagir. Ellis made him a first-class jagirdar for the same reason that the Talpurs had issued the sanad in the first place: he was head of the Chandio tribe, on the border with Baluchistan, and it was essential for him to be allied to the Government of Sind.[24] Similarly, the Numrios' jagirs predated the Talpur government but they had no sanads to prove it. Ellis doubted whether their Sardar could have retained any of his jagirs if normal procedures had been followed.[25] On a lower level, Saiyid Ghulam Rasul Shah of Jhangara, near Sehwan, was included on the roll of Sind Sardars in recognition of his family's influence, even though the date on his sanad qualified him for no more than a third-class jagir.[26]

Ellis studiously avoided introducing any changes into the rural power structure. He confirmed the high status of certain families and allowed others to drift into obscurity. Third and fourth-class jagirdars with zamindari interests were not seriously affected when their jagirs lapsed to government. Their incomes did not depend wholly on jagir revenues since they had farms of their own, within their jagirs or elsewhere. When Mir Jam died in 1904, his life jagir was resumed by government but his heir, Mir Ali Akbar Khan, was not reduced to penury. Mir Jam held the land within his jagir as a zamindar and so, instead of a large jagir, Ali Akbar inherited an estate of 15,594 acres, ample to safeguard his family's wealth and influence. Ali Akbar's nearest rival in taluqa Hyderabad was Saiyid Zainalabadin Shah, with a relatively paltry 778 acres.[27]

On the other hand, jagirdars who had no zamindari interests, and who lacked the means or acumen to acquire any in the meantime, lost their position: although, in line with traditional practice, the government often softened the blow by granting compassionate allowances to their immediate dependants. Ali Gohar Laghari's life jagir had been worth Rs 5,004 per year, but he had no zamindari interest. When he died in 1882, his only survivor, a daughter, was left destitute until government granted her a compassionate allowance of twelve rupees per month. Ten years later, Ali Gohar's younger brother was also given a monthly allowance of twelve rupees.[28]

Gradually, therefore, the less important jagirdars faded reasonably painlessly from the scene, leaving the men of substance in the top rank of society as first and second-class jagirdars or as Waderos. Only a ninth of the total occupied area of Sind was therefore alienated in jagir by 1900. All third and fourth-class jagirs had been resumed, while a lack of surviving male heirs had cut the number of hereditary jagirdars almost by half. Forty-seven Sind Sardars held 66,110 acres and twenty-six representatives of the four great Talpur families held 418,252 acres. The number of first-class jagirs had increased to sixteen through the creation of two new jagirdars. One was a tribal grant in Upper Sind Frontier which was treated as a first-class jagir and the other was awarded to Seth Naomal Hotchand for services rendered during the conquest of Sind.[29] First-class jagirdars held 249,266 acres altogether and no other sanads were issued.[30] Ellis' policy of reducing jagir lands to a minimum had been eminently successful.

III

Most of the jagirdars were Baluchis and the government did not redress the balance by appointing more Sindhis. The British had no use for jagirdars per se. The most important tribal chiefs, the Talpurs and the Sind Sardars had been confirmed in their jagirs, not to give them power, but in recognition of the power they already had and to prevent them from feeling aggrieved. Maintaining their privileges helped to attach them to the government, but they had no formal functions as jagirdars. Naturally, they were expected to show their appreciation of the government's generosity by supporting the administration whenever possible, but this was not a duty – although they would lose their jagir if they were actively disloyal.[31]

What the government needed was people with local influence who could assist its district officers. Jagirdars had their part to play but, for all their status, there were not many of them. Waderos supplied the deficiency. Within their domains they were no less powerful than jagirdars and in one sense they were more important: they were more numerous. In 1900, 1,741 zamindars held estates of over 500 acres each, but there were only eighty-nine jagirdars.[32] As the third and fourth-class jagirs lapsed to government, jagirdars became ever more thinly spread over the province, but almost every village had its Wadero.

Waderos held no sanads or other titles of authority. The word, 'Wadero,' was a term of respect and not the designation of an office or class. A Wadero's position depended entirely on his landed wealth, his personal status and the deference he could command from his neighbours. He might also be a jagirdar, but that hardly affected his status. Most first and second class jagirdars were Waderos in any case

– that was, indeed, one of the criteria for confirming their sanads. As to the third and fourth class jagirdars, those who were Waderos suffered no loss of standing when their jagirs lapsed, while those who were not had enjoyed no social significance in the first place.

Waderos maintained patriarchal authority over their *raj* (community) and agriculturists looked up to them as their leaders. Captain Wallace, an experienced revenue officer, commented in 1862 that, 'The Wuddera is able to exercise a most beneficial influence over the residents in his Deh.'[33] Forty years later, conditions had not changed. H.C. Mules, the Collector of Sukkur, praised Waderos in 1902 as 'the backbone of Sind.' On another occasion he explained that 'The peasant of Sind is not the class of man which . . . exists elsewhere, the "backbone" of the country, &c. The Sindhi peasant has not been accustomed to independence, and has always leaned upon the zamindars, "Waderas," and headmen.'[34]

Small zamindars were prompt to do Waderos' bidding. If bunds burst, canals were breached or floods occurred, each Wadero would bring out as many villagers as he could, set them to work, 'and by his presence and example, keeps them together, and makes them do what is required, and this frequently without payment or with only bare subsistence.'[35] A modern short story, 'The Deluge,' by Ghulam Rabbani Agro, puts flesh onto this nineteenth century quotation. Rabbani describes how a Wadero's anger is enough to terrify a peasant into helping to repair a breached bund, even though it means leaving his family to drown. No force is used, or even threatened; the peasant's instinctive dread is enough.[36] The children of peasants and haris have respect for the Wadero drummed into them at their mothers' knees, along with respect for their fathers. Some Sindhis even claim that mothers use the Wadero as a 'bogey-man,' to frighten their children into obedience. In this way, the rural population of Sind is still brought up to look to their Wadero for punishment and reward. Their deference is deep-rooted and almost unconscious. The Wadero's authority in rural Sind is so pervasive and unchallenged that it can only be compared with that of a tribal chief. It is in fact possible that, as formal tribal structures broke down when cultivation replaced pastoralism as the main occupation of Sindhi tribesmen, the latter transferred their tribal affiliations to powerful magnates, the local raj, with its mixture of tribes and families, replacing the more homogeneous tribal unit.

There were also sound practical reasons for smallholders to offer allegiance to Waderos. It cannot be explained away in terms of tradition and personality. Employing hundreds of haris on their vast estates, Waderos had the resources to turn out labour to construct and maintain irrigational works which were beyond the capacity of smallholders. Manual labour was a valuable commodity, supplementing the wealth represented by cash, land and crops. Smallholders looked to the Wadero to safeguard agricultural production.

Moreover, as a fertile frontier area, Sind had always been a source of plunder to aggressive nomads from the surrounding deserts of Baluchistan and Rajasthan. It was inevitable that agriculturists should come to rely on strong families who could protect them against the raiders. The Wadero's workforce provided security for himself and his neighbours. Throughout the nineteenth century, and up to the present day, cattle lifting was a regular industry in Sind and the haris could be used to track down or drive off cattle thieves and dacoits. Some Waderos were even in league with cattle thieves among their own haris. The Cattle Theft Committee stated bluntly in 1926 that a number of Waderos:

> think their prestige is enhanced by the influence they are able to exert upon badmashes [thugs], and feel obliged to keep a few thieves among their followers for the purpose of harassing a neighbour in the event of a quarrel.[37]

Similar accusations have been made by officials in Sind before and after that report.[38] It may not be too fanciful to suggest that, because protection was needed against the thieves, some harassed their weaker neighbours to remind them how indispensable it was to be well protected.

Smallholders and peasants were not comparable with haris. They were not employees or tenants of Waderos, nor were they dependent on them financially, but they had to keep in their good books. It was not just a question of being physically protected or harassed. The Wadero was, in every way, the focus of rural life. The village mosque was almost certainly built with the Wadero's money and the imam and mullah were his pensioners. Any education the villagers could hope for was given by the mullah. The Wadero presided over important religious festivals and social occasions, providing food and entertainment for the villagers. Cock fights, the national sport of Sind, could be held in his *autaq* (guest house), the only place where large numbers of people could conveniently gather to watch, gamble and organize the day's play – since cock fighting is now illegal, this facility is even more highly prized today, the Wadero's compound being a secluded spot where the police are unlikely to interfere. The Wadero could also arrange wrestling matches and other contests between villages and could invite strolling players and musicians to entertain his raj at his own expense. In modern Sind, some Waderos act as local cinemas, showing the villagers videos of Pakistani and Indian films in their autaqs.

These reveal the lighter side of a Wadero's duties and responsibilities. More seriously, agriculturists required his assistance with the many problems which arose in their lives. Someone whose cattle had been stolen would seek the Wadero's help to trace and recover them. A family might want the Wadero to stand surety for them when they borrowed from a bania, or to intercede on their behalf if the bania was threatening to foreclose on a mortgage. If any dispute arose with the revenue authorities, the Wadero might petition government on behalf of the local landholders. Agriculturists squabbling over women or water might appeal to their Wadero for arbitration. This would be particularly important if the disputants were under the protection of different Waderos, for smallholders could not address themselves directly to so lofty a personage as a strange Wadero. They had to ask their own Wadero to approach the neighbour for them. If there was a gap in status between the Waderos themselves then the junior one, in his turn, might have to seek a reference from a senior Wadero, jagirdar or Pir.

An example from contemporary Sind will help to illustrate how Waderos acted, and act still, on behalf of their raj. The episode, a routine incident in the life of the rural community, took place in 1977 while I was staying with a prominent Wadero on his village lands. Cattle, stolen from some petty holders of the Wadero's raj, had been traced to the house of a man owing allegiance to a neighbouring Wadero. Following the custom of the twentieth as well as the nineteenth century, the animals had duly been ransomed back by the rightful owner. This should have ended the matter but some bitterness remained because the offender's father had been a follower of my host and the latter felt the thief had added insult to injury by leaving his raj and then stealing from his former associates. My host therefore made his anger known in ways that were never explained to me. Whatever the details, the technique was effective. In desperation, the culprit and two other petty zamindars implicated with him appealed to their own Wadero to intercede on their behalf. And so it happened that the neighbour arrived at my host's autaq one evening, with his three protégés in his wake. There followed a fairly tense half-hour. The two Waderos sat on chairs on the verandah. The petty men sat on a mat, a little distance away, looking distinctly uncomfortable. With my ambiguous status, I merited a chair, but was placed apart from the rest of the gathering. Various servants and retainers sat on the ground, beyond the verandah. All those on the verandah were served tea and snacks. The Waderos chatted for a while before coming to the point. After ticking the three men off, rather like a slightly amused headmaster, my host assured them that he harboured no grudge. Their relief was visible. They burst into smiles and thanked him profusely. Soon after, the whole party left, well satisfied. My host told me his anger had partly been intended as a warning to other would-be defectors. It demonstrated that they needed his good will, even if they joined a neighbour's raj. It also gave notice to cattle thieves that he would not tolerate harm to families under his protection.

Two points are worth noting. One is that my host had gone to some lengths to avenge the petty holder whose cattle had been stolen. He would not have done this unless the person in question was widely known to be faithful. The object of the exercise was, after all, to demonstrate the practical value of loyalty. The second point is that the three culprits must also have paid conspicuous homage to their own Wadero since they had, when one considers it, put him to a good deal of trouble: he had to make the effort to see a neighbour whom he did not normally visit socially and, however much he tried to laugh it off over sips of tea, he had been obliged to ask a favour. It was an awkward position to ask him to put himself in. A smallholder could expect this kind of help from a Wadero only if he remained steadfast. This involved a host of social obligations, such as attending the marriages and funerals of the Wadero's family and paying courtesy calls on him. Carrying out various jobs for the Wadero – like mending a bund – was another way of earning his good opinion. In addition, smallholders gave him small gifts, like milk, *ghee* (clarified butter) and honey. Some smallholders maintained regular funds to remunerate their Waderos. It was not that the Wadero needed these gifts. They were symbolic, tokens of respect.[39]

For haris and smallholders, Waderos were the real power in the land. The British authority, with its police and lawcourts, was remote, spiritually and also physically – the nearest police station might be several miles away: a long and tiring journey on poor roads, with little certainty of justice at the end of it. In the late twentieth century, the Wadero's importance in this respect has perhaps increased, his jeep often being the most effective way of reaching a hospital in an emergency – or a polling station in an election.

Rather than waste time trudging to the office of an unknown policeman, a hari or petty zamindar – now as a hundred years – ago was even more likely to turn to the familiar Wadero in times of trouble. In 1893, a hari named Budho found his brother, Nawaz, dying after being hit during a quarrel. Budho went straight to the village of Wadero Tharo Khan Lahori and told him what had happened. Only after reporting to the Wadero did Budho go on to Larkana and inform the police. The most significant point is that the murder did not take place in an isolated area, but on the outskirts of a large town. The Lahoris' village was only a mile or so from the Deputy Collector's office, so the nearest police station was quite accessible. Moreover, Tharo Khan's son had already investigated the background. While making his rounds that morning, he had come across Nawaz lying on the ground and heard the whole story from him. He then found the attacker and demanded an explanation. He took no further action because he had not realized how serious the injury was; Nawaz' liver had been ruptured, so there was no external bleeding.[40] Not only, then, did the Wadero hear of the murder before the police, but his son had already looked into it as part of his normal duties. If it had been a simple assault rather than murder, the Wadero would probably have sorted it without involving the police.

Many cases are on record in which Waderos and jagirdars acted as the de facto civil authorities. A remarkable one happened on the night of 29 December 1889. A gang of dacoits broke into the houses of two wealthy families in a village in taluqa Tando Allahyar, wounding six people. Wadero Allah Bakhsh, who lived nearby, was told about the burglary while it was still in progress. He set out at once with about thirty armed men but arrived too late. The dacoits had escaped. As the villagers were frightened, he took control. He sent men in different directions to warn the neighbourhood and arranged for the care of the wounded. Fateh Khan Khokhar, a jagirdar, responded to his call and brought some of his followers. At daybreak, Allah Bakhsh, Fateh Khan and their men rode off after the dacoits and captured several of them. This all happened before the police put in an appearance. The whole operation was organized by the Wadero and the jagirdar. Indeed, when the police finally arrived, they found it difficult to get any useful information out of the terrified villagers and had to rely on evidence gathered by Allah Bakhsh.[41]

The only role of the police, therefore, was to collect the prisoners brought in by Allah Bakhsh and write up the evidence he had collected. The Wadero had turned out a large body of armed men, at no notice, in the middle of the night and had rounded up members of a gang of violent criminals. This was the reality of Waderos' local influence. Allah Bakhsh must have cut a more impressive figure among the local people than the police officers who turned up after the action was over. The outlook was bleak for anyone who was, in Wadero Allah Bakhsh's eyes, a wrongdoer.

The significance of this last inference is reinforced by an incident in Upper Sind Frontier District in 1896. A boy named Safar was raped while tending cattle. He told his family that the assault had been carried out by someone from the village of Wadero Tajo Khan. The family complained to the Wadero who promptly ordered his men to turn out all the villagers for an identity parade. Safar picked out Piru and Tajo Khan sent his people to investigate the scene of the crime. They found signs of a struggle, along with drops of dried blood and semen, all of which confirmed Safar's story. They also identified Piru's tracks. Tajo Khan advised the boy's family to go to the police, who naturally proceeded to work up a case against Piru.

Later, however, Tajo Khan had second thoughts. He told H.C. Mules, Deputy Commissioner of Upper Sind Frontier, that the true culprit was Piru's brother, Ditto. This was good enough for Mules and he ordered the police to drop the charges. The police objected. They alleged that Tajo Khan was shielding Piru, but Mules overruled them. Tajo Khan was 'an old and reliable zamindar of the highest respectability' who could have no motive for helping one brother at the expense of the other. Mules condemned the police criticisms as an attempt to discredit the Wadero. He conceded, though, that the case could not be tried in a regular court where the laws of evidence would be applied with inconvenient strictness, so he sent it before a council of elders. They understood the weight which should be attached to Tajo Khan's statement and duly convicted Ditto.[42]

The police, quite literally, do not figure at all in this scene of law enforcement in British Sind. They were no more than a faint voice offstage. The crime was reported to the Wadero. He investigated it, discovered a suspect and supervised the detective work. The police came in at the end to rubber-stamp his efforts. The entire body of evidence was then set aside at the instigation of the very Wadero who had set it up, as a result of uncorroborated hearsay evidence produced by him. When the police attempted to protest, the British district officer removed the case from their jurisdiction and put it before an Assembly of Waderos presided over by himself. The lesson was simple: the police were all but irrelevant; agriculturists should take heed of their Waderos when it came to law and order.

These cases indicate that a Wadero's word was enough to bring a person to court. An unscrupulous Wadero could have people charged almost at whim. In 1891, Ghulam Mangrio claimed that he had been seized by the police who, instead of taking him to the police station, brought him to the autaq of Saiyid Murid Shah, a local jagirdar. Ghulam Mangrio said the Saiyid had him hanged by the hair until he agreed to pay Rs 200 for his release. Colonel Mayhew, the Collector of Shikarpur, ordered an enquiry but it was inconclusive. Mayhew believed this was because the local people were too frightened of the Saiyid to give evidence against him. He declared angrily: 'The Police were the servants of this Troublesome Jaghirdar and Disturber of the Public Peace.'[43]

It followed that a person whom a Wadero wished to shield was safe from justice, while Waderos themselves were virtually above the law. Since the police relied on the Waderos' help to find criminals, there was little they could do if a Wadero himself was implicated. This was certainly Colonel Mayhew's belief and, a few years after the controversy over Saiyid Murid Shah, he had to deal with an even more dramatic episode.

On 1 November 1896, Wadero Ghulam Murtaza Bhutto visited Jeramdas Dharamdas, the Mukhtiarkar of Ratodero. Jeramdas was known to be preparing a report against Ghulam Murtaza for Mayhew. The Wadero may have been hoping to persuade him to change his mind. Jeramdas refused to see him immediately. He made Ghulam Murtaza wait outside in the sun for an hour or so, then granted him only a short interview. It was a great dishonour for a Wadero to be treated so shabbily and a witness claimed to have heard Ghulam Murtaza say that the Mukhtiarkar 'gives me no proper respect. I shall "see" him.'

The following morning, Jeramdas was found murdered in his bed. It was reported that a hari employed by the Wadero's father, Khuda Bakhsh Bhutto, had been seen near the house where the Mukhtiarkar was staying, along with a khaskheli (hereditary servant) of Ghulam Murtaza. Ghulam Murtaza was charged with instigating the murder. He was refused bail and remanded in custody. However, the evidence was circumstantial and the Wadero was acquitted after the trial.[44]

The acquittal occurred despite strenuous efforts by Colonel Mayhew to secure a conviction. Mayhew had no doubt of Ghulam Murtaza's guilt. He assured the Commissioner in Sind that Jeramdas had fallen victim to the Wadero because of his efforts:

> to bring this man Ghulam Murtaza Khudabux Bhuto to his senses and to make him mend his wicked and dissolute and infamous ways and to give up his evil practices which are dishonest and criminal – so has brought down upon him without question the wrath or revenge of this powerful rascal.[45]

Ghulam Murtaza was a wealthy man with estates in the Shikarpur and Upper Sind Frontier Districts. His grandfather, 'the legendary Dodo Khan Bhutto,'[46] was one of the most important zamindars in Sind – 'and the family one and all have for years been notorious for their influence for Evil,' according to Mayhew. The Commissioner in Sind was convinced and persuaded the Bombay Government to offer a reward of Rs 1,000 for information leading to the arrest and conviction of the murderers or instigators. The murder, the Commissioner explained to the Governor of Bombay, had terrified the local officials and he warned that Ghulam Murtaza 'is well-known to have instigated other murderous attacks if not murders.'[47] Only the previous year, a man had accused Waderos Rasul Bakhsh and Ghulam Murtaza Bhutto of complicity in the murder of his brother.[48]

Rs 1,000 was an enormous amount of money in nineteenth century Sind, but no witnesses came forward and the case collapsed. This represented a shattering blow to British prestige. The government could not afford to take on so formidable an opponent as Ghulam Murtaza Bhutto and lose. Mayhew was furious. He demanded that the Frontier Regulations should be extended to Shikarpur District so that suspects could be convicted on circumstantial evidence. The ordinary courts could not cope with cases of this sort, involving an influential Wadero, because of their pedantic approach to the rules of evidence – they required corroboration of the facts. The normal process of law should be suspended and extraordinary courts established. If the Frontier Regulations had been in force, said Mayhew, Ghulam Murtaza and the other Bhuttos would have been behind bars. He declared angrily that it was 'the talk of the Bazaar that this is the 13th murder these Bhuttos have perpetrated and got off scot free.'[49] The Commissioner in Sind sympathized but warned that the Governor of Bombay could not justify introducing Frontier Regulations into a non-Frontier district.[50] Presumably, wreaking revenge on the Bhuttos would not constitute justification for such a policy departure.

There is a striking ferocity about Mayhew's account of this episode. This may partly have been his individual style. His signature at the foot of documents suggests a choleric nature – in green ink, the letters boldly formed, it is stamped at a sharp, angry angle across the page.

However, in *Daughter of the East*, Benazir Bhutto suggests a more personal motive for Mayhew's dislike of Ghulam Murtaza, her great-grandfather. According to her, Ghulam Murtaza had fallen in love with an English woman. Appalled by this violation of the racial code,

Mayhew tried to warn him off and eventually threatened to flog him: but Ghulam Murtaza caught the whip and thrashed the Colonel instead. He fled to Bahawalpur, followed by the English woman, who was killed during a skirmish with the police. The British declared Ghulam Murtaza an absconder and auctioned his possessions, but later agreed to allow him back to Sind.[51]

This story is implausible when set against the deafening silence of the contemporary record. Mayhew's personal antagonism towards Bhutto was clear, but his colleagues betrayed no more than a degree of irritation. That would not have been the case if he had been implicated in the dishonouring, abduction and killing of a white woman. It would have been a burning scandal. It could not have been hushed up. The righteous rage of the English would have blazed through every passing reference to Ghulam Murtaza.

Stanley Wolpert, in *Zulfi Bhutto of Pakistan*, gives a more convincing account, derived from the papers of Sir Shah Nawaz Bhutto, Ghulam Murtaza's son.[52] According to Shah Nawaz, the woman was Mayhew's Sindhi mistress, who left him for Ghulam Murtaza. This rings more true because it would explain the more measured response of the other British officials. Mayhew would have had to keep his native mistress secret if he wished to preserve his job and his pension: so his colleagues would have known nothing of the murky undercurrents of his vendetta against the Bhuttos.

Nevertheless, whatever his personal motives, there were sound political reasons for Mayhew's alarm over Ghulam Murtaza's acquittal. Imperial authority depended to a large extent on fostering an illusion of effortless invincibility to deter any challenge from even being considered. By throwing the weight of the administration behind the prosecution, Mayhew had ensured that the trial would be viewed as a contest between himself and the Wadero – a contest which the Wadero, clearly, won. There could be only two interpretations of the outcome: the government had hounded an innocent man and failed to crush him; or else Ghulam Murtaza had got away with the murder of a senior government officer. Either way, the government seemed impotent. It was the writ of the Bhuttos which ran in the Ratodero region, not the writ of the British administration.

In the end, according to Wolpert, Mayhew had Ghulam Murtaza's house burned to the ground. The shock killed his father, Khuda Bakhsh, and Ghulam Murtaza himself was eventually poisoned. That may have satisfied Mayhew's desire for revenge, but it hardly amounted to a reassertion of imperial authority. There is none of the olympian detachment of the British Raj about it. It smacks more of gang warfare. The sense of the administration losing its grip, and losing its face, is reinforced by an episode which took place the year after Ghulam Murtaza's acquittal. While Mayhew was in camp at Kambar, four of his clerks were robbed and a bania waylaid within sight of his camp. These were not ordinary crimes, explained Mayhew. They had been organized by the Waderos to insult him and proclaim that government was helpless. The Waderos could do as they pleased, right under Mayhew's nose, without fear of detection or punishment. This was an extraordinary admission of inadequacy from a representative of the imperial government. It might be fanciful to detect personal dislike behind the incident, a desire by the Waderos to teach a lesson to a discredited official who had lost his *izzat* (prestige) through his persecution of the Bhuttos, but if they intended to humiliate Mayhew, they succeeded. The Waderos of Kambar were, blustered Mayhew, 'the instigators of thefts and harbourers of thieves and scoundrels of every sort and description.' He added that the police did as the Waderos bid, and the people feared the Waderos more than the government. Anyone, said Mayhew, who testified against the Waderos or their 'parasites' would suffer sooner or later – a man's house might be broken into or set on fire; his cattle might be stolen; his crops might be burned; or his wives' or daughters' heads might be shaved. Nobody dared to come forward and give evidence against them. The government, confessed Mayhew, was virtually powerless.[53]

It was true that the government could not do much about such people. In 1884, the Collector of Hyderabad received evidence which convinced him that two Saiyids were instigating most of the criminal activity around Matiari. No witnesses were prepared to give evidence, so it was futile to initiate criminal proceedings against them but the Collector felt they should at least be asked to resign from the local Municipal Board. Even this seemed unwise to the Commissioner in Sind, who pointed out that it would be impossible to enforce the demand if they refused, and the government would lose face. The strongest action he could suggest was to strip them of their government honours.[54]

Mayhew resorted to a similar stratagem to confront the Waderos of Kambar. He instructed his officials not to accept hospitality from those suspected of disrupting his camp. The prestige of Waderos was boosted when British officers joined them as guests for a shooting party or were given presents of game or sheep. If officers refused such tokens, it was a mark of disfavour which would damage the Waderos' standing.[55] In effect, he was telling his subordinates to cold-shoulder recalcitrant Waderos.

At the same time, Mayhew issued a general reminder to his Deputy Collectors that they should not accept invitations from Waderos indiscriminately. Many officers, he complained, kept on good terms with Waderos who had been deprived of their honours by government, even if they were known criminals.[56] This was a remarkable admission. It was hardly worth the trouble of disgracing Waderos in the first place if British officers persisted in fraternizing with them. Since Sind was excellent hunting country, the hospitable Waderos presumably knew how to keep sporting British officers content. Moreover, Waderos were essential to the administration and officers had little choice but to maintain diplomatic contacts in the hope of encouraging their co-operation, even if they disapproved of them.

The Waderos' influence therefore affected both high and low. Deputy Collectors were susceptible to it, while haris were at their mercy. Government could not always guarantee the safety of its own officers and yet it relied on Waderos for the administration of the country. It is small wonder that smallholders and peasants obeyed the Waderos without question, looking up to them as their leaders.

IV

Since Waderos' power depended on their own wealth and prestige, they had no need of government support. A jagirdar who misbehaved could in theory be threatened with the loss of his jagir, even if the threat was rarely translated into action. In 1869, Khairo Khan Karmati, of Mirpur Sakro, was deprived of half of his jagir after an enquiry concluded that he had blocked police investigations into a murder. However, since the government was reluctant to take such extreme action against one of its leading citizens, the jagir was restored only three years later, with a warning that he could not expect similar leniency in the future.[57] No such action could be contemplated against a Wadero. So long as he paid his land revenue, he could not legally be thrown off his estate. Government had no hold over Waderos. Nevertheless, their need to maintain their prestige could make them vulnerable to pressure on occasions. If Waderos lost face when they were snubbed by government officials, their standing was increased when they were honoured. By the end of the nineteenth century, the Sind government had developed a remarkably effective system of bribing Waderos with honours to secure their cooperation.

Waderos' preoccupation with prestige was not mere vanity. It was of practical importance because it helped to determine the extent of their influence. Each Wadero had to compete with his neighbours for the allegiance of the great mass of smallholders. He had to impress upon the lesser folk that he was a powerful and formidable person, so that they would join his raj rather than his rivals'.

The smallholders would give their loyalty to the man for whom they had most respect, and they would respect the man whose *izzat*, or prestige, was greatest. Izzat remains to this day a critical part of life throughout Pakistan and northern India. Maintaining izzat is a driving motivation for vast numbers of people, from all communities and classes and in every walk of life. Many will go to great lengths to avoid the shame of losing face. Izzat was once defined as 'consideration in the eyes of one's neighbours.'[58] In the case of a Sindhi Wadero, it boiled down to 'looking the part.' A large estate and plenty of retainers were prerequisites, but less tangible aspects were almost as important, to provide the trappings of power. Lavish entertainments and the ostentatious provision of charity to faqirs, beggars and hangers-on gave a display of wealth and hinted at greatness of soul. Hunting parties, with multitudes of haris acting as beaters, further testified to a Wadero's prosperity, besides demonstrating his power over men. A modern zamindar compared a Wadero's prestige to a balloon: one pinprick, and it would burst. He explained that if a Wadero was summoned by a local officer and made to wait all day, or if he was made to sit on the ground in the presence of an officer, then his izzat would be destroyed. The bubble would burst. People would realize he was not such a great man as he claimed and they might resist his authority. Smallholders would desert him and transfer their allegiance to a rival. He would lose their services and gifts, and he might find himself being harassed by more powerful Waderos. He might even have difficulty collecting his share of the crop from his haris at batai. The only way to avoid these dire consequences would be to put on a show of force to emphasize that he was still as strong as ever. Mayhew's case against Ghulam Murtaza Bhutto in 1896 had been constructed on an understanding of these imperatives. The allegation had been that Bhutto murdered the Mukhtiarkar as revenge for being made to sit in the sun. This would have been a profound and potentially dangerous humiliation. It was not just a matter of injured pride. Izzat was vital for the survival of any Wadero. Bhutto's acquittal did not invalidate the credibility of the motive attributed to him.

Many Waderos felt their izzat was enhanced if they collaborated with government and were rewarded for it. A man loaded with honours would appear to have the ear of senior officials: it might be dangerous to cross him and advantageous to be on good terms with him. There was certainly some truth in this. When Wadero Tajo Khan changed his mind about the guilt of the man accused of raping the boy in 1896, the Deputy Commissioner had accepted his testimony on the ground that he was a 'respectable' zamindar (see above, page 93) – and one of the ways he measured respectability was by looking at Tajo Khan's past record of cooperation. Tajo Khan, then, really did have the ear of the highest official in the District, and could influence him in a spectacular way. One can understand why, as one officer put it contemptuously in 1854, Waderos displayed 'an almost ridiculous anxiety' over favours from government.[59] There was in fact nothing ridiculous about it. Honours were proof of government trust and, like the knighthoods coveted by British officials, they carried tangible benefits with them. The honours most highly prized by Waderos included swords, *lungis* (strips of cloth worn over the shoulders like a scarf), gun licences, seats in darbars, *afrinamas* (letters formally acknowledging services rendered) and small grants of rent-free land (*seri* and *mamuli* grants).

An honour the government was able to manipulate most effectively concerned the right to be seated in the presence of a British officer. It was loosely referred to as a 'chair' and recipients were known as 'kursi nishin' zamindars or 'chairholders.' A chair was a high distinction. Three zamindars who had been recommended for rewards in 1889 lobbied for chairs, but the Commissioner in Sind considered they not sufficiently important and gave them lungis in open darbar instead.[60] A lungi indicated that a man had once performed a valuable service: but a chair proved that government regarded him as valuable in himself. It was an even greater honour to be on a Collector's darbari list or – better – the Commissioner's. This guaranteed invitations to official darbars: a mark of real distinction. An additional complexity was that some people could sit while others had to stand. And somebody who merited a chair at the local Collector's darbar might have to stand in the company of the truly great and good at the Commissioner's. Such subtle refinements transformed an apparently straightforward function into a battlefield of protocol and status. It must have had instant appeal for colonial officers brought up in the feudal atmosphere of English public schools, where minute gradations of seniority could make all the difference between privilege and degradation. Most British administrators played the honours system perfectly, through sheer instinct. After all, it also reflected the arcane social rituals, observed by themselves and their wives, through which the hierarchy of Anglo-Indian society was enforced.

A chair, a position on a darbari list, or a gun licence was not a permanent right. They were held at the pleasure of the Commissioner in Sind. They accordingly carried with them a degree of responsibility. A man had to prove he remained worthy of the government's good opinion. This gave the government a handle on Waderos: a privilege could be withdrawn if the holder misbehaved. The evidence of witnesses before the 1917 Rasai Committee confirms the value Waderos attached to these honours. When asked about their positions, many mentioned that they were Honorary Magistrates or Presidents of District Local Boards, but several added that they were chairholders, were on a Collector's darbari list, or held a gun licence.[61] This showed that they put being a chairholder on a par with performing a function in local government. It was a mark of great status.

The British government, too, took the award of a chair very seriously. In 1875, the Collector of Karachi explained that he gave all schoolmasters a chair when they visited him or attended his darbars. This demonstrated his respect for teachers and encouraged the people to develop a similar respect for education. He suggested that the Commissioner in Sind should turn his idea into a general policy.[62] His letter provoked a lengthy debate. Many Sind officials were reluctant to confer such honour on so relatively inferior a class as schoolteachers. The matter was resolved when the Educational Inspector proposed that the privilege should be confined to head teachers.[63] Even this was too much for the Deputy Collector of Larkana. He complained that the headmasters of vernacular schools were usually young and poorly paid. Responsible officers like Head Munshis would resent having to stand or squat while a young man drawing less than half their salary was permitted to sit.[64] The Commissioner, though, was unmoved and rebuked him for raising the question after it had been settled.[65] This emphasizes the importance the government attached to the award of a chair. It was a privilege which was not conferred lightly.

Government was accordingly careful to ensure that an honour did not enhance a man's izzat more than he deserved. Pir Sahibdino Shah of Guni was recommended for an afrinama and a sword in 1894, for his help in detecting crime. When he was given the news, he volunteered to contribute some money of his own, so that government could buy an especially valuable and highly finished sword. The District Superintendent of Police was taken with the idea but the Commissioner in Sind dismissed it. The Pir, he wrote tartly, must be content with whatever mark of distinction government was pleased to bestow on him and could not 'fictitiously enhance the recognition of his merits.'[66] The value of swords and lungis could be adjusted to match the importance of the honour – better steel or workmanship on a sword, or finer cloth or embroidery on a lungi, reflecting greater merit on the recipient. As with the hierarchy of chair-holders, the government considered the matter fully before making the award. There was never anything accidental about the quality of the article presented.

An interesting insight into how the honours system worked in practice is given in an account by the District Superintendent of Police, Shikarpur, of his efforts to track down a gang of dacoits in 1893. The episode began in January when two dacoits were arrested by Wadero Rasul Bakhsh Bhutto, grandson of the famous Dodo Khan. The Superintendent gave Rasul Bakhsh 'not the slightest credit' for the arrest because he believed the Wadero had been hiding the men, turning them in at the last moment to throw suspicion off himself. Far from being rewarded, he was deprived of his gun licence and other privileges. The rest of the gang were still free, though, and they carried out a series of robberies in Naushahro Abro the following month. Wadero Ghulam Kadar Drakhan made some more arrests and the police were able to extract the information they needed to set off in pursuit of the gang. By March the Superintendent was hot on their trail, leading a patrol into Kalat territory. Several local dignitaries were, more or less willingly, pressed into the expedition. Ghulam Kadar Drakhan was an obvious choice, and Allah Bakhsh Pathan was another Wadero who, the Superintendent believed, knew something about the gang. In addition, because they were going into tribal territory, the Superintendent brought along Lashkar Khan, chief of the Jamali tribe, and his son, Yar Muhammad. The Superintendent reckoned that Lashkar Khan could put him on the scent of the dacoits if he wanted to, but he doubted whether the mere promise of reward would do the trick. A practical display of generosity was needed. The Superintendent called an impromptu roadside darbar. With much pomp and circumstance, he wrote out an afrinama for Ghulam Kadar Drakhan, thanking him for his efforts so far, and announcing that he would be presented with a sword later. Ghulam Kadar became the hero of the hour and the others were duly jealous. The Superintendent wrote triumphantly that 'The effect was instantaneous.' Lashkar Khan provided information, his son accompanied the police on their enquiries and within days two more dacoits were arrested.

This left only one member of the gang at large, a man called Mehra. He was hiding in British territory, possibly under the protection of two Waderos, Gul Muhammad Drakhan and Gauhar Khan Jamali. The Superintendent returned to base and summoned them to his office. He told them that if Mehra was not produced shortly, they would both be stripped of their honours. To show he meant business, he reminded them what had happened to Rasul Bakhsh Bhutto. The Superintendent thought Gul Muhammad was the prime mover in this affair and persuaded the Commissioner in Sind to intervene. The Commissioner sent a stern personal warning to the Wadero. With the weight of the whole government bearing down upon him, Gul Muhammad must by now have been thoroughly alarmed. A fortnight later, he brought Mehra in, and that was the end of the dacoit gang.[67]

With a judicious mixture of rewards and punishments, the Superintendent had cajoled a number of Waderos into assisting him. Not all had been volunteers. One, Rasul Bakhsh Bhutto, had been disgraced and another, Ghulam Kadar Drakhan, lavishly honoured *pour encourager les autres*. An interesting point is that although Allah Bakhsh Pathan was at one stage threatened with the Commissioner's displeasure, he was nevertheless given an afrinama when he did what was required.[68] The government spared neither carrot nor stick when it came to demanding cooperation from Waderos.

One does not, of course, need to accept the Superintendent's opinions of the Waderos to appreciate his approach. There is no evidence that Gul Muhammad Drakhan was actually harbouring Mehra, and it hardly mattered. Once the Commissioner in Sind had decided that he would be disgraced, it was up to him to redeem himself by finding the suspect. Honours were held at the Commissioner's pleasure, and no judicial process was required to remove them. Gul Muhammad had no option but to comply. He may have produced Mehra because he really was an accomplice, or because he had used his local influence to hunt him down. Either way, it illustrates the somewhat uneasy balance between Waderos and government. The government could not find the criminals without the assistance of the Waderos; yet the Waderos were not always anxious to assist. The government relied on the threat of punishment or the promise of reward to press Waderos into its service. So long as the result was the same, either approach was satisfactory from government's point of view.

The trick only worked, though, if the Wadero was looking for official favour. Ghulam Murtaza Bhutto's acquittal over the murder of the Mukhtiarkar in 1896, in the face of government's strenuous efforts to secure a conviction, must have boosted his prestige more than any number of honours. Again, as with Gul Muhammad Drakhan, the question of guilt or innocence was immaterial. One is talking here about prestige, not justice. The issue was success – to show, as it were, who was boss – and Colonel Mayhew recognized the damage done to administrative effectiveness when the government lost face after Bhutto was freed. Being stripped of one's honours in these circumstances was almost a distinction in itself. That is to say, if the government distinguished one man by presenting him with a chair, it distinguished another when it struck him off the Commissioner's darbari list. Both were men to be reckoned with, with whom lesser mortals would not wish to cross swords. The izzat of both would be enhanced. There is no evidence that the Bhutto clan lost any respect or authority when Rasul Bakhsh and Ghulam Murtaza were disgraced. Subsequent history, on the contrary, suggests the opposite. Similarly, Saiyid Muhammad Shah of Sann was singled out by the Collector of Karachi in 1895 as 'without exception, the most troublesome and evil-dispositioned zemindar in the Sehwan Sub-Division.' His chairs, gun-licences and all other privileges had been withdrawn 'on account of the systematic aid and refuge afforded by him to notorious thieves and outlaws & the systematic obstruction offered by him to all Government officials.'[69] It takes an exceptional person to earn such strong enmity from senior government officials and get away with it. Attempts to undermine his izzat had no effect. Not only was it impossible to collect enough evidence against him to bring him to trial, but government pressure failed to bully him into changing his ways. Muhammad Shah was someone for whom government favour held no attraction. Ten years later, he continued to defy the government and the Superintendent of Police returned to the attack. Although he still could not find any evidence which would stand up in court, he had no doubt that Muhammad Shah 'causes thefts, housebreaking, dacoities & murders to be committed.' The Superintendent gathered together a list of influential people who were willing publicly to proclaim the Saiyid's bad character. Besides prominent government officers and Sardar Muhammad Yakub, the Vizir of Khairpur State, who was a former civil servant, the list included Malik Sobdar Khan, chief of the Numrio tribe; Maliks Essab Khan and Dodo Khan who were also Numrio notables; and Seth Vishindas, one of Sind's most famous and wealthy merchant-zamindars. In the event the list did not have to be used because the Saiyid was, somewhat conveniently, murdered.[70]

Luckily for the government, people like Muhammad Shah were

the exceptions. The majority of Sindhi Waderos valued the support they received through the honours system or, simply, were more frightened of confronting the British than he was. However, despite the rewards, some found that supporting the police could have its drawbacks. Once a suspect had been arrested, the matter was passed to the lawcourts where izzat counted for nothing. A Wadero was treated like any other witness. He could even suffer the humiliation of cross-examination by a Hindu lawyer. And though judges had due regard for the respectability of witnesses' characters, they could not convict defendants on the word of some Wadero, however much Waderos – and British officials – wished they would. A court appearance could be a blow to a Wadero's dignity, especially if the suspect was eventually acquitted.

It had been different during the first twenty years of British rule in Sind, when justice was administered by district officers. They had wide-ranging and arbitrary powers and they knew the Waderos. They recognized the weight that should be given to Waderos' testimony. The system suited both Waderos and officials, although it put a heavy burden of work on the latter.

This was all swept away in 1866. The Bombay Code was introduced to Sind and properly constituted courts were set up. District officers continued to exercise magisterial powers for minor offences, but prisoners could appeal to superior courts.[71] Judges did not have the same powers of discretion as district officers, nor did they want them. They were accustomed to respect established court procedures, to adhere to laws of evidence and, particularly, to presume the innocence of the accused. Their attitude was incompatible with that of the Waderos, who felt their prestige could not endure the dishonour of having their word questioned in public.

The judges' attitude was also incompatible with that of the district officers, who took much the same view as the Waderos. Within a few years of the introduction of the Code, Sind officials chafed under its restraints. Judges, they complained, understood nothing of local conditions. They stuck to the letter of the law, without regard for the customs of the people – by which they meant the standing of the Waderos. In 1870, Sir William Merewether, the Commissioner in Sind, reprimanded R.H. Pinhey, his Judicial Commissioner, for reducing on appeal sentences passed on cattle lifters by magistrates. Pinhey's response was couched in legalistic language, citing precedents and conventions. Merewether brushed all this aside. The magistrates, he pointed out to Pinhey, were district officers who, because of their contact with the people, were the best judges of what punishments were appropriate. He concluded: 'Local experience is the only safe guide, applied of course within the limits assigned by law.'[72]

Friction between judges and administrators persisted. In 1888, the Sessions Judge of Shikarpur was transferred back to the Presidency proper after pressure from the Collector of Shikarpur and other officers. They had complained that the judge's ignorance of Sind led him to misinterpret the testimony of witnesses and acquit people who ought to have been convicted. He had, for example, dismissed as 'unreliable' evidence given by the wife of a man accused of murdering her lover. She had confessed to adultery but the judge believed she was just protecting her husband. Anyone acquainted with the country, exclaimed the Collector of Shikarpur, would have known that nothing short of torture would have wrung such an admission from her if it had been false. After her husband's acquittal, the Collector had been forced to protect him from the wrath of the victim's relations.[73] It would have been simpler and more convenient for all concerned if the man had, as everyone had expected, been hanged.

The judge's successor was no improvement. He believed it was his duty to keep Sind sentencing practices in line with the rest of the Presidency. This led him to reduce many sentences imposed by district officers and even to set convictions aside on occasions. Like Pinhey nearly twenty years earlier, he was particularly concerned about sentences for cattle lifting. And, like Merewether before them, the Collector of Shikarpur and the Deputy Commissioner of Upper Sind Frontier protested that the administration of justice would be impossible if such leniency persisted. On this occasion, however, the Judicial Commissioner was on the side of the officials. Cattle stealing, he explained, was more common in Sind than elsewhere and sterner measures were required. Besides, the Judicial Commissioner could see no reason why the Presidency proper should be used as a standard for Sind.[74] The controversy was brought to an abrupt halt a year after the judge's appointment, when he died of overwork – brought on, the Judicial Commissioner said darkly, by the harsh summer of Upper Sind, aggravated by excessive study of Presidency law reports.[75] The judge was replaced by a Sindhi, Dayaram Gidumal, who understood Sind officials and gave them satisfaction for many years.[76]

These disputes were not prompted by sheer obscurantism on the part of district officers. At the heart of the matter was their anxiety to preserve their working relationship with the Waderos. One of the charges Merewether had brought against Pinhey in 1870 was that interfering in a magistrate's sentence reduced him in the eyes of the people, making him less effective as an administrator.[77] In other words, district officers were losing face. If British officers felt their own izzat might be in jeopardy, Waderos must have been even more concerned. Officers frequently claimed that the excessively legalistic attitudes of judges were discouraging Waderos from helping the police. The complaints increased towards the end of the century. The Collector of Larkana stated the Waderos' case in 1904:

> "What is the use," they say, "of our helping the police in catching thieves if we are disgraced in the eyes of the people and made the laughing stock of all the badmashes [thugs] in the country by having our word disbelieved by the Court at the instance of a petty Bania vakil [lawyer]?" That is the attitude of many respectable and loyal zamindars.[78]

Two years later he repeated his warning: 'Each time a thief is acquitted in spite of the zamindar's efforts to bring him to justice the latter's influence is diminished. The thief comes back and laughs at the zamindar.' Anything which caused a zamindar to lose his prestige or become apathetic about assisting the police weakened government's capacity to deal with crime.[79] It is interesting that it seems not to have occurred to the Collector that courts might sometimes be justified in acquitting suspects despite the evidence of Waderos. He took it for granted that anyone accused by a Wadero was surely guilty.

The Collector suggested that the problem could be solved by introducing the Frontier Regulations to his District, so that he could commit cases where the evidence was circumstantial or uncorroborated to a *jirga* (council of elders) instead of a court. A jirga was not a substitute for a court, because it did not have the power to sentence. It acted rather like a jury, establishing guilt and recommending a punishment or compromise to the magistrate. The advantage of a jirga for a district officer was that it cut out the long-winded procedures and tiresome formalities of regular courts. It also avoided much argument since lawyers could not plead before a jirga, simplifying its deliberations immensely. Its members established the facts according to their own lights, using their personal knowledge and experience as tribal leaders in a way that would be unthinkable in a regular court. And they always gave proper deference to the word of important Waderos.[80] Various Sind officials, on various occasions, demanded that the jirga system should be extended to Sind, and they always received the same dusty answer: the British government was only prepared to tolerate such a compromise with legal principles in frontier regions where tribal customs hindered the normal administration of justice. Elsewhere, like it or not, the solid panoply of lawcourts had to be maintained.[81]

Since the legal system could not be changed to suit the Waderos, the alternative was to change the constitutional position of the Waderos themselves. This had become apparent to Bartle Frere when he was Commissioner in Sind in the 1850s, before the Bombay Code had even been introduced. He had seen how useful village *patels* (headmen) were to local administrators in the Deccan and he believed the administration would benefit if Waderos could be persuaded to perform a similar function. Patels had well-defined obligations and remuneration, and their authority depended partly on local influence and partly on the support of government. They were village officers who had an obligation to support the local police and revenue administration.[82] Many Waderos did help with the day-to-day business of revenue-collection and justice but, unlike patels, they were not accountable to government. This was so unsatisfactory that Frere complained that the province lacked 'all that frame work of villages and other municipalities which keeps society together.'[83] He wanted to formalize the position of Waderos to remedy the deficiency in Sind's social machinery but he was advised that, as a class, they could not be trusted with heavy responsibility. Accordingly, he did not attempt to set up a regular system of patels.

Instead, he gave *seri* grants to a limited number of Waderos as a first step towards a more universal system. Seri grants were small allocations of rent-free land, originally given to stimulate cultivation. Frere changed their purpose by making them dependent on the aid grantees regularly provided the administration.[84] The intention was to tie the Waderos into the government, bringing them into partnership, as it were, with district officers.

Frere's scheme was not a success. In the first place, officers could not find enough Waderos who were both suitable and willing to accept the grants. Seri grants were only twenty to thirty acres. In the Deccan, where holdings were small, they had considerable value.[85] But their economic significance to Sindhi Waderos was negligible and government could not make them large enough to attract big landholders without depriving the state of more land revenue than it could afford. As a result, seri grants in Sind had no intrinsic worth beyond whatever importance Waderos chose to attribute to them as favours from government. When they discovered that these tokens carried with them a whole burden of obligations and duties, few were interested. Patels were therefore introduced into only a few dehs.

Indeed, it may be misleading to refer to seridars (seri grantees) as patels at all. It was a foreign word, borrowed from the Deccan. Seri grants could not turn Waderos into village officers. At best, they could encourage them, in a general way, to co-operate with government. This hardly made them more effective, in terms of prompting help from Waderos, than chairs in darbars, and they were much more expensive.

The disadvantages of the system became increasingly apparent and in 1874 the Bombay government decided no new seri grants should be awarded. At the same time, a committee was appointed to look into the possibility of introducing village officers on a large scale. Its recommendations, presented in 1877, led to the passing of the Sind Village Officers Act in 1881. This provided for the appointment of patels in every deh, to be paid through seri grants, and it laid down their duties.[86] A report published the following year hailed the Act as the beginning of a new village system,[87] but in the event it was scarcely an improvement on Frere's scheme. The only sections which could be implemented were those establishing a comprehensive network of subordinate revenue officers (tapedars) in every village. This proved successful since tapedars had not previously been spread evenly across the province. The provisions relating to patels were still-born because nobody of real influence was prepared to accept patelships which involved statutory obligations and so reduced their independence. The Commissioner in Sind decided to stay with the old informal honours system.[88]

Seri grants were therefore allowed to lapse as the incumbents died, except in Thar and Parkar, where Frere's patel system had taken root and proved useful to government.[89] It was never clear why seri grants should have proved so popular in the desert – perhaps the extreme uncertainty of cultivation made seridars more appreciative of any concessions made to them. Whatever the reason, by the end of the century seri grants in Thar and Parkar still retained 'a value in the eyes of the people altogether out of proportion to the amount of assessment which in many cases does not exceed two or three rupees.'[90]

In 1899, the Bombay government put forward fresh proposals for a patel system. Officers in the Secretariat in Bombay, accustomed to the chartered functionaries of Deccan villages, were unhappy with the seemingly haphazard arrangements on which Sind thrived. They felt village headmen with defined functions were necessary – although they had learnt their lesson sufficiently to concede that it would be difficult to do this in 'a province like Sind where no villages in the

Indian sense of the term exist.'[91] To make the idea more attractive to Sindhi ears, the government suggested seridars should be known by the familiar term of Wadero, instead of patel. Robert Giles, the Acting Commissioner in Sind, nipped the plan firmly in the bud. 'Wadero,' he explained to his colleagues in Bombay, was a title of respect given to large zamindars. It could not be conferred upon lesser men. Besides, he did not agree that the system was deficient. In his experience, Waderos 'already recognize their responsibility as regards crime and assistance to Government while in no way regarding themselves as Government servants.' He saw little chance of grafting the 'village system' onto the 'zamindari system,' though he conceded it might be useful to appoint some smallholders as patels in those few areas where there were no recognized headmen.[92]

When Evan James, the substantive Commissioner, returned to his post a couple of months later, he disagreed with his locum tenens. The present arrangements were too vague to be satisfactory. The feudal system, he believed, could not last for ever and some replacement must be found for it. He decided to nominate a few of the best Waderos as seridars and present their sanads in open darbar. He might award them lungis as well, to add to the sense of occasion. At the same time, he would read out their duties under the Village Officers Act, expressing confidence that these would always be borne in mind. He was sure that by appealing to their izzat, he could persuade Waderos that it was an honour to be given responsibility by the government. James hoped sanads would soon be eagerly sought after: 'And gradually a defined sense of responsibility for the specific duties recited in the sanad will replace, or rather supplement, the indefinite traditional feeling that Government requires aid on certain occasions.'[93]

The great feudal spectacle envisaged by James was a far cry from the tidy management solution the Government of Bombay had in mind and it never went ahead. The following year, the government dropped it. Accepting defeat, government conceded that Waderos were already sufficiently alive to their responsibilities. There was no need to appoint patels except in places where there was no local magnate, or it was clear the appointment was a sinecure. J. Muir-Mackenzie endorsed this policy as Commissioner in Sind in 1904, reiterating the arguments of his predecessors. He thought Waderos might be used more often in the investigation and trial of petty cases, but warned that government should proceed with the utmost caution.[94] Like Frere's officers fifty years earlier, he was chary of giving formal powers to the Waderos.

By the end of the nineteenth century, the experiment with patels was concluded and the wheel had turned full circle. Government did not feel Waderos could be trusted with statutory powers, while Waderos refused to compromise their independence by accepting subordinate positions. There was still no niche for the Waderos within the administration. The makeshift honours system trundled along, with varying success. In 1926, the Cattle Theft Committee commented on yet another proposal for appointing village headmen. The members went over well-trodden ground. They doubted whether big zamindars, 'of the class who are *de facto* village headmen in Sind,' would take the posts either with or without remuneration – while headmen of lower status would not be able to report offences against the wishes of more powerful neighbours. In short, it would not work.[95] With that, the ghost of Frere's patel system was at last laid. The question was not raised again during the two decades that remained of British rule in Sind. The Waderos continued to enjoy their power, with little or no responsibility. They had no need of government patronage, and so the Sind authorities were never able to acquire control over them, beyond the vague threats and promises implicit in the honours system.

Towards the end of the nineteenth century, the government did take a tentative step towards delegating legal responsibilities to landed magnates: it appointed some Waderos as Honorary Magistrates. The idea seems first to have been raised in 1864, but the Commissioner in Sind of the day felt no good would come of it. Three Sardars had been appointed Honorary Magistrates as an experiment, but he said they had turned the administration of justice into 'a complete farce.' One had been reluctant to send cattle thieves to prison for more than a week, while the magistrate a few miles away was giving them two years.[96] The punishment of cattle thieves, it will be recalled, was a sore point with Sind officials. The experience was not repeated until 1887 when a Parsi, Byramji Jehangirji Rajkotwalla was appointed Honorary Magistrate for the Karachi municipal area.[97]

Two years later, government took the step of appointing a jagirdar, Mir Abdul Hussain Khan Talpur, as magistrate. Although he was from one of the four great Talpur families, the Judicial Commissioner in Sind was reluctant to proceed. He did not believe that people like the Mir, who spoke no English, should serve as magistrates, and he doubted whether he had much knowledge or experience of legal administration. Furthermore, since his jurisdiction would fall in villages belonging to himself and his relations, the Judicial Commissioner doubted whether defendants would feel free to appeal against him. However, after much soul-searching by the Judicial Commissioner and the Commissioner, the Mir was appointed.[98] Their opinion seems to have been influenced by an appeal from the Mir himself and the strong personal recommendation of the Collector of Hyderabad. The Collector added that it would be good policy to encourage the Mirs to take an interest in public affairs instead of burying themselves in their families.[99] The appointment of Mir Abdul Hussain was followed by the installation of four more Talpur jagirdars as Honorary Magistrates.[100]

The five appointees worked successfully. In May 1892, Evan James, the Commissioner in Sind, agreed to take another step by appointing two non-jagirdars. The Deputy Collector of Naushahro Feroze, Kadirdad Khan, had recommended Saiyid Gambal Shah of Naushahro and Ghulam Rasul Jatoi of Moro. Their Sindhi education, explained Kadirdad, was as good as that of any government official, their Persian generally better, and they had been studying the law in preparation for their appointment.[101] James welcomed the proposal. Their appointment would not just help the local administration but would have:

> distinct political value, as showing that Government desire to utilize the voluntary services of landowners & native gentlemen of position, who have qualified themselves for the powers by education & by setting a good example of prudence & forethought in the management of their estates to the Zemindars around them.[102]

For James, then, the Honorary Magistracy was a way of showing government's appreciation for well-disposed and intelligent men. Appointments might inspire other Waderos to improve themselves through education and better husbandry, in the hope that they too might be honoured. It is interesting that farming ability should have been regarded as a qualification for a legal position. James was pleased to hear the following year that the two Waderos had discharged their duties satisfactorily.[103]

The creation of Honorary Magistrates had political advantages, besides helping to ease the burden of work on district officers. It involved local magnates in the administration, without turning them into public servants as patelships threatened to do. On the contrary, an Honorary Magistracy conferred great honour on the holder because it gave him substantial powers and responsibilities. Mir Abdul Hussain Khan, for example, assured James that, 'I am doing judicial work for the sake of gaining your good will.' He declared that men either worked for gain or fame, and that he himself was working for fame, adding: 'We covet honor for honor's sake and I believe the Government approves of and encourages this idea.'[104]

If someone acquired honour by accepting an Honorary Magistracy then, by the same token, he could not afford the disgrace of losing it. Ghulam Rasul Jatoi became alarmed when he was deprived of his magisterial powers in 1902. It was through no fault of his own but because of bad health. Ghulam Rasul complained that it 'would affect me most prejudicially in the eyes of my neighbouring Zemindars and fellow subjects, and lower me entirely in their estimation.' The Commissioner saw the justice of his argument and restored his powers, even though he could not actually perform the functions.[105] The following year, the Collector of Larkana complained that Wadero Tharo Khan Lahori, another Honorary Magistrate, 'has never tried a case and has neither the necessary knowledge nor fitness to try one.' He asked for Tharo Khan to be deprived of his powers, unless Honorary Magistracies were intended to be entirely ornamental posts. The Commissioner did not agree because, as with Ghulam Rasul Jatoi, he sympathized with the Wadero's predicament. He noted in the margin of the Collector's letter: 'Leave him the powers. It would be a slight on him to withdraw them.'[106] Rather than remove Tharo Khan from the list of Honorary Magistrates, the government appointed Wadero Illahi Bakhsh Bhutto as a second magistrate for Larkana, to try Tharo Khan's cases for him.[107] Striking off Tharo Khan's name would have undermined his izzat. Politically, this was useful to the government and well worth the slight inconvenience of doubling posts: the men appointed were at its disposal. As Robert Giles, the Collector of Karachi, remarked while putting forward the name of Malik Sobdar Khan, chief of the Numrio tribe: 'The young fellow . . . will gain prestige and we – I trust – a hold, for good, over him.'[108]

Sobdar Khan was appointed as an Honorary Magistrate,[109] but it proved difficult to find other men of substance who were capable of taking the responsibility. Magistrates had vital duties to perform. Powers could not be lightly handed out in the pursuit of political expediency. Many Waderos were ill-educated and few had any legal knowledge. The problems encountered by government in looking for a few men suitable to act as Honorary Magistrates shed light on its reluctance to invest Waderos as a whole with – considerably lesser – statutory powers as village headmen.

Tharo Khan Lahori was a case in point. He had first been recommended by Robert Giles, when he was Collector of Shikarpur, in 1893. Giles frankly admitted that he intended the post as an honour, because Tharo Khan was the leading zamindar of the District, rather than as an opportunity for him to dispense justice. Giles explained that, in the unlikely event of his actually having to try a case, a Munshi could be sent over from the nearby government offices for legal advice. Tharo Khan, though no doubt deserving recognition from a grateful government, was hardly magisterial material and the Judicial Commissioner objected to Giles' proposal.[110] In 1898, Giles' successor put Tharo Khan's name forward again and was successful, the Judicial Commissioner of the day apparently being unaware of the objections.[111] As has just been shown, the original suspicions of Tharo Khan's suitability were only too well founded. Giles appears to have been particularly struck by the political advantages of Honorary Magistracies. In 1896, while Collector of Karachi, he recommended Wadero Dital Khan Chandio as a magistrate on the ground that he was the premier zamindar of the Delta region, who had proved his personal worth by his readiness to assist government in every way. It was a drawback that he was old and uneducated, but he could pay for a qualified Munshi while his sons, who were educated, would help him. Government did not take up Giles' suggestion,[112] and similar problems arose with other recommendations made by local officers. Giles' predecessor as Collector of Karachi had not been prepared to name anyone in the whole District as 'fit to be invested with magisterial powers.' The Assistant Collector of Sehwan had put forward three names, but the Collector endorsed only Nawab Hassan Ali Khan Laghari – only to discover he was ineligible because he held land within the area where his jurisdiction was to lie.[113]

Even when suitable people were discovered, insuperable obstacles often arose because, as one British officer exclaimed, 'Sind is the home of feuds, enmities and false complaints.'[114] Waderos tended to be drawn into rivalries with one another as they competed for the allegiance of smallholders, and this raised doubts about their impartiality. Giles complained in 1896 that it was hard to find men who were both worthy of appointment and free from involvement in local jealousies. There was just one in the whole of Thatta Division, and he was too old and sick.[115] The Assistant Collector of Jherruck had been impressed with Saiyid Nawaz Ali Shah. He was an influential landholder from a good family, he was well educated and he had looked up the law in preparation for his appointment. It turned out, though, that his family had a long-standing feud with a neighbour, Shaikh Bakardar, so any power the Saiyid possessed might be deployed against the Shaikh's followers.[116] Similar problems were revealed when the Assistant Collector of Hala recommended Akhund Yar Muhammad of Matiari. He had known the Akhund for twenty-five years and had the highest opinion of him. He was an excellent farmer, which was a good start. He was wealthy, his annual land revenue bill coming to no less than Rs 2,000. He was a just landlord who was liked and respected by his people. Indeed, concluded the Assistant Collector, 'There are few native gentlemen in Sind better fitted for the honour and who could be trusted to make use of the powers of a Magistrate more judiciously and uprightly.' Nevertheless, the Judicial Commissioner opposed the appointment. The people of Matiari would interpret it as setting the Akhund up over his rival, Saiyid Muhammad Shah. No matter how honest the Akhund might be, there would be continual complaints of injustice and demands for cases involving the Saiyid's followers to be transferred to other courts. In the event, the decision not to appoint him was interpreted as a triumph for the Saiyid's faction. In 1895, they petitioned the Commissioner in Sind that, since government had recognized the Akhund's bad character by refusing his appointment as a magistrate, it should follow through by dismissing him as a Municipal Commissioner and turning down his application for a gun licence.[117] The petition, being purely malicious, had no effect on government but it confirmed the Judicial Commissioner's fears that appointing the Akhund would have created complications.

Once it became clear that government was looking for Honorary Magistrates, the mere rumour that someone might be selected could prompt his rivals to protest to the Commissioner.[118] Government was not usually concerned with the substance of the accusations. But the existence of enemies would prevent him from carrying out his duties without controversy. With so many petitions and counter-petitions flying across the province, the very institution of honorary magistracies may have caused curious tremors in the political balance of the countryside. Many a Wadero must have celebrated imaginary triumphs over hated rivals who, had he but known it, had never actually been in the running. And many others must have nursed groundless resentments against the enemies who had supposedly thwarted their hopes of advancement. And so enmities were fed and intensified by fictitious victories and defeats.

James' experiment, then, in which he tried to use Honorary Magistracies to involve the leaders of the community in administration was not a success. When in 1896 he asked his district officers for more names, they displayed no enthusiasm. The Collector of Hyderabad thought Honorary Magistrates were unnecessary and the Deputy Commissioner of Thar and Parkar agreed. The leading zamindars already made themselves useful to the administration in various ways but, being generally uneducated, they could not perform magisterial duties which would in any case be irksome for them.[119] Of all the district officers, only Giles, as Collector of Karachi, gave a positive response, as a result of which Malik Sobdar Khan Numrio was appointed. By 1899, there were still no more than thirteen Honorary Magistrates in Sind, of whom six were jagirdars and two were zamindars; the rest were professional men with jurisdiction over urban areas and retired Mukhtiarkars who had previously exercised magisterial powers.[120]

At the close of the nineteenth century, therefore, the Government of Sind was still unable formally to involve Waderos in the administration. Waderos were unwilling to accept positions as village headmen because they feared their izzat might suffer if they appeared to compromise their independence. They would probably have welcomed greater powers and responsibilities as Honorary Magistrates, but government did not trust them sufficiently. It preferred to play safe by appointing ex-officials, and also jagirdars – from the old ruling family especially – who were so high in rank as to be reasonably aloof from the rivalries which played so large a part in the lives of lesser jagirdars and Waderos.

Consequently, the government had been unable to develop beyond the situation which had prevailed when the British first occupied Sind: the success of its administration depended on the cultivation of an informal relationship with the landed magnates. It was not so much *governing* the governors, as *courting* them – they had to be persuaded it was in their interests to assist government. Distributing honours was an improvised system but effective. Most Waderos coveted such honours and feared their prestige would suffer if they were deprived of them. There was the drawback that those Waderos who did not prize government patronage had nothing to lose and might even flout the administration, but they were a minority and in the absence of an alternative the inconvenience had to be endured. Attempts to make Waderos more accountable by giving them seri grants failed because seridars never regarded their grants as anything but marks of distinction. If government had seriously tried to gain economic control over Waderos, it would have had to alienate an unacceptably large amount of land to them. In some ways, the appointment of Honorary Magistrates was a refinement of the honours system in that it demonstrated government's faith in Muslim notables as a class. To this extent, it was as much a political as a judicial scheme, designed to boost the izzat of Waderos.

As well as persuading Waderos to co-operate, government had to ensure that they were able to deliver the goods. It had to be certain they were still the governors: that their izzat was high and their estates intact. The honours system bolstered their izzat but Waderos' real power came from their economic strength. They could only be useful if they were wealthy. The Sindhi countryside must continue to be dominated by the great Muslim landholders.

Rumours that power might be slipping from their hands therefore caused consternation among the officials charged with governing Sind.

Chapter 4

Holding by the Paternal Acres[1]

I

Many British officers believed, in the latter decades of the nineteenth century, that the Waderos' estates were breaking up. Unable to make a living from their sprawling holdings, poorly cultivated as they were by disinterested haris, Waderos had been forced to raise money by mortgaging their property to bania moneylenders. Gradually their land passed to their creditors or was bought up by the more efficient smallholders. An anxious government acted to avert the ruin of its allies and the policy appeared to be successful. As Table 6 shows, largeholders were still well established in Sind at the end of the century. In almost all of the thirty-five taluqas for which figures are available, the proportion of land held by largeholders was either holding steady or increasing during the last two decades of the nineteenth century and the first two of the twentieth. Only seven registered a decrease of more than five percent in largeholders' share of the occupied area, while twenty-three showed increases of over five percent – including three with increases over one hundred percent. Nevertheless, the government remained nervous. As late as 1908, a Bombay report expressed apprehension that the demise of the Waderos had been postponed, not averted.[2] In the event, the Waderos of Sind continue to flourish at the end of the twentieth century despite successive Pakistani land reforms. Their resilience in the face of deliberate political attack leads one to approach tales of their travails under the British with some scepticism. Yet, surprisingly, the nineteenth century controversy also arose out of early attempts at land reform. The failure of these attempts, and the change in political direction they provoked, illustrate the practical constraints under which the colonial government operated, while raising critical questions about the scope for reform in contemporary Sind.

Table 6 Largeholders in Sind around the turn of the century

Zamindars holding estates of 500 acres and more 1869/70–1913/14

Taluqa	*Year*	*No. of largeholders*	*Average area of estate of each largeholder (acres)*	*% of total occupied areaheld by largeholders %*
Upper Sind Frontier				
Jacobabad	1885–86	44	2,384	76
	1893–94	59	2,445	82
	1903–04	59	2,733	92
Kandhkot	1894–95	66	1,762	63
	1902–03	83	1,627	66
Kashmore	1894–95	37	1,737	50
	1902–03	49	1,983	69
Thul	1893–94	78	1,944	75
	1902–03	91	1,898	73
Shikarpur				
Ghotki	1885–86	5	1,177	8
	1893–94	10	1,469	15
Kakar	1881–82	8	1,056	15
	1890–91	7	1,096	12
Kambar	1882–83	13	1,346	16
	1886–87	14	1,532	19
	1891–92	15	1,314	18
Larkana	1869–70	16	1,178	16
	1880–81	12	979	14
	1891–92	13	1,265	19
Mehar	1892–93	12	898	11
	1900–01	18	1,213	20
Nasirabad	1882–83	8	784	11
	1895–96	16	793	15
Naushahro Abro	1884–85	20	1,273	29
	1897–98	21	1,347	28
Ratodero	1882–83	8	1,479	18
	1891–92	19	1,344	32
Sukkur	1889–90	9	1,566	24
	1897–98	13	1,759	31
Hyderabad				
Badin	1898–99	22	910	14
	1906–07	28	888	17
Dero Mohbat	1887–88	15	1,063	23
	1907–08	17	1,328	22
Guni	1882–83	31	1,791	41
	1892–93	43	1,188	38
	1904–05	33	1,678	44
Hala	1883–84	42	1,309	54
	1892–93	59	1,198	59

Taluqa	*Year*	*No. of largeholders*	*Average area of estate of each largeholder (acres)*	*% of total occupied areaheld by largeholders %*
Hyderabad	1896–97	9	679	5
	1904–05	9	2,264	21
Johi	1887–88	17	1,034	26
	1896–97	27	988	19
Kandiaro	1881–82	16	687	11
	1894–95	21	796	16
Moro	1881–82	9	994	12
	1894–95	19	817	15
Naushahro Feroze	1881–82	20	884	10
	1894–95	44	1,194	22
Shahdadpur	1892–93	26	1,370	25
	1904–05	37	1,328	29
Tando Allahyar	1890–91	21	1,379	18
	1904–05	26	1,511	22
Tando Bago	1898–99	34	1,420	42
	1906–07	34	1,517	38
Thar and Parkar				
Sinjhoro	1892–93	7	1,205	27
	1904–05	7	1,262	27
Karachi				
Ghorabari	1888–89	24	669	33
	1902–03	15	862	27
Jati	1887–88	18	1,021	33
	1897–98	19	972	34
	1913–14	16	1,196	27
Kotri	1889–90	4	915	26
	1897–98	4	1,046	29
Manjhand	1885–86	8	1,074	26
	1893–94	11	1,484	44
Mirpur Bathoro	1883–84	3	747	3
	1895–96	12	1,034	19
	1913–14	8	1,699	19
Mirpur Sakro	1888–89	24	974	40
	1902–03	11	808	19
Shahbandar	1886–87	19	905	29
	1897–98	17	946	39
	1913–14	15	1,312	34
Sujawal	1883–84	12	1,084	25
	1895–96	9	1,682	29
	1913–14	8	2,277	32
Thatta	1882–83	10	1,092	22
	1898–99	10	1,022	22
	1902–03	7	1,102	19

Source: Calculated from nominal lists of largeholders appended to some Settlement Reports

The Waderos' predicament in the nineteenth century was said to have its roots in the British revenue settlement. In the 1860s, the Bombay government had introduced the raiyatwari settlement of the Deccan into Sind. This had been designed for smallholders and was considered ill suited to the largeholders of Sind. Critics alleged that it was driving the Waderos to debt and dissolution.

II

Land revenue was a sensitive issue in India. It was the one aspect of government policy which had a direct and immediate impact on the mass of the population. The levying and collecting of the revenue preoccupied rulers and subjects alike. Even cultivators for whom the British government was little more than an abstract concept, and who never saw a British person in their entire lives, had to pay (or take steps to evade) their taxes. As to the government, land revenue was its main source of income. Sorting out the revenue system usually provided the first peace-time contact between the people of a freshly conquered province and their new administration. As soon as the fighting was over and the military position was reasonably secure, the government' thoughts would turn towards its long term survival: towards collecting its revenue. Settlement Officers would spread into the countryside to 'settle' the land revenue – that is, to establish the basis on which tax was to be paid and set the rates. They began by surveying the province, to provide accurate maps. Then they got down to the details of agricultural production. They familiarized themselves with the various types of soil and the crops they could support, the irrigational system, the methods of cultivation and any other factors which affected production, such as susceptibility to floods, droughts or pests. Their research enabled them to estimate yields per acre, the costs of cultivation and, in the light of prevailing prices, to predict farmers' profits. From this, they recommended the rates per acre at which the government assessment should be levied.[3] Since it was a time-consuming business, which could hardly be repeated each year, Settlement Officers had to predict future trends and set the assessment for a fixed period. In the Bombay Presidency, settlements were revised every thirty years, every twenty years in the Punjab. Finally, they studied the tenancy system to decide on whom the revenue should be settled. The decision to collect land revenue from one class of person rather than another could be critical. In Sind, two revenue models were considered – the village-lease system of the North-Western Provinces and the Punjab, and the raiyatwari system of the Deccan. From 1863, government committed itself to the Deccan model. It was in many respects a surprising choice.

Under the village-lease system, the revenue was settled on an entire village or community and the headman was responsible for its payment. In Sind, this would have meant identifying the Wadero as headman and requiring him to pay the revenue on behalf of his raj. This system was cheap to administer since it entailed a minimum of bureaucracy. The government just calculated its total claim and took a lump sum from the leaseholder. Wasteland was included in the lease and the villagers were left to decide among themselves how much land should be cultivated and by whom. Government noted the rights of inferior holders but had no direct dealings with them. So long as the leaseholder paid his revenue, it was no concern of the authorities what proportions the inferior holders contributed – although it could intervene if requested.[4] The system left responsibility with local magnates, and was suited to a region – like Sind – dominated by powerful landholders.

The raiyatwari system had emerged from experience of regions where peasant holdings predominated. It was based on a detailed field survey. The area was demarcated into 'Survey Numbers' (fields). Each was mapped, its boundaries clearly marked on the ground and its holder's name registered as the occupant. As Survey Numbers could be 'resigned' (given back to the government) or taken up at the start of each cultivating season, agriculturists could vary the size of their farms according to their resources. Assessment was levied per Survey Number, whether or not it was cultivated. Evidently, the more farmers could cultivate in fewer Survey Numbers, the greater their profits would be. The raiyatwari system, therefore, encouraged intensive, efficient, small-scale agriculture, penalizing large estates where land was wasted and cultivation relatively inefficient. Revenue was collected from individual landholders, however small their holdings.[5] The raiyatwari settlement had not been devised with people like the Sindhi Waderos in mind.

Before the British conquest of 1843, there had been a village-lease settlement in Sind, government collecting its revenue in kind from the Waderos.[6] Napier, however, was suspicious of great landholders. He encouraged his officers to bypass them and deal directly with the smallholders.[7] His instructions did not amount to a coherent revenue policy but he was steering Sind towards a raiyatwari system and the traditional arrangements started to fall into disuse. When Sind was annexed to the Bombay Presidency in 1847, R.K. Pringle, its first Commissioner, halted the drift by ordering a return to the village leases. At the same time, he replaced the batai assessment (assessment in kind) with a cash demand.[8]

Pringle's leases were disastrous. They were imposed hastily, without preliminary enquiries. Village boundaries were neither demarcated nor investigated – only in Thar and Parkar were any reliable maps drawn.[9] In the absence of information about the property included in the leases, officers appear to have relied on guesswork: many leases in the Hyderabad Collectorate were given to people who were not even landholders.[10] The leases were fixed for seven years. No remissions were allowed except under particularly serious circumstances.[11] Rents were based on the average value of the government share in previous years, but prices had been unusually high in the late 1840s because political instability in the Punjab had disturbed agricultural production and boosted demand for Sindhi grain. Punjabi agriculture revived after the province was annexed in 1849, and prices fell. The average price of grain in Sind fell from thirty or thirty-five rupees per kharar in 1847 to nine rupees twelve annas in 1852.[12] Many Sindhi leaseholders found they could not pay their revenue. By the time Bartle Frere succeeded Pringle as Commissioner in 1852, the leases were universally unpopular and the system was in a shambles. Frere accused Pringle of 'leasing out the entire country without any idea of what we were leasing, or to whom, at excessive rates.'[13]

One of the reasons for the failure was government's ignorance of Sindhi agriculture. It would be impossible to introduce a long-term settlement until the province had been fully surveyed – something which should have started years before. Since this would be a lengthy process, Frere initiated a 'rough' survey as an interim measure in 1855. Officers were to obtain a general picture of the province, and use this as the basis for a correspondingly 'rough' settlement. Their results would provide the groundwork for a more accurate survey later.[14]

Meanwhile, a makeshift system based on crop-rating replaced Pringle's leases. Local officers attempted to calculate the government demand from an estimate of cultivation at each harvest but, without maps, it all came down to guesswork and haggling in the end. When Frere toured Sehwan Division in 1857, he was shocked to learn just how rough a 'rough' settlement could be. He received 'vociferous complaints' from the zamindars, but with no reliable records, 'I could rarely ascertain whether just grounds for complaint did or did not exist.' [15] The one redeeming feature was that government no longer attempted to take more than the zamindars actually had.

While disapproving of the way Pringle's leases had been introduced, Frere supported the principle of the village-lease system.[16] He wanted Waderos to be involved with the local administration.[17] Village-leases would reinforce their position, whereas a raiyatwari settlement might leave them without a role. However, four years of a raiyatwari model under Napier had accustomed smallholders to pay revenue directly to government, while the hardships caused by Pringle's leases had made Waderos wary of taking on financial commitments on behalf of other people. These two factors reduced enthusiasm, among both large and smallholders, for village-leases. Besides, none of the Settlement Officers working in Sind had experience outside the Bombay Presidency. Despite Frere's recommendations, they almost automatically based their work on the familiar Deccan pattern, with its minute field-survey.[18] They were encouraged by John Jacob who, acting as Commissioner during Frere's absence on leave in 1856, ordered officers to go into more detail than Frere had envisaged when commissioning the rough survey.[19]

Both systems existed side by side for a while, some smallholders paying revenue to government, others paying through their Waderos. In 1862, Samuel Mansfield, Frere's successor as Commissioner in Sind, took a further step towards the formal introduction of the Deccan settlement. He ruled that all land belonged to government. Zamindars could not exercise rights over land unless they paid revenue on it.[20] The declaration was against the spirit of the village-lease where all land, cultivated or not, was in the lease, but it reflected practice in the Deccan, where government had asserted its proprietary rights over wasteland. It followed from the assumption, which dominated official thinking at this time, that the State was the sole landlord in India and that agriculturists were its tenants. It is debatable whether this was a correct interpretation of Indian law, although it was certainly expedient for government.[21] Certainly, Mansfield's interpretation was not accepted without protest in Sind itself. Evan James, writing in 1872, insisted that before his pronouncement, 'The Zemindars were the owners of the soil in the strictest sense of the word.'[22] His opinion was unchanged twenty years later when he returned to Sind as Commissioner.[23] The non-official members of the 1926 Fallow Rules Committee, who were all zamindars, also denied that zamindars had ever been the 'occupants' of Bombay official parlance; they had always been 'the proprietors of the land.'[24] Whatever the rights and wrongs, though, Mansfield's decision was never reversed. Government continued to exercise proprietorship over wastelands in Sind long after the British had left India.[25]

By establishing government's claim to wasteland, Mansfield's declaration anticipated a field assessment, under which every Survey Number was at the disposal of government and paid for by the holder. It coincided with the secondment to Sind of Major J.T. Francis, a Bombay Settlement Officer, with a brief to devise a system of settlement for the province. A Deccan-style field-survey had been under way for several years and Mansfield had just adopted a Deccan-inspired policy towards wastelands. It was hardly surprising that, when Francis submitted his report in March 1863, he recommended the introduction of a Deccan-type settlement.[26]

Francis did modify the basic Deccan model, most importantly by introducing a flexible approach towards wastelands. Most Waderos included tracts of uncultivated waste in their holdings. This enhanced their *izzat* by swelling the acreage of their estates, and gave them a steady income from letting out grazing and woodcutting rights. After Mansfield's decision, all waste had to be assessed. Zamindars had to pay revenue on it or surrender it as 'government waste' which could be given out to other zamindars.[27] This made sense in the densely populated Deccan where, because land was scarce and holdings were small, farmers intensively cultivated every acre: but in Sind, land was abundant and fields were left fallow for at least two years out of three. Believing government would unnecessarily antagonize zamindars if it interfered with their long established habits of cultivation, Francis borrowed an ingenious, not to say bizarre, expedient devised by John Jacob in Upper Sind Frontier to accommodate fallows.[28] This model, which became known as the 'diffused rate' system, required land to be divided into large Survey Numbers of twenty to thirty acres each. It was assumed that the zamindar cultivated only one-third every year, leaving the rest fallow. If one imagines a thirty-acre field assessed at three rupees per acre then, with ten acres cultivated every year, its annual assessment could be fixed at thirty rupees, giving it a 'diffused rate' of one rupee per acre per year. After three years, each acre could have paid the 'full rate' of three rupees.[29] A zamindar who cultivated more than ten acres would derive a clear profit from the extra cultivation. This was a bonus for making good use of the land.[30]

The 'diffused rate' system was, for government, a disaster. Zamindars realized that if they cultivated the entire Survey Number for a year, then resigned it as government waste, they could get away with paying only a third of the revenue. In a word, their farming became more efficient and intensive, but the government lost money.

This was not the reward for good husbandry which Francis had in mind. It was first noticed in taluqa Sakrand in 1865,[31] but the pattern became familiar throughout the province. The occupied area of Dadu declined from 78,455 acres in 1867 to 59,333 acres in 1877, and in Naushahro Feroze from 153,367 acres to 94,230 acres.[32] The Commissioner in Sind tried to check the abuse by ordering zamindars who reoccupied land to pay the assessment during the period during which it had been left unoccupied.[33] This had little effect. Wasteland was abundant and there was no need for zamindars to take up the precise plots which they had previously resigned.

Luckily for government, Francis had limited Sindhi settlements to ten years, to allow the rates to be increased. In 1874, a conference of Settlement Officers in Hyderabad abolished the 'diffused rate' system.[34] Under their revised system, Survey Numbers were smaller, at four and a half acres on average, and liable to the full rate each year – but only if the field, or part of it, was cultivated.[35] This enabled farmers to leave land fallow if they wished. Fallow Rules were introduced to limit the time fields could be left barren. After a certain period, fixed for each taluqa, zamindars had to cultivate, or at least pay assessment on, their fallow lands, or forfeit them to government.[36] These 'revision' settlements replaced the 'original' or 'diffused rate' settlements as they expired.[37]

Other difficulties remained. Assessment rates in the Deccan took account of such criteria as the quality and depth of soils and the proximity of lands to markets. On irrigated lands, separate rates were imposed as land-tax and water-rate. It was a tidy system, which could not be applied to Sind. All soil in Sind was alluvial. It varied so widely in quality that any attempt to classify it was doomed to failure. Instead, Francis adopted a rudimentary soil analysis. He identified the presence of sand or salt as serious 'faults' which impaired the productiveness of the soil, and worked out a scale by which Settlement Officers could gauge their importance. It was an imaginative solution, but Mansfield, the Commissioner, suspected that even this simplified scale would prove too detailed to put into practice.[38]

Francis also realized that it would be impossible to separate the land-tax and the water-rate. Departing still further from Deccan practice, he decided revenue should be payable per Persian wheel on 'lift' lands and per bigah on all other lands. The former, he remarked, could be regarded as a water-rate, the latter as a land-tax, but he warned against trying to distinguish between the two in an irrigated country like Sind: they were combined. The quality of the soil was 'a matter of secondary importance' to the nature of the water-supply.[39]

In the event, as Mansfield had predicted, Francis' soil classification was too complicated to be workable. Settlement Officers paid increasing attention to the irrigational facilities when calculating assessment rates, a habit not appreciated by the Government of Bombay. In July 1872, Alexander Rogers, a member of the Governor's Council, condemned the settlements in Sind. Too much emphasis, in his opinion, was laid on the water-supply, while such vital considerations as the proximity of land to markets, were ignored.[40] The Bombay government refused to sanction any more settlements until it had received a satisfactory explanation of the premises on which they were based.[41] In 1875, displaying a remarkable ignorance of Sindhi conditions, the government passed a resolution which insisted that 'purely irrigation and purely settlement questions should not be mixed together.'[42]

This comment was included in the resolution which abolished the 'diffused rate' system. Therefore, while doing away with the discredited 'diffused rate,' the 'revision' settlements introduced a new difficulty of their own. When deciding what assessment lands could bear, Settlement Officers were supposed to ignore important factors like the cost of canal clearances, which affected farmers' incomes, and the level of the country, which determined how well land was irrigated, and 'group' villages according to their 'natural facilities for water-supply' and their distance from markets.[43] But most land in Sind had no natural water-supply, being entirely dependent on artificial irrigation. In addition, towns tended to be situated on high-lying land, safe from floods, where irrigation was precarious; estates with good access to markets were often less valuable because they had poor water supplies.[44]

The solution came in 1881, when Colonel Haig, Superintendent of the Sind Revenue Survey, settled the taluqas of Mehar, Tigar and Labdaria. Their condition was too poor to stand a full assessment, so he introduced temporary settlements until they improved. Haig had argued strongly against Rogers' criticisms a decade earlier and he now threw caution to the wind by discarding all pretence of adherence to the Deccan model. Since the three taluqas suffered from an uncertain water-supply, Haig based his rates entirely on their irrigational facilities.[45] The experiment proved so successful that Haig's 'irrigational' settlements were extended to the whole of Sind as the 'revision' settlements expired in the 1880s and 1890s.[46] The main criterion for grouping villages was the quality of the water-supply, although other matters like access to markets were taken into account when appropriate. Rates were then set for the different types of irrigation and farmers were free to change their methods (and hence their assessment) according to circumstance. For example, because it was expensive to cultivate by means of a Persian wheel, rates were lower on 'lift' lands. A zamindar who had cultivated by 'flow' one year would pay less revenue the following season, if a poor inundation obliged him to depend on wheels.[47] It was an ideal system for an irrigated country, and Haig's 'irrigational' settlements remained in force until after the end of British rule in Sind.

When 'irrigational' settlements superseded 'revision' settlements, the Fallow Rules were suspended. For a while, zamindars holding lands under 'irrigational' settlements could leave their land fallow indefinitely. To remedy this, the Government of Sind introduced new Fallow Rules in 1887. The most important was Number 4, which provided that zamindars had to pay assessment on each Survey Number every five years or forfeit it to government.[48] It meant that zamindars could hold up to five times as much land as they cultivated.

The technical problems of the raiyatwari settlement, therefore, were not resolved until three decades after Frere initiated the 'rough' survey and settlement in 1855. The Deccan prototype had been altered out of recognition, with a water-rate substituted for the land-tax and with liberal provision for fallows. Only the field assessment remained to identify it as a raiyatwari system. But this was its most politically controversial feature. Many British officers believed that the field-assessment – however modified – undermined the economic viability of Waderos' estates.

The first, and most eminent, person to oppose the introduction of the raiyatwari settlement to Sind was Lord John Lawrence. He was Governor-General of India when Major Francis presented his report in 1863, and he took immediate exception to it. He was certain the system was unsuitable for large zamindars, and he doubted whether Francis had fully considered the issues. Before Francis' arrival in Sind, a third of the province had been subjected to a field survey and Lawrence suspected he had merely confirmed the *fait accompli*. He urged the Bombay government to think again, commending to them the village-lease system which had proved so successful among the largeholders of the North-Western Provinces – and of which Lawrence himself happened to have been one of the architects.[49]

Lawrence's arguments had no effect on either Francis or Mansfield, the Commissioner in Sind. Both maintained that the Deccan system was the finest in India. Francis, indeed, seemed able to find no defect in the Deccan settlement, nor any merit in that of the North-Western Provinces.[50] In the face of their intransigence, Lawrence agreed, in 1864, to let the Sind authorities go ahead with their raiyatwari system as they pleased, although he did so reluctantly: his final letter painted a glowing picture of the virtues of the village-lease system.[51] The Survey and Settlement Act passed into law in 1865, giving formal sanction to Francis' recommendations.[52]

Lawrence's defence of the great Muslim zamindars of Sind seems to contradict his wider reputation as an upholder of peasant rights. His distrust of the magnates of Oudh was well known, but it arose from his experience of the Rebellion of 1857. He was afraid they might rebel again.[53] The Sindhi Waderos, by contrast, had shown conspicuous loyalty during the rebellion, so Lawrence may have wished to reward them and preserve their beneficial influence. He may also, of course, have been concerned at the prospect of dispossessed largeholders whipping up rebellion – as had happened in Oudh in 1857.

Francis made no direct comment on the political implications of a raiyatwari settlement, except to emphasize that it should meet the needs of the majority: who were, naturally enough, smallholders.[54] He showed no interest in Waderos and gave only cursory attention to the impact of the settlement on them. He suggested that they should continue to take out leases on whole villages if they wished: but the liabilities of all inferior holders should be recorded, field by field, in readiness for a regular field-assessment if they declined to pay as a body.[55] This effectively killed off the idea. Largeholders would be held responsible for precise amounts of revenue under a detailed field-settlement, but were offered no corresponding advantages. It held none of the attractions of a village-lease, where inferior and superior holders were left to determine their liabilities among themselves. Furthermore, the lease would run for the full period of the settlement – at least ten years – and their experience of Pringle's leases had made Waderos unwilling to enter into long-term commitments with government.[56] In a province where irrigation was as uncertain as in Sind, nobody would want to act as guarantor for other someone else's cultivation. This had in itself been one of the strongest arguments against the village-lease system, as Francis had anticipated.[57]

In general, though, Francis seems to have turned a blind eye to the Waderos. His experience of Sind was limited – there is no record that he ever visited the province before 1862 – and he had only a few months in which to familiarize himself with local conditions and write his report.[58] He relied heavily on Malcolm Haig, the Karachi Settlement Officer.[59] Haig had been posted to the province in 1859 and, apart from short breaks for leave, was to serve there continuously until 1881. In 1874, he was put in charge of the Sind Settlement Department, with the title of Settlement Officer in Sind.[60] It may be significant that he voiced a marked antagonism towards the Sindhi Waderos. Writing in the *Sind Gazetteer* of 1876, Haig praised Napier for criticizing them. Napier had, in Haig's opinion, reduced the influence of great zamindars and given independence to the smallholders. He added that it was still the policy of the British administration to foster this desire for independence and put all landholders on the same footing.[61] Many of his colleagues would have resisted this interpretation and the compiler of the 1907 *Gazetteer*, reprinting Haig's remarks, felt obliged to set the record straight by appending a more conventional analysis of British policy.[62] Haig had been brought up in Ireland during the 'Hungry Forties,'[63] and his Irish background may have prejudiced him against landlordism; among the comments of Napier which he quoted approvingly was one comparing the Sindhi Waderos with the 'middlemen' of Ireland.[64]

Francis' report drew heavily upon lessons learned while helping Haig to settle taluqa Kotri in 1862. Captain Taverner, the Hyderabad Settlement Officer, remarked to the Commissioner in Sind that, 'Francis & Haig both write in great glee with regard to the Kotree Settlement.'[65] His experience here led Francis to the unexpected conclusion that, 'the Zemindaree tenure, as it exists in the Kotree Districts, differs in no material point from a Ryotwaree holding in the Deccan.'[66] Most of the zamindars in Kotri cultivated only a few acres, like Deccan raiyats, while the subdivision of land was quite as small as in the Deccan. Since the circumstances were similar, Francis felt no revenue system could work better in Sind than that which had proved so successful in the Deccan. He was aware that colleagues might disagree but concluded, in somewhat guarded language: 'I have no hesitation in saying that, in my opinion there is nothing in the nature of the Zemindaree tenure as it exists in the Kotree Talooka certainly, which precludes the general application of the Deccan form of settlement.'[67]

Yet Kotri was a curious taluqa on which to base the system. Holdings were exceptionally small. When Haig and Francis introduced the settlement, there were only three estates over 400 acres, the largest being less than 900 acres.[68] Table 6 confirms that this was unusual. In Sukkur, around this time, there were twenty-six zamindars with 500 acres each, including four with more than 2,500 acres, while in Naushahro Feroze, forty-four zamindars held over 500 acres, three with estates larger than 2,000 acres.[69] Kotri was hardly the obvious taluqa in which to test the applicability of the raiyatwari settlement to the great Waderos of Sind.

In 1872, Haig revised the Kotri settlement. His analysis of its effects confirms the suspicion that the raiyatwari system of Sind was actually intended to discriminate against largeholders. The number of smallholdings had increased, while the number of largeholdings had decreased. The average size of holdings had fallen from thirty-eight to nineteen acres, and no-one now held an estate bigger than 600 acres. Haig thoroughly approved of the trend towards smaller holdings. It would benefit the country, and he credited the settlement with producing this happy situation.[70] As further evidence of its good effects, he cited the career of Abdul Rahman Thebo who, when Haig had arrived with Francis in 1862, had been a hari, without an acre to his name. After the introduction of the settlement, he and two relatives borrowed Rs 600. They used Rs 366 to buy 185 acres of land which was being auctioned to recover arrears of land revenue. This was an inexpensive way of acquiring land. Prices were low at such auctions because 'respectable people' refused to bid, considering it 'a disreputable way of acquiring land.'[71] Abdul Rahman had no such scruples. He set the rest of the money aside for stock and seed. After two years, the partnership was dissolved and the land was divided between the three cosharers. Abdul Rahman supplemented his income by contracting to carry out canal clearances; he extended his holding and by 1872 was the largest holder in the taluqa, with 598 acres. Haig admitted the case was exceptional, but presented it as, 'an indication of the improvement in the condition of at all events the poorer classes of agriculturists, which may be looked for as a future result of the settlement.'[72]

Abdul Rahman might have flourished under any system, while the shrinking of largeholdings may have resulted from Waderos shedding excess waste or taking advantage of the 'diffused rate' system. Haig's position, though, was unambiguous. His settlements were tailored for 'the poorer classes of agriculturists,' and he was largely indifferent to the fate of the largeholders.

Evan James, a young officer appointed Deputy Collector of Sehwan in 1870, also believed that the settlement system was strengthening smallholders and he became convinced that it was seriously damaging the interests of largeholders. James, who was to return to Sind as Commissioner in 1892, served only two years in his first tour, but a report he produced just before leaving in 1872 had a far-reaching impact on its administration.

Kotri lay within James' Sub-Division, but it was the situation around his headquarters, in taluqa Sehwan itself, which caught his attention. Haig had settled Sehwan in 1864. By the time James took charge, a similar pattern to that at Kotri had emerged, but on a grander scale. Sehwan was more representative than Kotri, in that there was a greater proportion of largeholders. Twenty-three zamindars had held over 500 acres each in 1864, but by 1876, when the settlement was revised, only one remained.[73] James reported that most of the Waderos were hopelessly in debt to Hindu banias, to whom they were losing their estates. Worst affected were those holding land irrigated from the Manchar Lake.[74]

James saw in the settlement one of the chief agents of the Waderos' ruin. Mansfield's ruling on wastelands had presented them with the stark choice of surrendering their uncultivated waste, or paying for it before they had time to bring it under the plough. Unwilling to give up their traditional rights over uncultivated lands, the Waderos preferred to pay for them. They were driven to moneylenders to raise the cash, and so they sank into debt. James did not blame them for clinging to more land than they could cultivate. He defended them passionately:

> What course would an English squire adopt, if told to throw up a moor on his estate, or his lawn, or his park, or in default pay a heavy rent on it, commencing at once, though he knew that it would be some time before he could make the land fit to grow crops? Would he part with his paternal acres, or hold by them, trusting to scrape enough money from his cultivated farms to pay for them meanwhile? He would choose the latter alternative, I think, and so did the Muncher zemindars.[75]

James admitted that his ideas were influenced by conversations with the zamindars, and he may have been repeating their complaints.[76] He was apparently unaware how readily some of them had disposed of their 'paternal acres' when it suited their purposes under the 'diffused rate' settlements. James had been brought up on his family's estate at Barrock Park estate near Carlisle.[77] Coming from the Cumberland gentry, he may, unlike Haig, have been predisposed to sympathize with the landed families of Sind.

The burden of James' argument was that Waderos had to maintain their status and that government had prejudiced their interests by putting them on a level with peasants with regard to revenue payments. Peasants had no position to keep up, so they did not exercise authority over wasteland. Haig had kept no record of the *lapo* (a zamindari fee) which Waderos levied from farmers who cultivated land which had formerly belonged to them. James concluded angrily that 'all Zemindars' rights were treated as nullities' by Haig and the Settlement Department.[78]

It fell to Haig, as the senior Settlement Officer in Sind and the author of the Sehwan settlement, to answer James' criticisms. He vigorously defended the principles behind the raiyatwari system by denying that zamindari rights existed in Sind. He had not recorded the rights a zamindar could exercise over wasteland transferred to others, 'for the sufficient reason that I had not, as I have not now, the least idea of what they are, or that he has any rights at all over such land.' He refused to admit that there was a qualitative difference between a zamindar and a peasant. The distinction was, 'simply one of social standing, and generally (not always) of extent of occupancy.' If peasants had wasteland, they were free to levy whatever fees they wished, but neither they nor Waderos could do so unless they paid assessment on it to government.[79]

Haig's presented a straightforward enunciation of the principles behind Mansfield's decision of 1862. He had no compassion for people who clung to unprofitable land for sentimental reasons or to uphold their izzat. They merely caused large areas to lie waste, which other farmers could put to good use. The one largeholder in Sehwan who was prospering was Makhdum Dost Muhammad, who 'had the good sense to keep no more land than he could cultivate.'[80] Haig insisted that all complaints in Sehwan stemmed from a body of reckless and improvident zamindars, 'who under any circumstances would have steadily kept on the road to ruin, [and] find in the Settlement a convenient excuse for the pass to which they have brought themselves.'[81]

Haig defended the principle, but he did not defend the specific settlement which he had introduced to Sehwan. On the contrary, when he revised it in 1876, he declared, 'Nowhere has a Settlement so wretchedly miscarried as that which happily has terminated in Sehwan.'[82] He contended, though, that Sehwan was exceptional and that James, who had little experience of Sind, was not justified in applying to the rest of the province lessons he had learned there. He accused James of generalizing 'from a limited number of particular instances.'[83]

First of all, a change in the course of the Indus during the 1860s had silted up the channels feeding Lake Manchar, where most of their land was, preventing it from draining in time for crops to be sown. By 1875, less than half the original cultivated area could be cropped.[84]

Secondly, many of the leading zamindars were Saiyids whose exemptions from land revenue, granted by the Talpurs out of religious respect, had been stopped by the British. They therefore received higher tax demands just at the moment when the silting of the Manchar cut their incomes. According to Haig, their lifestyles made matters worse. They were quarrelsome, 'swift . . . to shed blood in miserable family brawls,' and the sums they squandered on prostitutes 'would suffice to redeem many a ruined estate.'[85] When he introduced the settlement in 1864, Haig had found that 'the idle class,' as he castigated the big zamindars, were all in debt, but he did not feel this entitled them to any concessions.[86]

However, the impact of the settlement was more harsh than Haig intended, for Maher, the Deputy Collector, refused to give adequate remissions of revenue. The rates were the same on cultivated as on uncultivated land, but Haig had never intended to penalize zamindars if circumstances beyond their control prevented them from cultivating – for example, as a result of flooding, water shortages or attacks by pests. Between 1864 to 1874, the occupied area fell from 79,465 acres to 55,627 acres. Since the reduction of the occupied area often accompanied the 'diffused rate' system, it cannot be taken in isolation as evidence of hardship, but Haig admitted that much of the best land had passed from largeholders to smallholders. The latter, he said, were scornfully referred to as 'Settlement Zamindars' by the old proprietors. Haig believed that the silting of the Manchar, the character of the Saiyids and Maher's unreasonable policy on remissions had combined to damage the fortunes of the Waderos. The settlement itself had nothing to do with it. After 1869, when Maher left, remissions were more generous and the Waderos started to recover.[87]

The Government of Bombay was not convinced. It did not accept that Sehwan was an isolated example. The failure of the 'diffused rate' system had long been obvious, and government was so unhappy about many aspects of the Sind settlements that it had refused to sanction new ones. It felt that James had made some points of general interest, and his remarks were added to the agenda of the conference of Settlement Officers which met at Hyderabad in November 1874.

The conference conceded that the 'natural dislike' of Waderos to relinquish their wasteland had probably added to their financial difficulties, and that it was 'only right and politic' for government to help them by respecting some of their claims. At the same time, the conference emphasized that zamindars had no legal titles to land they did not pay for; any concession on this point 'must be considered an act of grace.' The conference devised a novel expedient to effect this. Instead of paying assessment per Survey Number, Waderos would be able to take their entire estates on lease, at a reduction of up to 30% on the aggregate assessment the estates would otherwise have paid.[88]

This proposal remained a dead letter. There is no record of any zamindar applying to lease his estate on the terms offered. Giving zamindars one-third of their estates free of assessment was hardly a great favour. It would not even cover their fallows if they left two-thirds of their holdings barren each year. It certainly would not subsidize the vast tracts of wasteland which some Waderos possessed. The Fallow Rules which accompanied the 'revision' settlements were more generous, for they enabled zamindars to leave up to four-fifths of their estates uncultivated. Furthermore, Waderos had no desire to repeat their experience of Pringle's leases, when they had been made liable for the revenue on specified acreages and could not obtain remissions under any circumstances. A regular field-assessment was more flexible. They could cut their coats according to the cloth, resigning Survey Numbers if they could not afford to pay for them and taking them up again if conditions improved.

Moreover, the settlement did not in practice jeopardize Waderos' claims over wasteland. It was effectively a non-issue, saying more about district officers' relationships with Waderos than zamindari rights. It was generally recognized that certain lands belonged to certain families.[89] Whatever government might say, its technical ownership of the land could not set aside the Waderos' local influence, while the Fallow Rules gave them the opportunity to keep a title on fields which they could not immediately cultivate.

Officers' real fear was that a raiyatwari settlement was in itself incompatible with the existence of Waderos. This had been Lawrence's fear in 1863, when Francis submitted his proposals for the settlement system. James stated the case in detail in 1873, in a memorandum he prepared after leaving Sind. Under a raiyatwari settlement, every Survey Number was assessed. Someone who farmed intensively, without wasting any land, would have no difficulty in paying the revenue, but big zamindars were less able than peasant-proprietors to guarantee efficient cultivation because they had to depend on haris, who were notoriously shifty and disinterested cultivators. In addition, the field-survey took no account of the fact that, while peasants could keep all the crop for themselves, a zamindar had to make batai with the haris. That is to say, a Survey Number on a zamindar's estate had to support two sets of people, not one. At the same time, haris were beginning to be attracted by the prospect of acquiring cultivable wasteland on their own account and setting up as smallholders. The zamindar had to offer them higher rates at batai, to persuade them to stay in their jobs. James painted a grim picture:

> the zemindar, when he calls on his harees to engage for raising a crop, is told he must submit to getting almost nothing out of the land but the bare assessment, or the haree says "I will take up land for myself." The zemindar is thus reduced either to letting his land be cultivated for a song, or . . . he has to pay for it when he gets nothing out of it.

Thus Waderos, who had already taken out loans to retain their 'paternal acres' of waste, had to be satisfied with minimal returns on their cultivated lands. They were bound to fall further into debt. James warned: 'We have ruined such numbers of them in Sind that we ought to be careful to ruin as few more as we can.'[90]

There are few reliable figures against which to test James' assertion that zamindars could not afford to pay their assessments. However, the accounts reproduced in Table 4 (pages 63–64) do not support his case. Estates 1, 3 and 4 were contemporary with James' memorandum. The zamindars' net profits amounted respectively to forty per cent, forty-three per cent and twenty-four per cent of their gross incomes. These figures are no more conclusive than any other official statistics, but they indicate that, even after making batai and paying assessment, zamindars could still make reasonable profits.

Colonel Merewether, the Commissioner in Sind, disputed James' analysis. He commented on his inexperience and accused him of prejudice. James had, he said, formed 'hastily drawn conclusions' from 'a partial knowledge of the subject.' Instead, he recommended to the Governor of Bombay the counter arguments of Colonel Haig, whom Merewether praised as 'the oldest, most experienced, and most able Settlement Officer in Sind.'[91]

Haig maintained that James had started from a false premise. He agreed that largeholders received only a portion of the crop, but peasants were in precisely the same position. While Waderos had to divide their produce with their haris, peasants had to divide it with their cosharers. The field-survey could not discriminate in favour of either party on that score. Moreover, petty holders had less resilience than largeholders, for if the crop failed on their few acres, they had no others to fall back on.[92] The belief, held by James and many of his colleagues, that the batai system made largeholders uncompetitive was curious. It was ancient and practised throughout India. If the largeholders did not like it, they had only to switch over to the danai (cash rent) system. In fact, as discussed in Chapter 2, the batai operated in favour of the zamindars rather than against them and they were usually reluctant to adopt danai rents.

Although refuting much of the detail of James' case, Haig did not actually deny that haris were becoming more independent, and at the expense of the Wadero. He simply could see no harm in it:

> To a certain extent, indeed, the peasantry have everywhere become more independent, for they have prospered under the settlement. This is a change of circumstances unfavourable to the old proprietors but inevitable under the travelling tendencies of our rule.[93]

He clearly conceded James' point here, though he approached it from a different angle. While James was alarmed to see the Waderos weakened, Haig was pleased to see the peasants thriving. Abdul Rahman Thebo of Kotri, the hari who had profited from the misfortunes of an old proprietor to become a zamindar, must have been the essence of James' villain – the hari with ideas above his station. Haig, by contrast, admired him, seeing his success as a vindication of the system. The two attitudes complemented one another: whatever Haig might say, both men did believe that the raiyatwari system was ill suited to Waderos. Their argument recalls the exchange between Lord Lawrence and the Sind authorities in 1864.

A levelling tendency was intrinsic to the raiyatwari settlement. It was designed for petty holders. The field assessment, putting a premium on intensive cultivation, tended to put the holders of extensive estates at a disadvantage. It encouraged largeholders to give up excess land. At the same time, because Survey Numbers were small, people of the most limited means could afford to take up land and so the settlement promoted the development of a peasant class. With the size of Waderos' estates apparently diminishing, and the number of peasants increasing, it seemed that the Waderos would cease to exist.

The controversy surrounding the raiyatwari settlement came to a head over taluqa Larkana, in the 1880s. Larkana was an ideal laboratory. It was a complete contrast to Sehwan, where James had formed his opinions. No burden like the Manchar Lake hindered cultivation, nor did new canals improve it. From the time of the introduction of the original, 'diffused rate,' settlement in 1869–70, the irrigational facilities were consistently excellent. Prices remained constant. Apart from the occasional good or bad season, the only variable was the settlement.[94]

Larkana was known as the garden of Upper Sind. It was well situated for water and famous for the quality of its sugdasi rice, grown in the mail area in the western part of the taluqa. It had always been prosperous. When he introduced the original settlement in 1869, Haig was pleased to note that, in addition to its natural advantages, Larkana was 'happy in possessing a most enterprising and intelligent body of proprietors.'[95] Colonel Francis, who was still responsible for supervising settlement operations in Sind, believed the public spirit of the Larkana zamindars was without parallel anywhere in the Bombay Presidency.[96] Their greatest achievement was the construction of the Fordwah, a canal opened in 1855, over half the cost of which, amounting to Rs 23,000, had been met by the zamindars. In 1862–63, they had contributed Rs 86,177 for public works on top of their private expenses for canal clearances.[97]

Unfortunately, though irrigational works gave them a good return on their investment, some zamindars may been more generous than they could afford. In addition, Captain Ford, the Assistant Collector of Larkana, penalized zamindars who did not take advantage of the newly irrigated wastelands, forcing them to take on more land than they could afford to cultivate. The Collector of Larkana condemned Ford's 'forcing' system in 1869, but by that time all the leading zamindars were in debt except for Fateh Muhammad Lahori and his sons.[98]

When Haig revised the settlement in 1881, he found many of the Waderos in desperate straits. The most dramatic case was Khalifa Muhammad Panah, whose entire estate of 2,727 acres had been sold to his creditor, Seth Gokuldas. The 1,300 acre estate of Sardar Khan Abro had also been dispersed among his creditors. At the introduction of the settlement in 1869–70, the largest holder had been Shah Nawaz Abro, with 4,077 acres, but he had since been reduced to 1,182 acres – and no less than 1,439 acres of his land had been auctioned by government to recover arrears of land revenue. Other zamindars had lost similarly large amounts of land and were heavily in debt.[99] Table 7 shows the holdings of largeholders in Larkana in 1869, 1881 and 1892.

The settlement of 1869 had generated a substantial increase in revenue over the 'rough' settlement which had preceded it, but this was matched by an extension of the cultivated area, while the average rate of assessment per acre was less under Haig's settlement than under the 'rough' settlement. Haig refused to blame the settlement

Table 7 Largeholders in taluqa Larkana 1869/70–1891/92

Name of Zamindar	*Size of holding* *1869–70* *acres*	*1880–81* *acres*	*1891–92* *acres*
Shah Nawaz Abro	4,077	1,182	1,111
Muhammad Panah	2,727	–	–
Gokuldas	–	3,116	3,096
Mir Khan Abro & sons*	1,845	600	442
Pir Bakhsh Kalhoro & sons*	936	493	76
Muhammad Saleh Khizmatgar	904	175	188
Dost Muhammad Lahori	722	966	1,115
Tharo Khan Lahori	562	880	2,210
Lutaf Ali Abro & sons	571	422	247
Ghulam Shah	650	1,142	1,267
Ghulam Allah Abro	646	521	1,193
Sher Muhammad Sangi	447	511	459
Ghulam Ali Isran	177	652	1,990
Nangar Sangi	533	284	97
Shah Muhammad Kalhoro	1,597	691	376
Taj Muhammad Kalhoro*	530	274	151
Pir Sher Muhammad	675	138	574
Khalikdad Abro & others	569	569	964
Sardar Khan Abro	1,300	–	–
Khuda Bakhsh Bhutto*	–	919	238
Usman Ali Abro	–	–	560
Lakha Singh Amil	–	–	1,043
Pritam Singh	–	–	811
Muhammad Fazal Sangi	–	–	516

Source: *Larkana SR*, 1892

Note: Decreases in size of asterisked estates may be the result of family partitions.

for the Waderos' misfortune, attributing it instead to their 'neglect, dissipation and extravagance.' He had evidently revised his earlier, favourable, opinion of them. The settlement, he felt, had pressed too lightly on them. It had produced the familiar 'diffused rate' pattern of declining revenue collections and a reduction in the occupied area, without any corresponding decrease in production. Haig replaced it with a 'revision' settlement. The rates, he insisted, were reasonable, but they enhanced the revenue collections by an average of forty-one per cent over the next decade.

Haig's 'revision' settlement was given a trial in 1881–82. He had predicted that the revenue demand would be Rs 298,863, but it turned out to be Rs 330,160, over a *lakh* of rupees more than in the final year of the previous settlement. The increase was due to a good inundation and the growth of cultivation on the more highly assessed lands. The Government of Bombay believed the results proved that Haig's rates were judicious and did not strain the resources of the zamindars. In 1882, his settlement was confirmed for ten years, although the rates on lands near the town of Larkana were reduced slightly.[100]

Government's decision, so some zamindars alleged in a petition to the Governor of Bombay early in 1883, came as a shock to the inhabitants of Larkana. Over Rs 14,000 remained uncollected at the end of the year 1881–82 and they insisted it was beyond their capacity to pay Haig's rates. They begged the Governor to order a revision. Not only did the petitioners object to the particular settlement, but they condemned the whole settlement system, in terms which would have struck a sympathetic chord in the heart of Evan James. They complained that they had been forced to pay assessment on uncultivated land. In fact, all land was encumbered with such heavy rates of assessment that even banias refused to accept it in settlement of debts except at disproportionately low prices. Unable to sell their land, zamindars had no alternative but to relinquish it, or mortgage it at nominal rates. In the long run, they would all be ruined. If the Governor did not believe them, they advised him to send for the report of Robert Giles, the Assistant Collector of Larkana.[101]

Giles was indeed strongly critical both of the settlement and the system. He agreed with James that, because Waderos had to batai their crops and were defrauded by their haris into the bargain, they could not compete with smallholders under a field-assessment. This explained why revenue was more forthcoming on the mail lands, where holdings were small.[102] Other officials supported Giles. Thomas Hart-Davies, the Manager of Encumbered Estates in Sind, was adamant that, unless Haig's rates were reduced immediately, 'the Zemindars of the district will be totally ruined.'[103] Colonel Wallace, the Collector of Shikarpur, gave eloquent backing to these intimations of disaster. He looked beyond the present settlement in an apocalyptic restatement of James' vision of despair a decade previously. The zamindar was doomed, for he 'cannot maintain his position under a ryotwari system of settlement.' Zamindars beggared themselves by offering high batai rates which they could not afford, in a vain attempt to stop their haris deserting them to become petty holders. He produced no evidence to substantiate this claim. On the contrary, batai rates appear to have remained unchanged throughout the century. The Deputy Collector of Shikarpur had stated some years previously that the Larkana zamindars passed the burden of land revenue onto their haris if they had difficulty paying it themselves.[104] Nevertheless, Wallace lamented:

> It is hopeless to attempt to stem the tide and preserve the old Zemindar who has however done excellent service to the state. Sooner or later, one by one, the Zemindar will be obliged to lessen his holding until by degrees he, or as it is to be hoped, his descendants will sink into the position of a cultivator. We might reduce the Government demand upon him to stave off the evil for a time, but we cannot prevent the cultivator from setting up on his own account. Thus year by year the number of small holdings will increase until the larger holdings disappear altogether.[105]

Colonel Anderson, who had succeeded Haig as Superintendent of the Sind Revenue Survey in 1881, was unmoved by this barrage of criticism. It is interesting that he did not deny that the days of the great zamindar were numbered. Merely, like Haig before him, he had no regrets about it. A large estate, he maintained, could not be managed as economically as a small one – especially if the owner was a Wadero. Revenue which could easily be paid by peasants or banias, who seldom held more land than they could afford, pressed heavily on Waderos, who were notoriously unbusinesslike. Unable to compete, it was inevitable that the Wadero should see his estate slip into the hands of peasants and banias. If, 'for political or sentimental reasons,' government wished to 'bolster him up for a few more years,' the only solution would be to grant a special remission for the Wadero class. Anderson raised the question of special pleading by administrators. As they were the most influential people in the country, Waderos were in a position to make their grievances heard and many officials, 'ignoring the justice and difficulties of the situation,' sympathized with them. They blamed the raiyatwari settlement but really, said Anderson, the Wadero's demise was 'due to causes as natural as that man shall grow old and die.'[106]

Despite the petitions of the zamindars and the pleas of Giles and Wallace, the Bombay government refused to make any serious modifications to Haig's rates.[107] But the Larkana zamindars did not, as a class, 'grow old and die.' On the contrary, they survived and prospered. In 1883–84, government had difficulty collecting the revenue, nearly Rs 14,000 remaining in arrears, and a large number of warning notices had to be issued. However, less land than usual was actually forfeited for non-payment of arrears, since the zamindars managed to make up the deficit the following year. The Bombay government interpreted this as evidence that the zamindars were unwilling, rather than unable, to pay, and had deliberately withheld their revenue as a protest.[108] After 1884, the problem ceased, confirming government's suspicions. Even in the worst years of the 'revision' settlement (1885–87), the revenue demand was almost equal to the best years under Haig's original settlement, yet the zamindars had no apparent difficulty in paying.[109]

A slight rise in prices may have helped them. When Haig introduced his original settlement in 1869, the average price of uncleaned rice was Rs 1–5 per maund, but by 1882 it had fallen to between eleven to thirteen annas per maund. In 1884, prices climbed back to the 1869 figure, at Rs 1–4–9 per maund. This rise helped the zamindars but, when fixing the rates, Haig had assumed an average price of Rs 1–11 per maund, and this figure was not reached until 1892, the final year of the settlement. The average price of rice for the period of the settlement was lower than Haig had expected, at Rs 1–4–8.[110] The upturn of prices, though welcome, was insufficient to make the difference between ruin and prosperity.

For the Waderos did not merely survive, they positively thrived on Haig's settlement. Most extended their holdings, as Table 7 shows. When the original settlement was introduced in 1869–70, there were sixteen largeholders, with an average holding of 1,178 acres each. By the time it was revised in 1880–81, they had been reduced to twelve, with an average holding of 979 acres – though one should bear in mind that this was a 'diffused rate' settlement, under which some zamindars may have found it convenient to trim their estates. When Haig's controversial settlement was revised in 1891–92, the number of largeholders was thirteen, with an average holding of 1,265 acres. That is to say, the average size of a large estate had increased by a fifth under Haig's settlement. That hardly confirms the picture of suffering Waderos.

It was a development which ought not to have been unexpected. The arguments of Wallace, Giles and Hart-Davies in 1882–83 had centred on those zamindars who were badly in debt – people like Khalifa Muhammad Panah and Sardar Khan Abro. But their importance should not have been over stressed. Haig had mentioned other zamindars who had flourished under the original settlement in the 1870s.

He had singled out the Lahori family for praise, especially its head, Tharo Khan Lahori. His father, Fateh Khan, had been the only zamindar free from debt in 1869 and Tharo Khan followed his example, adding to his inherited wealth through purchases of good land in Larkana and Kambar.[111] Colonel Anderson, who betrayed no admiration for Sindhi Waderos as a whole, described him as:

> a man of some education and good address, has immense influence from his position, and energy of character amongst the other zemindars and is highly respected by the officials, both European and Native; he is a shrewd and careful man of business and altogether the most favourable specimen of the Muhammadan Zemindar that I have met.[112]

Tharo Khan's assessment had been raised by Haig. Both Anderson and the Commissioner in Sind believed that all the petitions against the settlement had been instigated by him.[113] Giles also held Tharo Khan in high esteem; some ten years later, he was anxious that Tharo Khan should be appointed as an Honorary Magistrate, as a mark of respect. Much of the opposition to the settlement, then, may be traced back to someone who was not in financial difficulties. It is surprising that, while prophesying the decline of the Waderos, Giles ignored the prosperous example of Tharo Khan Lahori, the leading zamindar of the taluqa, who virtually lived on his doorstep – the Lahori *autaq* being only a few minutes ride from the Assistant Collector's office.[114]

The Lahoris were not exceptional. Ghulam Ali Isran also made his fortune over this period. In 1869, he held only 177 acres in the rich *mail* lands. By the end of Haig's first settlement, which supposedly drove the great zamindars into debt, he had built up his holding to 652 acres. Ten years later, in 1892, he was one of the largest holders in the taluqa, with 1,990 acres.[115] His success was surely as dramatic as the collapse of Khalifa Muhammad Panah. In addition, Khuda Bakhsh, son of Dodo Khan Bhutto, the leading zamindar of taluqa Ratodero, bought 919 acres during Haig's original settlement. Clearly, this family of largeholders did not consider the rates of assessment to be prohibitive.

By 1892, therefore, there was evidence that several Waderos in Larkana were prospering: but it still did not seem conclusive either to Giles (now Collector of Shikarpur) or to Evan James, who had just been appointed Commissioner in Sind. The settlement was revised that year and the Settlement Officer proposed to enhance the rates of assessment. Giles disagreed. Instead, he reduced and rearranged the Settlement Officer's rates, to keep the total demand at its current level. James accepted Giles' recommendations.[116] In the event, the zamindars extended their cultivation and the revenue demand for 1893–94, the first year of the new settlement, was over half a lakh of rupees above the previous record. Since the total arrears for that year were no more than four annas, the zamindars evidently had no difficulty in paying and the collection went smoothly throughout the term of the settlement. It was due for revision in 1901 but Giles, now Commissioner in Sind, postponed it since he did not believe the taluqa could stand any augmentation of its revenue demand. Two years later, it was further postponed by the Collector of Larkana. By this time, Larkana was paying more revenue than any other taluqa in Sind.[117] At last, in 1907, the settlement was revised and the rates increased. The Settlement Officer, in his glowing account of Larkana's prosperity, paid scant heed to the warnings of the past. He insisted that 'the taluka is ripe for some enhancement of assessment.'[118]

The Larkana Waderos therefore thrived under a settlement which all had agreed would ruin them. That does not prove that the raiyatwari settlement met the needs of largeholders, nor that the assessment rates were moderate. It merely confirms that largeholders rested on solid economic foundations which could not be easily undermined. The estates may not have been cultivated efficiently, but they realized sufficient profits to keep their holders extremely wealthy. It would take more than a settlement system to make or break the Waderos.

People like Giles overestimated the impact which settlements could have on social conditions, and their belief in the imminent demise of the Waderos influenced their judgment. The correspondence relating to the revision of the settlement in Sukkur in 1898 sheds interesting light on this.

Sukkur, like Larkana, was a rich taluqa. It was the most thickly populated in the Shikarpur Collectorate. Yet the Settlement Officer reported in 1898 that all but five or six of the big zamindars were heavily in debt. He could find no natural circumstances to explain this, so he attributed it to their own extravagant and improvident habits.[119] Giles, who was Acting Commissioner in Sind, disagreed. With some justification, he called these reasons 'the stereotyped ones.' For him, as in Larkana, the settlement was the villain of the piece, and he urged the Governor of Bombay to reduce the assessment.[120] The Governor was not impressed with the arguments on either side. He doubted whether the Waderos were in such difficulties as was claimed. While thirteen Muslim largeholders held 15,385 acres in 1889–90, the same number held 22,465 acres in 1897–98: 'figures which by themselves do not support the alleged decline of the great families.' He refused to sanction the reductions proposed by Giles.[121]

Table 8 Largeholders in taluqa Sukkur 1889/90–1897/98

Name of Zamindar	*Size of holding* *1889–90* *acres*	*1897–98* *acres*	*Remarks*
Usif Mahar	2,058	2,535	Took up new land
Ghaos Bakhsh Mahar	33,306	5,629	Took up new land
Saiyid Nadir Shah	1,384	2,122	Took up new land
Abdul Rahman Pirzado	804	737	Forfeited fallow land
Lal Khan Pathan	1,891	2,677	Took up new land
Khair Muhammad Pathan	1,443	–	Transferred land to Faiz Muhammad Pathan
Sabal Hindu	357	356	
Motumal Hindu	282	249	Family partition
Khan Muhammad Mahar	915	884	Family partition
Hayat Phulpoto	1,256	2,110	Took up new land
Saiyid Ali Shah	310	359	Took up new land
Gulabrai Hindu	286	686	Took up new land
Ghulam Nabi Pirzado	247	1,394	Took up new land
Gelaram Hindu	264	342	Took up new land
Kimat Singh Hindu	–	548	Purchased land
Rahim Khan Khoso	441	338	Forfeited fallow land
Motial Mahar	378	738	Took up new land
Dipo Hindu	167	367	Took up new land
Faiz Muhammad Pathan	–	1,667	Purchased land from Khair Muhammad Pathan
Ghulam Haidar Khatian	354	1,118	Took up new land
Karim Khan Mughal	1,042	1,419	Took up new land

Source: Depy Collr., Sukkur, to Actg. Commr., Sind, 23 Dec. 1898, App. XXII (*B.N.S.* 328, *Larkana SR*, 85)

Table 8 confirms the Governor's impression. Apart from a few who had forfeited small amounts for the non-payment of assessment on fallow lands, and two who had transferred land to relations, all the big zamindars extended their holdings. The average holding of a Muslim largeholder increased from 1,183 acres in 1889–90 to 1,728 acres in 1897–98. Half a dozen Hindus were in a similar position, although they were building up their estates at a proportionately greater rate, their average holding increasing from 299 acres to 412 acres. It is reasonable to suppose that the Waderos must have had debts, for they could hardly have brought so much land under the plough without borrowing capital, but the evidence is that they were extending their holdings over the period when Giles and the Settlement Officer said their fortunes were deteriorating. The picture is much like that in Larkana.

Table 9 Muslim and Hindu largeholders in Sind around the turn of the century

Zamindars holding estates of 500 acres and more 1869/70–1913/14

		Muslims		*Hindus*	
Taluqa	*Year*	*No. of large-holders*	*Average area of estate of each largeholder (acres)*	*No. of large-holders*	*Average area of estate of largeholder (acres)*
Upper Sind Frontier					
Jacobabad	1885–86	35	2,523	7	2,375
	1893–94	50	2,569	9	1,755
	1903–04	49	2,941	9	1,802
Kandhkot	1894–95	55	1,858	11	1,279
	1902–03	66	1,712	17	1,295
Kashmore	1894–95	37	1,617	4	1,106
	1902–03	44	2,123	5	751
Thul	1893–94	68	2,054	10	1,196
	1902–03	80	1,971	11	1,366
Shikarpur					
Ghotki	1885–86	5	1,469	0	–
	1893–94	10	1,479	0	–
Kakar	1881–82	7	982	1	1,567
	1890–91	6	1,061	1	1,308
Kambar	1882–83	13	1,346	0	–
	1886–87	14	1,532	0	–
	1891–92	15	1,314	0	–
Larkana	1869–70	16	1,178	0	–
	1880–81	11	785	1	3,116
	1891–92	10	840	3	2,682
Mehar	1892–93	7	951	5	816
	1900–01	12	1,191	6	1,257
Nasirabad	1882–83	6	684	2	1,083
	1895–96	13	809	3	728
Naushahro Abro	1884–85	17	1,280	3	1,236
	1897–98	17	1,316	4	1,478
Ratodero	1882–83	5	1,609	3	1,262
	1891–92	14	1,323	5	1,403
Sukkur	1889–90	9	1,566	0	–
	1897–98	11	1,967	2	1,234
Hyderabad					
Badin	1898–99	14	887	8	949
	1906–07	17	933	11	816
Dero Mohbat	1887–88	11	1,174	4	757
	1907–08	11	1,634	6	768
Guni	1882–83	20	1,477	11	2,362
	1892–93	28	1,118	15	1,320
	1904–05	18	1,728	15	1,618
Hala	1883–84	37	1,351	5	997
	1892–93	49	1,238	10	1,002

Taluqa	*Year*	*Muslims* No. of large-holders	*Muslims* Average area of estate of each largeholder (acres)	*Hindus* No. of large-holders	*Hindus* Average area of estate of largeholder (acres)
Hyderabad	1896–97	4	760	3	570
	1904–05	5	3,641	4	542
Johi	1887–88	16	987	1	1,776
	1896–97	24	984	3	1,019
Kandiaro	1881–82	13	664	3	785
	1894–95	16	754	5	929
Moro	1881–82	9	994	0	–
	1894–95	18	810	1	938
Naushahro Feroze	1881–82	14	859	6	944
	1894–95	33	1,121	11	1,416
Shahdadpur	1892–93	15	1,421	11	1,301
	1904–05	20	1,163	17	1,521
Tando Allahyar	1890–01	17	1,430	4	1,161
	1904–05	19	1,499	7	1,546
Tando Bago	1898–99	22	1,505	11	1,380
	1906–07	21	1,536	13	1,486
Thar and Parkar					
Sinjhoro	1892–93	6	1,306	1	597
	1904–05	5	1,432	2	836
Karachi					
Ghorabari	1888–89	17	576	7	895
	1902–03	10	748	25	191
Jati	1887–88	14	901	4	1,464
	1897–98	12	912	7	1,075
	1913–14	8	1,355	8	1,037
Kotri	1889–90	3	617	1	1,811
	1897–98	3	559	1	2,058
Manjhand	1885–86	7	1,131	1	674
	1893–94	7	1,614	4	1,257
Mirpur Bathoro	1883–84	3	747	0	–
	1895–96	9	1,143	3	708
	1913–14	5	1,886	3	1,388
Mirpur Sakro	1888–89	13	1,061	11	872
	1902–03	7	725	4	954
Shahbandar	1886–87	15	973	4	652
	1897–98	13	1,002	4	765
	1913–14	10	1,439	5	1,060
Sujawal	1883–84	10	1,121	2	895
	1895–96	8	1,799	1	743
	1913–14	8	2,277	0	–
Thatta	1882–83	9	1,077	1	1,228
	1898–99	9	146	1	805
	1902–03	6	1,182	1	623

Source: Calculated from nominal lists of largeholders appended to some Settlement Reports

Indeed, it is hard to find concrete examples of Waderos in decline. Tables 6 and 9 show that zamindars with 500 acres and more were still firmly established in Sind in the last decades of the nineteenth century. Table 6 confirms that there were not many taluqas in which the Waderos' share of the occupied area fell. One was Johi, in Hyderabad Collectorate, where the area occupied by largeholders dropped from twenty-six per cent of the total to nineteen per cent between 1887–97, although the number of largeholders increased. Table 9 reveals few taluqas in which Waderos were losing ground to Hindus. The apparent exceptions were in Hyderabad Collectorate, where Hindus were investing in cotton lands as the development of railways made exports more profitable. In some of these taluqas, notably Kandiaro, Naushahro Feroze, Shahdadpur and Tando Allahyar, their holdings were bigger than Muslims': but the Waderos do not appear to have suffered correspondingly for, except in Shahdadpur, they also expanded their estates and the number of Muslim largeholders increased.

The most significant evidence of largeholders declining in relation to smallholders was in Mirpur Sakro, of the Karachi Collectorate. As in Sehwan, the causes were natural, and the pattern was similar in the neighbouring Delta taluqas Ghorabari, Jati, Thatta and Sujawal.

Mirpur Sakro was one of the poorest taluqas in Sind. The cultivated area was shrinking and by 1901–02, all the zamindars were deeply indebted both to government and to banias. The Settlement Officer doubted whether either would get their money unless there was a rapid improvement in the water-supply.[122] Table 10 sets out details of largeholdings for the period 1889–1903. The average size of a Muslim largeholding fell from 1,061 acres to 725 acres, while the number of big Muslim zamindars almost halved. Many lost huge amounts of land under the fallow rules. Others had sold, often to Hindu creditors. Their Hindu competitors were not faring much better, though, for out of eleven with over 500 acres in 1889–90, there were only four in 1902–03. Nevertheless, three new largeholders were prepared to invest in Mirpur Sakro by purchasing land – and two of them were Muslims. As in Larkana, so even in this miserable taluqa, if some Waderos were losing land, others were buying it.

In the nearby taluqa of Sujawal, whose largeholdings are reported in Table 11, conditions were less desperate and most Waderos extended their holdings. There was, though, one spectacular example of an ambitious hari. In 1883–84, Shaikh Imam Bakhsh held only 83 acres. Ten years later, he had 2,087 acres, having bought out his 'former master,' Nawab Pir Bakhsh Khan Talpur.[123] The latter's

Table 10 Largeholders in taluqa Mirpur Sakro 1889/90–1902/03

Name of Zamindar	*Size of holding* 1889–90 acres	1902/03 acres	Remarks
Fateh Chand	1,203	835	Forfeited fallow land
Chuto	720	264	Forfeited fallow land
Teju	590	355	Forfeited fallow land
Chato	680	11	Sold land
Ahmad	561	–	Sold land to Jot Singh
Jot Singh	1,395	1,409	Forfeited 1,034 acres fallow, bought 1,048 acres
Vario	1,210	791	Forfeited fallow land
Gul Hassan	1,541	265	Sold land
Khilandas	699	56	Sold land
Umar	726	352	Sold land
Ghazi Khan	728	920	Bought land
Chato	646	613	Forfeited fallow land
Bhim	720	252	Sold land
Jan Muhammad	1,401	555	Family partition
Mataro	1,689	418	Family partition
Saleh Muhammad	1,049	602	Forfeited fallow land
Muhammad	1,352	189	Sold land
Mariam	620	240	Sold land & forfeited fallow land
Kadu	1,515	101	Sold land & forfeited fallow land
Mangharam	691	173	Forfeited fallow land
Nanikram	886	128	Forfeited fallow land
Akil	1,695	1,010	Forfeited fallow land
Shivandas	566	384	Forfeited fallow land
Achar	506	252	Forfeited fallow land
Basarmal	–	958	Bought land
Imam Bakhsh	–	628	Bought land
Ibrahim Shah	–	573	Took up land

Source: Settlt. Offr. to Commr., Sind, 22 June 1904 (*B.N.S.* 332, *Mirpur Sakro SR*, 15)

estate had fallen from 3,238 acres to 509 acres. A similar fate befell the heirs of Saiyid Saleh Muhammad Shah, who lost their property to a Muslim moneylender, Mohab Ali Miano.

These appear to illustrate the decline of the Muslim landed gentry, yet several Waderos were flourishing. Three increased their holdings by over a thousand acres each. Their success was a contrast to the misfortunes of the big Hindu zamindars. Though one of these, Deval, built up a substantial holding between 1883–96, another, Navalrai, lost half of his, while the third Hindu, Basarmal, sold his entire estate to a Muslim.

The net result was that, instead of twelve estates with more than

500 acres in Sujawal in 1883–84, there were only nine in 1895–96. In 1913–14, there were still nine large estates. Meanwhile, the size of largeholdings increased, from an average of 1,084 acres in 1883–84 to 1,682 acres in 1895–96, to 2,277 acres in 1913–14. In other words, after 1883, there were fewer estates, but larger ones.

Table 11 Largeholders in taluqa Sujawal 1883/84–1913/14

Name of Zamindar	Size of holding 1883/84 acres	1895/96 acres	1913/14 acres	Remarks
Asiat & Mithial	2,016	–	–	Wife & daughter of Saleh Muhammad Shah; sold land to Mohab Ali Miano
Basarmal	991	–	–	Sold land to Muhammad Kamil Shah
Mohab Ali Miano	–	3,273	3,328	Bought land from Asiat & Mithial
Saiyid Muhammad Kamil Shah	1,379	2,385	3,067	Bought land from Basarmal
Khair Bakhsh Khan Laghari	585	1,929	2,825	
Umed Ali Khan Laghari	783	487	287	Died; heirs sold land to Saiyid Haji Hashim Shah
Sohrab Khan Laghari	503	340	344	
Pir Bakhsh Khan Talpur	3,238	509	678	Sold land to Shaikh Gahi Khan
Shaikh Gahi Khan	83	2,088	1,541	Bought land from Pir Bakhsh Khan Talpur
Shaikh Pinial	773	796	790	
Muhammad Pario Khizmatgar	542	185	307	
Navalrai	799	333	366	
Saiyid Kaderdino Shah	645	2,548	4,507	
Gul Muhammad Sumro	750	864	1,480	
Devan	–	743	9	Died; heirs sold land to Damoderdas
Saiyid Haji Hashim Shah	–	–	180	Bought land from heirs of Umed Ali Khan Laghari
Damoderdas	–	–	474	Bought land from heirs of Devan

Source: *Sujawal SRs*

Note: Original holders were dead by 1913/14; figures in this column refers to heirs.

None of this evidence supports the hypothesis that the raiyatwari settlement damaged the interests of Waderos, nor is there proof that the great estates were breaking up. Some estates certainly did disintegrate, but others replaced them. It is tempting to see 'traditional' Waderos, like Khalifa Muhammad Panah of Larkana and Nawab Pir Bakhsh Khan Talpur of Sujawal, giving way to 'settlement' Waderos like Abdul Rahman Thebo of Kotri, Ghulam Ali Isran of Larkana and Shaikh Imam Bakhsh of Sujawal: but these are isolated cases. The majority of estates remained in the same families, fluctuating in size but, as often as not, enlarging themselves. To stretch Colonel Anderson's metaphor, it was inevitable that some Waderos should grow old and die – but not all at once. It was equally inevitable that others should be born and that Waderos as a class should live on.

III

Overall, therefore, Waderos did not suffer in consequence of the raiyatwari settlement. The question remains whether peasants, for whom the system had been designed, prospered under it. Lewis Mountford, the Manager of Encumbered Estates, brought the earlier analyses up to date in 1901. He explained that, after big zamindars had been forced to throw up their wastelands in the 1860s and 1870s, irrigational improvements made the wastes cultivable: but, by then, the Waderos were too deeply indebted to take advantage of the situation and so their haris seized the opportunity: the Wadero 'lost not only his land and his rent therefrom, but also his tenantry.'[124]

Mountford's scenario, though neat and widely accepted at the time, does not fit the facts for, as shown above, many big zamindars did extend their holdings. If haris were indeed leaving the great estates, the Waderos were carrying on without them. It may even have been the Waderos who pushed their haris off their estates. Under the fallow rules, zamindars' land could stay uncultivated for four consecutive years. If haris were not available, there was nothing to pay. But, the moment even a small portion of a Survey Number was cultivated, the full assessment was levied on it. With remissions available but not guaranteed, farmers may have become reluctant to engage haris for the poorer Survey Numbers: so the settlement system may actually have encouraged zamindars to cut their work-force to the minimum.

Whether they quitted their employers voluntarily or were dismissed, haris could not lightly embark on careers as landholders.

It was not such an easy option as commentators like Mountford implied. It was an expensive and risky step, and many would-be peasants must have been daunted by the prospect. Waste was given free by government, but it had to be made cultivable before it was any use. Water-courses had to be dug to bring water from the canal to the field, *jungle* (natural vegetation) had to be cleared, the soil had to be broken up. If the land was irrigated by 'lift,' as most was in the nineteenth century, a Persian wheel had to be constructed and the prospective smallholder must have a team of bullocks to drive it. He had to have a plough, a seed-drill and other equipment. He had to obtain seed to sow the soil and feed his cattle and his family. Finally, sufficient profit must remain after the first year's cultivation, to pay the government assessment.

Table 12 shows the incomes of two peasant families in taluqa Sukkur in 1873, giving an indication of the expenses involved in smallscale cultivation and the amounts of money an aspiring peasant would have to borrow. Malcolm Haig presented these figures to demonstrate the feasibility of living on minute holdings, but he admitted that the families involved were 'rare exceptions.' They had no dealings with moneylenders and sold their produce to the highest bidder, getting better prices than most peasants. With unusually high yields, their food consumption was larger than for others of their class.[125]

If one imagines that the first family were haris who had just taken up their land then, at the prices quoted by Haig, they would have needed Rs 14–4 to buy nine and a quarter *maunds* of seed (Rs 1–15–2 per acre). However, Haig's price, of Rs 1–8 per *maund*, was the rate at which they sold the grain. If they had been buying, they would have paid more. The average price per *maund* of wheat in Sukkur at this time was as 2–8–8; *juari* was Rs 1–15–2 per *maund*.[126] At these traders' prices, their seed would have cost Rs 20–9–3 (Rs 2–13–6 per acre). The second family would have needed Rs 27–9–3 (Rs 2–10–8 per acre), or Rs 11–8–2 (Rs 1–12–5 per acre) at the cheaper rate.

Therefore, an outlay of two or three rupees per acre was required for seed – an investment of twenty to thirty rupees on a ten acre plot. When one recalls that it had been considered plausible that a debt of twenty rupees could have induced a hari to commit murder on behalf of Ghulam Murtaza Bhutto in 1896, and that *taqavi* loans of ten to twenty rupees were considered sufficient to tie haris to their zamindars, then one can appreciate that these sums were, for a hari, enormous. On top of these commitments, the family had to discharge their existing accumulation of debt to their zamindar.

Table 12 Incomes of two peasant families in taluqa Sukkur, 1873

FAMILY No 1

Family members: 2 men, 2 women, 1 young son, 2 young daughters.
Property: 4 bullocks, 2 cows, 1 cart, 7.25 acres of land.

Cultivation:

	acres	*maunds*
Wheat	4	52
Juari	2.25	29
Total cereals	**6.25**	**81.50**
Cash crops	**0.75**	48

Consumption of cereals:	*maunds*
Food	*60*
Seed	*9.5*
Balance for sale	*12*
Total	**81.5**

Income from crops:

	maunds	*Price per maund*	*Value*
Cereals	12	Rs 1–8 annas	Rs 18
Sugar cane	30	Rs 6	Rs 180
Tobacco	18	Rs 5	Rs 90
Total income from crops			**Rs 288**

Other income	*Value*
Sale of butter @ 1 anna per day	Rs 11 – 4 annas
Spinning by women @ half anna each per day	Rs 24
Carting for two months @ 8 annas per day	Rs 30
Total income from other sources	**Rs 65 – 4 annas**
Total income from all sources	*Rs 353 – 4 annas*

Expenses	
Seed, manure, assessment, etc	Rs 144
Provisions (fish, meat, spices, etc)	Rs 51
Clothing	Rs 35
Total expenses	**Rs 230**
Net income from all sources	*Rs 123 – 4 annas*

FAMILY No 2

Family members: 2 men, 1 woman, 2 young sons, 2 young daughters, 2 working daughters.
Property: 6.5 acres of land.

Cultivation:

	acres	*maunds*
Wheat	3	39
Juari	1.75	36
Total cereals	**4.75**	**85.00**
Cash crops	**0.75**	Not given

	Annual consumption of cereals:		*maunds*
	Food		*57.75*
	Seed		*7.75*
	Balance for sale		*12.50*
	Total		85

Income from crops:

	maunds	*Price per maund*	*Value*
Cereals	12.5	Rs 1 – 8 annas	Rs 18 – 12 annas
Tobacco and sugar cane	Not given	Not given	Rs 270
Straw	Not given	Not given	Rs 10
Total income from crops			**Rs 298 – 12 annas**

Other income	*Value*
Sale of butter @ 1 anna per day	Rs 11
Spinning by women @ half anna each per day	Rs 12
Total income from other sources	**Rs 23**
Total income from all sources	*Rs 321 – 12 annas*

Expenses	
Seed, manure, assessment, etc	Rs 146
Provisions (fish, meat, spices, etc)	Rs 46
Clothing	Rs 30
Total expenses	**Rs 222**
Net income from all sources	*Rs 99 – 4 annas*

Source: Settlt. Offr. to Collr., Shpur., – Sept. 1873 (*B.N.S.* 201, *Sukkur S.R.*, 56–7

These calculations take no account of the cost of making land cultivable, nor do they enable the families to buy food. The first family spent fifty-one rupees on provisions such as fish and spices and ate grain to the value of ninety rupees, for which they would have had to pay Rs 139–6–5 at the market price. The second family spent forty-four rupees on provisions, and their food grain was valued at Rs 86–10 (or Rs 130–1–2 at the market price). Finally, the calculations exclude money to purchase seed for cash crops like tobacco and sugar-cane, on which both families depended for their living. The first family earned only Rs 2–12–4 per acre from cereals, while the second family made Rs 6–0–12 per acre from the sale of cereals and straw. The average assessment in Sukkur was Rs 2–10–6 per acre and so, without the cash crops, the first family would have nothing left with which to repay their debts and prepare for the following season.

This was only the beginning. The inundation in Sind was so uncertain, that a family with just a few acres had no security. They would be exceptionally lucky to get two good crops in succession, while a couple of bad seasons would bring them to the end of their meagre resources.[127] Having run up debts to obtain their land, then, many ex-haris fell further into debt to survive. It is hardly surprising that, as Evan James remarked in 1897, the number of haris who had become successful landholders could be 'counted on the fingers.'[128]

James had predicted this result two decades previously, in 1873, when he asserted that no agriculturist could make a living from a farm of less than twenty acres. Such holdings, he believed, were only cultivated every two or three years, as a prop to the holders' main livelihood, which came from sheep, goats or cattle.[129] The Collector of Karachi agreed, saying, 'It is impossible for a holder of anything under 15 acres to be more than a slave to some money-lender.'[130] If one goes back to the figures in Table 11, one can appreciate that the peasant families' solvency, marginal as it was, depended on cultivating their entire holdings. The loss of only a few acres would have destroyed their profits. They were extremely vulnerable to the vagaries of the inundation. The Collector of Sukkur estimated in 1902 that farmers had to be certain of cultivating forty or fifty acres annually if they wished to amass sufficient resources to tide them over the inevitable bad seasons. Anyone who could not do that extent would be ruined after a couple of poor inundations. In Sind, that meant holding at least 100 acres, half of which might be cultivable each year. Anyone with less, believed the Collector, was worse off than a hari.[131]

It is unfortunate that no investigations into peasants' circumstances were carried out in nineteenth century Sind, to test these theories but the summary of landholdings in Table 13 seems to confirm the Collector's impression that holders with more than 100 acres were making the best progress. Their number increased by half over the fifteen years from 1880 – 1895, whereas the total of holders with less than 100 acres grew by only 18%.

People with the smallest means, then, could not rely on their plots for their livelihood. Many supplemented their income: and the most readily available source of employment in rural Sind was as a hari.[132] A modern study by Luther Gulick sheds some useful light on this hypothesis. He showed that three haris on a farm near Hyderabad in the 1970s owned small plots of four, five and seven acres each, which they had inherited. Their income was derived from a combination of their shares at batai, their livestock (buffaloes, goats and chickens) and their produce. Their holdings were, in effect, kitchen gardens.[133] Tiny holdings, therefore, may not always have been proper peasant occupancies, but kitchen-plots for fortunate haris. It follows that even when haris became smallholders, zamindars did not necessarily lose their services. Apart from the tiniest holders, larger petty holders also needed to hire out their labour on occasions, when their crops failed or they were unable to sow their land. For example, the water-supply at the tail of a canal might fail, forcing peasants with land there to work as haris for a zamindar whose estate (or part of it) was at the head, or whose land was irrigated from a different canal. Alternatively, members of a family who had recently acquired land might take on extra work as haris to reduce their debts. Anyone holding under about twenty acres was, potentially at least, a hari.

Moreover, an aspiring peasant had to obtain capital from somewhere and the village bania was the most likely source. The average hari family had no security but their cattle. This might be enough: but if even Waderos sometimes complained of haris absconding without paying their debts, then a bania, with none of the Wadero's authority, must have been all the more afraid that an ex-hari might bolt if the crop failed. Some haris may have mortgaged their land before taking it up, as a form of future security, but banias were bound to give preference to those who already had land to mortgage. E.W. Trevor, Deputy Collector of Sehwan, confirmed in 1882 that applications for the smallest plots invariably came from people who already had small holdings of their own. When plots of less than ten acres were given out, he explained, it did not mean that the number of petty holders was increasing, but only the size of petty holdings.[134]

The allegation that haris were taking up wasteland at the expense of their employers is therefore unproven. There is a further, simple consideration: it is not credible that haris should have grabbed up land in defiance of their zamindars. A Wadero would have no difficulty in trumping up charges against any bold spirits who defied him, or burning their crops. At the very least, they would lose his protection. Middling zamindars, with holdings of 100 to 500 acres, might find it more difficult to assert their authority over their haris yet it appears, from Table 13, that they formed the most successful group of landholders in Sind; their numbers increased by 65% over the period 1880–1 to 1894–5. They do not appear to have suffered from the loss of their workforce. If some haris left their zamindars to become smallholders, they did it with the zamindars' tacit approval. There was enough land to go round and the zamindars could afford to lose them.

Many British officials believed that the peasant was a creation of British rule. Lewis Mountford, the Manager of Encumbered Estates, referred to peasants, somewhat fancifully, as 'exotics needing cherishing, if they are to exist at all.' Since government policy had created the peasant in Sind, he must be protected, or else government

Table 13 Landholdings in Sind 1880/81–1894/95

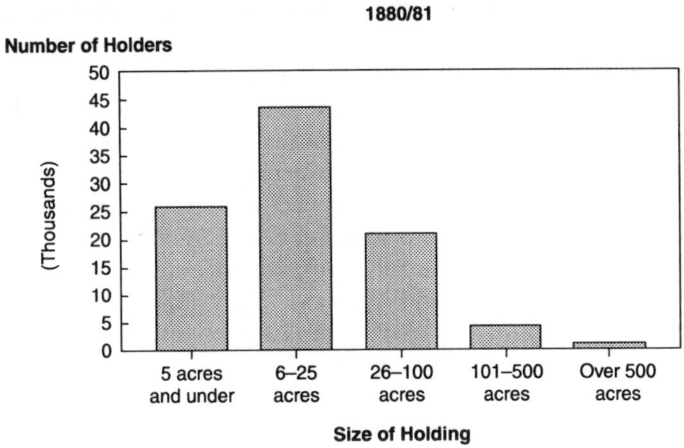

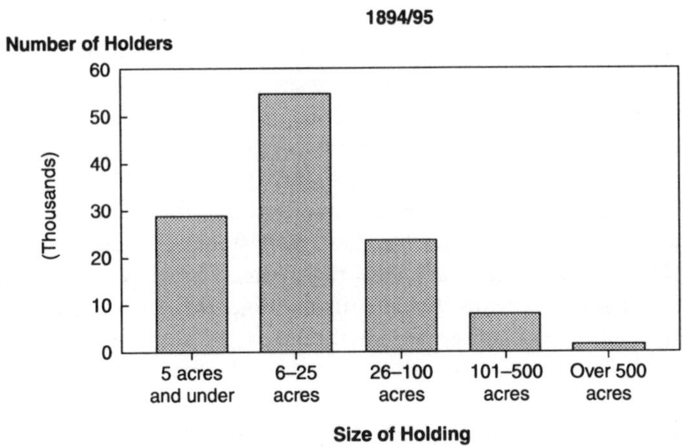

Size of Holding	*Number of Holders*		
	1880/81	*1890/91*	*1894/95*
5 acres and under	25,873	25,716	28,974
6–25 acres	43,728	50,055	54,760
26–100 acres	21,066	20,514	23,285
101–500 acres	4,738	6,885	7,810
Over 500 acres	1,132	1,216	1,297
TOTAL	**96,537**	**104,386**	**116,126**

Source: Commr., Sind, to Govr., Bombay, 12 Aug. 1896, Note A (P.G.B., R.D.L., 1899 (Jul.–Dec.), Confl. Pr., 797)

must 'stop creating him altogether.'[135] H.C. Mules, the Collector of Sukkur, was more cynical: 'The petty holder in Sind is a creation of our rule and a great mistake we made in creating him.'[136] There are no figures to indicate how substantial a body of peasants existed in Sind at the time of the conquest. At the end of the century, when reasonably accurate statistics were available, there is no evidence that haris were setting themselves up as landholders on a large scale; holders of plots of under five acres were the most slowly advancing section of agriculturists, their total increasing by only 12% between 1880–95. In that respect, the raiyatwari settlement does not appear to have injured the interests of Waderos. They may have lost some ground to middling zamindars, but not to any significant extent. The number of largeholders increased by only 15% between 1880–95, but that is not tantamount to a decline. Table 6 confirms that largeholders still held a substantial proportion of the occupied area and many were enlarging their holdings.

British officers' anxiety about the fate of the Waderos was a natural result of the special relationship they had built up with them. Relying on Waderos to assist the local administration, and knowing there was no alternative to them, they were extremely sensitive to any hint that their collaborators were in difficulties. Their fears may have been fuelled by a misplaced confidence in their own statistics. Nineteenth century settlement reports included many pages of tables which have a seductively authoritative appearance but, like most statistics, must be treated with caution. Among them were statements comparing the sizes of holdings at the various settlements. These were worse than useless: they were positively misleading, for they consistently exaggerated the number of smallholders. The information was collected according to the area held in each deh, not according to the aggregate area of each holding in the taluqa. That is to say, someone with five one-hundred acre holdings in five dehs was recorded as five holders of one-hundred acres, not as one holder of five hundred acres.[137] Officers frequently interpreted such figures to indicate that smallholders were more important than they really were. Malcolm Haig in 1873 expressed his pleasure that Kotri contained no estate larger than 400 acres. He was quoting from the table of landholdings and apparently did not notice that elsewhere in the same report he himself mentioned that Abdul Rahman Thebo held 598 acres[138] – presumably not in a continuous tract, so that he figured in the table as more than one landhold*ing* (as opposed to landhold*er*). The figures for Larkana in Table 14 illustrate the point.

The message of this table seems unambiguous: the number of

Table 14 Landholdings in Larkana, 1870–1892

	Size of Holding (acres)					
Year	*Under 20*	*21–50*	*51–100*	*101–500*	*Over 500*	*Total*
1870	3,764	712	183	134	26	4,819
1881	5,902	672	216	170	7	6,966
1892	9,641	707	224	191	5	10,768

Source: Sup., Sind Rev. Survey, to Commr., Sind, 8 March 1892 (*B.N.S.* 315, *Larkana S.R.*, 35)

people holding less than twenty acres was rising dramatically, while the number of largeholders was falling – equally dramatically. The largeholders were declining and the smallholders growing. The figures, though, do not allow for the fact that some of the largeholders in 1870 held blocks of over 500 acres in different dehs, while in 1892 several Waderos held blocks of under 500 acres. The nominal list of largeholders attached to the report in which this table appears (see Table 7) shows that in fact only sixteen individual zamindars held over 500 acres in 1870, but there were twelve in 1881 and thirteen in 1892 – a different story altogether. Unfortunately, there are no more reliable sources, along the lines of the nominal lists of largeholders, against which one could check the progress of smallholders. One can at least speculate that misinterpretation of statistical evidence may have been led some officers to exaggerate the significance of petty holders.

Those haris who crossed the great divide to become smallholders were financed by banias.[139] Even before they took up their new land, the would-be peasant family were deeply in debt and when they added to their holdings, they added to their debts. During their early years as landholders, they depended on banias for subsistence and bad seasons forced them to borrow more. The Collector of Shikarpur remarked disparagingly in 1902 that the petty holders were perpetually engaged in litigation with banias, 'eventually being sold up and relapsing to their natural condition of "hari."'[140] This was an exaggeration, for the petty holders did survive as a class, but it was true that their whole existence was bound up with debt.

What was true for the peasant was true for the Wadero. Without capital he could not extend his estate. He pledged his land as security and found in the bania a ready source of credit. Like the peasant, he borrowed freely. The growth of indebtedness among both large and smallholders reflected their need to borrow to increase their landed wealth. One of the main beneficiaries from the extension of the occupied area was therefore the bania, who financed the agriculturists and took interest from their profits. Banias may even have benefited more than their clients.

Chapter 5

The Omnipresent Bania[1]

I

After revisiting Sind in 1876, Sir Richard Burton wrote, 'The Hindu's reed-pen is a rod of iron and abjectly the unhappy Sindi trembles before it.'[2] By Hindu, Burton meant the Hindu bania, the trader and moneylender, and by 'Sindi' he meant the Muslim zamindar, the perennial debtor. The creditor, he was saying, tyrannized over the debtor, imposing ever harsher and more inequitable terms. It is interesting that Burton scarcely appeared to recognize the Hindus as Sindhis at all. It was a colourful summary of the average British official's attitude towards debt. Twenty years later, Evan James, the Commissioner in Sind, quoted Burton's remark to support his own argument that debt was an intolerable burden on Sindhi Muslims in general and the Waderos in particular.[3]

Rural debt was the bugbear of nineteenth century administrators throughout India. In Sind, its social effects were aggravated because the creditors were almost all Hindu, the debtors almost all Muslim. There was nothing new in this, but British rule initiated critical changes in the relationship between debtors and creditors, especially by conferring full property rights on landholders. They could mortgage, sell or otherwise transfer their property as they wished. This put them in possession of a valuable asset which increased their creditworthiness, enabling them to raise more capital than before – or to run up ever greater debts. The catch was that creditors could seize their land to recover their money, a power which was unthinkable in pre-British times.[4] This gave creditors the opportunity to acquire land cheaply. Waderos did not generally have a strong business sense. They did not appreciate the commercial value their land had acquired. Expressing their status through the size of their estates rather than the efficiency of their husbandry, they often sacrificed profits to buy up additional tracts of unproductive land, mortgaging themselves in the process. According to British officials, this left them prey to predatory banias. Forbidden by their religion to lend money on interest, Muslims had traditionally left all financial affairs to the Hindu minority. The latter, like minorities elsewhere, had established a reputation as shrewd merchants and bankers, wealthy but disdained by the majority community. Before the conquest, they had not been able to take up land and they took advantage of the protection provided by British rule to establish themselves as landholders: but, it was claimed, they did it at the expense of indebted Waderos and other Muslims.

Evidence was provided in 1896 by an investigation into six 'representative' villages from each of the forty-seven irrigated taluqas in Sind.[5] Regrettably, the report did not state the criteria for selecting the taluqas, so one cannot be sure how representative they were in practice. It did, however, provide a rough indication of the situation. It estimated that Hindus held twenty-eight per cent of the occupied area in 1895–96. This represented a revolution in land ownership for, half a century before, they had held virtually nothing. Moreover, of the 30,839 acres which they had acquired in the selected villages between 1890–91 and 1895–96, only 7,683 acres, roughly a quarter, was new land taken up by them: the rest, 24,143 acres, they had taken from Muslims. They also enjoyed the produce of a further fifteen per cent of the land, which was mortgaged to them. Altogether, then, by 1896, Hindus had the benefit of forty-two per cent of the occupied area. Evan James commented in his review of this report:

> No one could possibly object to the Hindus taking up land on their own account. It is a free country, and enterprise should be encouraged . . . . What I do object to is that they should be allowed to obtain by usury land belonging to others, and to reduce the former owners to a state of abject dependence. The feeling of injustice engendered by this tyranny strikes at the foundations of our rule.[6]

In this context, the growth of indebtedness could have serious political consequences. People who lost their land or witnessed the suffering of indebted neighbours might lose faith in the British Raj. They might cease to co-operate over crime and taxation; they might even oppose the British authorities. British officers developed a jaundiced view of banias, regarding them as a troublesome complication, bent on eroding the foundations of the British administration. The political sensitivity of debt increased with time. It became explosive in the twentieth century, when Muslim indebtedness fuelled resentment against Hindu banias, boosting the popularity of the Pakistan movement.

In the nineteenth century, British antipathy towards moneylenders was reinforced by prejudices imported from Europe. The arguments frequently revolved around stereotypes borrowed from anti-semitic folklore, officials viewing the relationship between debtor and creditor in simplistic terms, through a haze of racial and cultural preconceptions. The archetypal caricature of the grasping Jewish usurer was transferred to the Hindu bania. He became 'the eastern Shylock.' The honest – but somewhat obtuse – agriculturist was helpless in the moneylender's hands, enabling 'the cunning practitioner of the market-place to swindle the dull peasant out of his land.'[7] It is refreshing to come across an observer like Malcolm Haig, who lampooned the conventional wisdom as early as 1869:

> Nothing was bad enough to be said of the Bania, the sole representative of thrift and prudence in the community. He is called "*the Sind extortioner*" – "*the source of all evils*" – "*the curse of the cultivators*," but it is conceded that he is "*perhaps in a measure a necessary evil*."[8]

Haig had his own prejudices, particularly when it came generalizing about the extravagance of Muslim zamindars, but he did appreciate the significance of credit in economic development. No doubt, some moneylenders were rapacious: but money had to be lent if cultivation was to take place. Agriculture had to be financed. Loans had to be advanced. To appreciate fully both the benefits and the damage brought about by banias, it is necessary to examine their operations and motives in greater detail.

II

Banias were, first and foremost, businesspeople. Their interest in land grew out of their trading activities. Some may, like Waderos, have hoped to boost their izzat through large holdings, but they were more interested in land as an investment. It guaranteed access to raw materials. Hindu merchants were keen to start up their own farms. Much of the profit they realized from the growth of Sind's export trade, based on the produce of Sindhi farms, was invested in land.

To keep their overheads down, they preferred smaller, more intensively cultivated holdings than Muslims. Much of the literature of the period assumes that banias had no real interest in cultivation, and that land passing to banias was lost to agriculture. They were commonly referred to as 'non-agriculturists,' and the habit of sloppy generalization was so engrained in the official correspondence of nineteenth century Sind that the terms 'bania,' 'Hindu' and 'non-agriculturist' were virtually interchangeable. This was misleading because many banias were efficient farmers, 'the Hindu money-lender being often considerably more of an agriculturist than the kind of Mahomedan who loses his land.'[9] Approaching farming as a commercial venture, banias were keen to get value for money out of their land. If land passed from inefficient debtors to efficient creditors, the overall effect on the agricultural economy would have been beneficial.

The main concentration of Hindu landholders was in the cotton-growing areas of eastern Sind. These came within reach of market centres like Hyderabad, Shahdadpur and Tando Allahyar when railways developed in the seventies and eighties. Many traders set up cotton gins and rice-husking factories to process their produce.[10]

An episode from the career of one of the most prominent of these Hindu capitalists illustrates the nature of their operations. Seth Vishindas Nihalchand was the son of a great Kotri merchant. By the time of his death, he had multifarious business interests. He was a forest contractor and he owned two fleets of boats, plying as far as the Persian Gulf, the Malabar Coast and Madras. He put a substantial amount of his capital into the land. In 1892–93, he held 697 acres in Hala and he was the largest holder in Kotri, with 1,811 acres in 1889–90. He established cotton-gins, cotton-bale presses and rice-husking machines near his lands.[11]

When, in 1885, the zamindars of taluqa Manjhand, adjoining Kotri, wanted to reopen an old canal, Vishindas stepped into the breach with his capital reserves. The Irrigation Department had opposed the scheme as too expensive. Vishindas offered to carry out the works and keep the canal in order at his own expense, provided he could take up 3,000 acres of the newly irrigated land and was given the right to collect all government revenue on lands directly watered by the canal while it was under his management. After six years, he handed it back to the Irrigation Department as a regular government canal.[12]

Vishindas was exceptional: but, though few could afford to take up thousands of acres of barren land, all over Sind banias were investing in the land according to their means, specializing in cash crops such as oilseeds, cotton, tobacco, wheat and vegetables. Even village banias, who could not be compared with the great merchants of

Karachi, Sukkur and Shikarpur, were often people of substance. One claimed to have had no less than a thousand rupees on him when he was mugged in 1897 and others, whose houses had been burgled, alleged losses as high as ten to twenty thousand rupees.[13]

A network of agents linked the large European, Bombay and Sindhi trading houses of Karachi with the village banias. Most firms had agents in Hyderabad, Sehwan, Jacobabad and other market centres, and by the end of the century at smaller towns like Tando Allahyar and Tando Adam. They bought produce from the village banias and forwarded it to the main offices. Since they did not have direct contact with the agriculturists themselves, the village banias were the linchpin of the system. They occupied a pivotal position as merchants and moneylenders.

As merchants, they were middlemen. They bought produce from the cultivators at the threshing floor. Some they kept for retailing locally, the rest they sold on to the dealers. Their circumstances as traders made them a natural source of credit, and so most were in addition moneylenders, providing, among other things, the investments which enabled agriculture to develop.

The system had evolved to suit those engaged in trade. It saved the great merchants from employing a large body of agents to go shopping round the farms, while it provided the banias with secure trading contacts.

It was less advantageous to the producers. If they had sold directly to the agents, they might have obtained better prices: but this was extremely rare. Malcolm Haig said in 1876 that he knew of almost no instance of agriculturists going beyond their own or a neighbouring village for a buyer, nor trying to make a better bargain than they already had with their usual bania.[14] It was reported some years later that it was simply 'not the custom' to seek a better bargain.[15] Shepherds in Kohistan did not even go to the trouble of shearing their sheep, but sold the fleeces on the sheep's back to the banias, who made their own arrangements for shearing and no doubt lowered their buying prices accordingly.[16]

The system appears highly unsatisfactory for the agriculturists, but they had little choice. They did not have connections among the large dealers, so could not afford to cart their produce to town on the offchance of finding good prices. Some British administrators thought that the coming of the railways would change the picture. Occasionally, big firms set up agencies at railway stations so that they could buy from agriculturists at better rates. A Settlement Officer wrote enthusiastically in 1901 that 'the railway comes to the rescue of the cultivator in his most uneven struggle with the money-lender and trader.' No longer was the cost of sending produce to market beyond cultivators' means: 'Already, one hears of the cultivators hurrying off with their grain to the station to sell it while the price is high and pay off the season's debt.' He hoped that agriculturists would no longer play into the hands of local banias who knew and exploited their family circumstances when knocking down prices or negotiating loans.[17] However, these expectations were not fulfilled and the banias preserved their traditional roles. When Settlement Reports were written in 1929 and 1930, it was still rare for agriculturists to take their produce to the railway stations. The majority handed it over the village bania as they had always done.[18]

Agriculturists did not feel free to sell on the open market because they were not simply selling their produce: they were regulating their accounts at the same time. Before they could sell their produce on the open market, they had to pay off the season's debts. Many, though, found themselves as impoverished at the end of the season as the start, if not more so.

The problem lay in the mixture of transactions that took place when farmers sold their produce. First, their banias established the value of the crop, with reference to the price they expected to sell it for in the market. This they compared with the debts outstanding. The price credited to the agriculturist represented the difference between the value attributed to the crop and the debt owed. The calculations were complicated by fluctuations in price throughout the year. An agriculturist who borrowed seed at the beginning of the season, when prices were high, would repay at harvest time, when prices were low. The bania had to maintain a record of the prices prevailing at the different times. As one can imagine, the arithmetic could be extremely confusing, 'even if the *bania* were honest and not addicted to taking unfair advantage of the complication.'[19] With illiterate clients who were ignorant of business, the temptation was strong for banias to twist the record to their own advantage, and they sometimes succeeded in buying produce at excessively low rates which bore little relation to those quoted on the markets.[20] In 1901, after five years of investigation into the debts of hundreds of zamindars, L.J. Mountford, the Manager of Encumbered Estates in Sind, produced a lengthy catalogue of banias' sharp practices and zamindars' gullibility. On one occasion, he recalled:

> the zamindar, an old man of 65, seemed very much amused during the enquiry, and when, after the Banya had produced his

> accounts and I had examined them, I asked the zamindar what he had to say to a debt of Rs 500, he smilingly produced a receipt on pink paper, saying he had discharged the amount of Rs 500 in his grain-yard last year, and that this was the receipt. He could not read, and when I told him that the receipt was for Rs 200 and not Rs 500, his system received a shock.[21]

Even if the client were literate, it made little difference since accounts were kept in a specialist 'bania' Sindhi script which was incomprehensible to most non-banias.[22]

Waderos were theoretically in a better position to bargain with banias than other farmers, but in practice this was not always the case. According to Mountford, they were curiously susceptible to flattery along the lines of, 'how can a poor weak Banya cheat' a powerful Wadero. They seldom insisted on receipts and were not inclined to look at the small print.[23]

The client's account was recorded in a ledger. On the right-hand side the bania entered all debits such as grain supplied, household articles and cash provided, bonds taken out and interest charged. The credits – mainly the value attributed to the client's produce – were entered on the left-hand side. Every so often, the two columns were balanced out and the client acknowledged the debt which usually emerged at the end of the calculations. Acknowledging the account was generally a formality since the agriculturists knew they might lose their credit facilities if they contested it.

An account opened with a loan advanced by the bania. This consisted of two items. First was the actual sum required. This might represent the value of grain, cash or other articles advanced, or it might be composed of old debts and interest which had been rescheduled. The figures normally did not refer to cash as such, but the value attributed by the bania to the client's produce and articles supplied to the client.

The second portion of the loan was a fee known as *panjot*. *Panjot* may have originated as a device to encourage prompt repayment, for the bond would carry no interest up to a certain date. In one case, the client borrowed Rs 400 and the bond, dated 15 July 1896, was made out for Rs 688. The bond was interest-free for three years. On 16 June 1898, the client repaid Rs 144. A year later, however, interest was imposed at the punitive rate of 2 annas in the rupee per month, equivalent to 150 per cent per year. By 4 January 1900, the client owed Rs 1,142–6–6. If he had not repaid any money before the interest charges commenced, he would have owed Rs 1,395.

In this case, the interest mounted at a particularly vicious rate because it was levied monthly. A full year of charges would have brought the debt to some Rs 2,600. Even when interest was charged annually, though, the *panjot* had a harsh multiplier effect. In another case, a client borrowed Rs 1,800 and the bond was made out for Rs 1,942. It carried no interest for eighteen months but thereafter interest was taken at thirty-seven and a half per cent per year. Three years after the bond had been signed, the capital sum had doubled, the debt standing at Rs 3,778.[24]

The account was secured by a mortgage on part of the client's land. The zamindar remained as proprietor but paid all or some of the produce of the mortgaged plots as interest. The creditor usually, took responsibility for an appropriate proportion of the government assessment. Large sums could be borrowed against small areas. Details of mortgages in Mehar between 1887–91 show that one zamindar borrowed Rs 300 against four and a half acres, the creditor taking three-quarters of the produce as interest and paying three-quarters of the assessment. Another farmer pledged eight and a half acres for only Rs 100, the creditor taking all of the produce and paying all the assessment.[25] The differences may reflect the quality of the land, or the extent to which the client, being more powerful, more commercially astute or less indebted, was able to bargain with the bania. Mountford quoted an extremely unsatisfactory arrangement when a zamindar mortgaged sixty-eight acres for only Rs 250, the entire produce to be paid as interest. The zamindar agreed, if he defaulted or the crop was insufficient, to pay a penal rate of twenty rupees per acre. Mountford did admit, though, that this was not a typical case.[26]

No term was usually assigned to the mortgage, so this could continue indefinitely. Less commonly, once the debt had mounted up, banias pressed for a usufructuary mortgage in which they stipulated that they should have full control of the land until the debt was paid. These mortgages sometimes carried a time limit, a clause being inserted to stipulate that the bania could foreclose if the debt was not repaid within a certain period. The zamindar remained the nominal *khatedar* (registered occupant) but the bania had effective possession and was legally regarded as the superior holder, with the zamindar a mere tenant. It was the bania who was responsible for paying the assessment, clearing the water courses, arranging *taqavi* loans for the haris.[27]

The bania was at the same time supposed to set the profits against the debt and interest to pay off the loan. The bania also, if necessary, provided an allowance for the zamindar who, depending on how much of the estate had been mortgaged, might by now be virtually dispossessed. Mountford alleged that, by concealing profits, exaggerating expenditure, manipulating the account and giving the zamindar a generous allowance, most banias succeeded in showing a steady loss, so as to remain in constant possession of the land.[28]

In 1875, for example, some Baluchi zamindars mortgaged land to a bania for Rs 2,800. At the same time, they acknowledged past debts to the value of Rs 12,100 – of which Rs 7,700 was interest. Five years later, the bania insisted on amalgamating the two debts into one usufructuary mortgage bond for Rs 14,000, on terms entitling him to cultivate the whole area and reimburse himself at twenty-four per cent interest per year until the debt had been paid off. The balance of the profits was to be divided equally between himself and the debtors. This arrangement did nothing to diminish the debt. On the contrary, the bania claimed in 1886 that it had swelled to Rs 68,123 as a result of the losses he had made on cultivation, for which he held the zamindars responsible. He added another Rs 59,121 as interest, bringing the total debt to Rs 127,244. He then sued the zamindars in court for a round Rs 110,000, remitting part of the interest.[29] That is to say, the principal debt of Rs 7,192 increased eightfold over eleven years and the zamindars were threatened with the loss of their land. Luckily for them, the threat was not carried out because the District Judge of Shikarpur established that the bania had falsified the accounts. Mountford, though, insisted it was a typical case. He could think of only two examples out of the hundreds he had investigated where any profit had been shown and the original debt diminished. Such mortgages, he alleged, invariably led to the sale of the land.[30]

This last assertion, however, does not ring entirely true. Normally, there was no need for a bania to foreclose because the deal suited both parties. Many zamindars were, to the despair of their champions in the British administration, remarkably complacent about their mortgaged state. The fact was, it had its advantages. It saved them from worrying about tedious matters like cultivation and estate management, and there was a feeling among the great families that it was beneath their dignity to concern themselves with such sordid affairs. Besides, the burden of finding cash for the assessment was transferred from their shoulders to the banias' along with the mortgage bond.

Estates were not, therefore, administered by banias as a consequence of debt alone. Many zamindars deliberately leased their estates to banias for their own convenience. This was confirmed by a modern Sindhi zamindar. When he inherited his estate in 1935, all of its affairs were in the hands of a bania who arranged the sowing, cultivation and harvesting of crops and dealt with the haris, giving them *taqavi* loans and dividing the crop with them. For his services, he charged the zamindar one *seer* per *maund* (two and a half per cent), and the haris ten *seers* per *maund* for the *kharif* harvest (twenty-five per cent) and five *seers* for the *rabi* harvest (twelve and a half per cent). This was a long-standing arrangement. It had nothing to do with debt, but was purely for the convenience of the zamindar. The current holder, an astute commercial farmer, did away with the practice in 1941.[31]

Not all zamindars succeeded in striking such advantageous bargains with their banias and a Settlement Officer commented in 1919 that he had heard zamindars claim to have leased their lands on terms which sounded more like usufructuary mortgages.[32] No doubt, zamindars' motives were often mixed and it may have been difficult to distinguish where leasing ended and mortgaging began. Mountford, as one might expect, found several instances of unprofitable leases – one zamindar lived on an allowance of Rs 500 per year although the bania admitted to an annual profit of at least Rs 2,000; another received Rs 553 when the bania's profits came to Rs 1,435.[33] A Settlement Officer exclaimed in disgust in 1909 that through such arrangements, 'the zamindar reduces his income in half and gains in return nothing except a complete freedom from all risk and responsibilities of his position.'[34]

But, at face value, this does not sound like nothing. Many people would pay a high price for freedom from risk and responsibility. When he served in Sind soon after the British conquest, Sir Richard Burton noticed that many zamindars were bankrupt and mortgaged to banias precisely because they were not concerned about their solvency provided they could maintain their life-style:

> As long as the Zemindar could procure his daily bread and dose of Bhang [hemp], support a wife or two, and possibly a dancing girl, wear a sword, and ride a horse, he would rarely, if ever condescend to think or care about his property.

Burton added that this was not a new phenomenon. It was a way of life.[35]

In other words, the Waderos wished to maintain their izzat and their comfort, leaving the profits to the banias. One of the creditors of Mir Ghulam Muhammad Khan Talpur explained in 1899 that the Mirs:

> are not very careful in carrying on their expenses & in the disposal of their income. For instance, Mir Mahomed Khan enjoys a very large income, but he is quite indifferent as to how his affairs are managed. His officials . . . spend his money in any way they please, & have been squandering it. The Mir Saheb is himself devoted to hunting, & knows nothing.[36]

Apart from his land, which was all mortgaged, the Mir received a political pension of Rs 10,800 per year, so he need not have been in straitened circumstances.[37] Like many a zamindar, he was content to muddle through: though effectively bankrupt, he was able to live in the manner to which he was accustomed.

If such arrangements suited the zamindars, they suited the banias too. Banias had no *izzat*, however wealthy they might be. Without the zamindars behind them, they might find it difficult to obtain from the haris 'that respectful assistance which is so essential to success as a zamindar.'[38] So long as the zamindar was still nominally in control of the estate and enjoyed high status in the countryside, the haris would co-operate with the bania as the zamindar's representative. A zamindar's backing was so important that even when land was actually sold to a bania, the latter often kept the zamindar in place as a figurehead, to provide moral authority. In such cases, the zamindar would technically be a tenant, but would retain all the trappings of zamindari status. All that was lacking was the substance – the title deeds.

Giving the zamindar a generous pension, to enable the family to keep up appearances, was a sound investment. Whether the land was mortgaged to the bania or leased back to the zamindar, there was no reason for either party to disturb the relationship. So long as the bania enjoyed the profits and the zamindar family enjoyed their lifestyle, they could co-exist in reasonable harmony. Problems normally arose only when trust broke down, and one side suspected the other of playing false. For example, a bania who suspected a zamindar of cheating him by making private arrangements with the haris over batai might refuse to pay the government assessment, and the zamindar might retaliate the following year by seizing the entire outturn. The next step would be a court case and the zamindar was almost certain to find himself facing the loss of his land.

This was the new factor, which entered the equation to threaten the balance of power. The risk of losing land had not existed before the British conquest. Under the Talpurs, creditors could seize crops and movable property, but they could not deprive people of their livelihood by taking away their land. The British gave creditors the power to foreclose on their debtors' property.

In the early days, the device was used sparingly. Until 1866, the law was administered by Deputy Collectors who, as district officers relying on Waderos for support, were reluctant to grant possession orders which would throw their allies off their estates. Moreover, it took time for creditors themselves to appreciate the power which had been granted to them. When the Collector of Karachi investigated debt in Sehwan in 1859, he found only one case in which a bania had stipulated that the land would become his property if the mortgage was not repaid, and he suspected this was because the Mukhtiarkar of Sehwan, who was a relation, had given the bania advice about British law.[39]

The Bombay Code, introduced in 1866, deprived local administrators of their jurisdiction over civil cases. These were henceforth decided in formally constituted civil courts by judges who were given little discretion. Discretion was particularly significant with respect to the law of contract. Provided a creditor could prove that the client had acknowledged the account then that was the end of the matter and the debtor must pay the debt. No principle of equity could come into play.

The Civil Code put enormous power into the hands of creditors and many debtors despaired of obtaining justice under its provisions. A few years after its introduction, Evan James reported that zamindars regarded the civil court set up under the Code as a calamity:

> destined to bring their ancestral property to ruin, their ladies to dishonour, and themselves to imprisonment and disgrace. It was a plague which every one of them told me must have been sent upon them by God as a punishment for their sins.[40]

Furthermore, there was no restriction on interest charges. Interest could be levied at any rate: the Subordinate Judge of Shikarpur ruled in 1899 that 37.5 per cent per month 'is not heavy.' The sole proviso ruled out penal interest: but if a clause was inserted to allow heavier interest in case of default, that was no longer, technically, penal interest. It was simply part of a contract to which the debtor had agreed. In 1895, the Subordinate Judge of Sukkur enforced a claim for Rs 1,481 which had grown out of a principal debt of Rs 650 on the ground that, since the bond contained a 300 per cent penalty clause, the amount claimed was not excessive.[41] As Evan James remarked in 1900, civil courts appeared to work on the assumption that 'every

Indian debtor, when he signed his bond, had an English solicitor at his back advising him.'[42]

Since it was difficult for debtors to win suits brought by their creditors, most cases were undefended. Having received a decree for the execution of the bond, the creditor could apply for an attachment of the debtor's movable or immovable property. Even the lesser evil – the attachment of movable property – was an unpleasant business which could cause serious economic damage. In 1870, Akhund Saiyid Khan complained on behalf of some zamindars of taluqa Naushahro that their farming implements, including Persian wheels and bullocks, were frequently seized in satisfaction of their debts:

> The wheels come to a standstill and cultivation suffers. In this manner, the cultivators are deprived of their means of support & we zemindars are subject to a loss by having to pay the assessment when nothing was cultivated & produced.[43]

The execution of civil court decrees under these circumstances could lead to little but further debt. It is not surprising if debtors preferred to cut out the civil courts and come to some agreement with their creditors, even if it did mean unfavourable mortgages.

There was another reason why Muslim largeholders in particular were anxious to avoid civil suits. It was mentioned in Chapter 3 that Waderos were sometimes reluctant to assist with law enforcement because they feared that being cross-examined in criminal cases would damage their prestige. A civil suit was even more damaging. A proud Wadero would have to suffer the indignity of being hauled up in court by some lowly bania, his private affairs bandied about in public and, in the end, a decree would be made out against him. This seriously reduced his standing in the eyes of his neighbours, but worse could follow. The execution of a civil court decree was a still greater affront to family honour. A zamindar from Sehwan explained in 1872:

> a bailiff of the Court who is perhaps a Hindoo shall forcibly enter and search the recesses of your house. The privacy of your ladies, who have never left the house since they were children, shall be violated, under pretence of collecting your household furniture, and then your character and reputation are blasted for ever.[44]

Such a calamity had to be avoided at all costs if a man was to preserve any standing in the country. In Upper Sind Frontier in 1882, 'the simple threat of being sued in the Civil Court is quite enough to induce a Beluch to execute a bond on whatever terms his creditors may wish to execute.'[45] The Baluchis explained that debtors were in no position to contest cases when the banias were educated and assisted by counsel. They themselves were illiterate and legal advice was not readily available. They did not trust Hindu pleaders, the few Muslim lawyers in Shikarpur took advantage of their rarity to charge exorbitant fees, and there was no guarantee that they would win. In fact, since they would probably be contesting a bond to whose terms they had signed up, the chances were that they would lose. In the long run, it was easier, cheaper and less risky to avoid a suit and sign another bond.

This was also the preferred solution of the bania. A civil suit was expensive for creditors as well as debtors. They too had to pay lawyers and court fees, and they were reluctant to throw good money after bad. Banias in Mirpur Sakro complained in 1873 that it could cost them as much as fifty rupees to recover a debt of twenty.[46] Other banias alleged that court proceedings could ruin both debtors and creditors.[47] Like creditors across the world and down the ages, banias' chief concern was to maintain their cash flow. A civil suit was a last resort.

Even when they had obtained a judgment, banias seldom went to the extreme of executing it. Between 1877–81, the Jacobabad Civil Court issued decrees against 103 zamindars, but only three were executed. In the other cases, the decree-holders contented themselves with extracting fresh bonds.[48] The decree was just another stage in the negotiating process, to step up the pressure. Banias preferred a compromise, using the decree as a lever to negotiate a new lease. Again, this is a familiar pattern in debt proceedings the world over. The creditor's objective is to recover the money, but executing a judgment involves more fees. It is to the advantage of both parties to reach a private agreement. The main value of the civil court to a bania was that the threat of a suit, and then the threat of executing a decree, were useful sticks with which to cow a recalcitrant debtor.

The case of Mir Ghulam Muhammad Khan Talpur illustrates the position. For several years he allowed debts to accumulate, caring 'not for the morrow.' By 1899, he had run up a debt of Rs 25,632 and had several judgments outstanding against him. He was shocked when a creditor threatened to execute one of these decrees. He appealed to Evan James as Commissioner in Sind and 'protector of nobles,' to prevent the loss of his honour. When he realized that the Mir's entire household property might be sold at auction, James agreed to intervene. He was nervous of the political consequences of such a disaster striking Sind's leading family. Various officers suggested schemes whereby part of the Mir's income could be set aside to pay off his debts, but the Mir refused to contemplate them, protesting that he could not afford it. He begged several times to be saved from the dishonour of having his goods seized, but was reluctant to concede that the simplest way out of his difficulties might be to try and pay the money back. Eventually, James lost patience with him. People in the Mir's position must not be allowed to be 'absolutely irresponsible' about their financial affairs, he declared, refusing 'to make the slightest effort to discharge their liabilities.' James threatened to remove the Mir's name from the privilege schedule unless he agreed to make a deal with his creditors. In the end, a compromise was sorted out, whereby repayment was stretched over so long a period that it can hardly have been satisfactory from the creditors' point of view.[49] It was, though, better than nothing, and nothing was all that was on offer until the Mir, and Evan James, had been sufficiently alarmed by the impending action. One can understand why, on a different occasion, James sympathized with banias who had to recover their dues in the face of 'the bad debts, the constant attempts to evade solemn promises, the attempted brow-beating.'[50]

Against this, Mir Ghulam Muhammad justified his refusal to honour the debt on the ground that it consisted entirely of interest. His creditors, he declared, 'went on charging repeatedly interest and compound interest & including it in the principal which consequently went on increasing. They have not only received the whole principal from me but also a portion of the interest.'[51] This reveals a slightly eccentric view of the relationship between interest and principal, but there may have been some truth in his allegation. It was common for banias to bundle up old debts and interest into new bonds. A Rs 650 bond written up for a zamindar in 1893 consisted entirely of an old debt and its interest. By 1895, interest on it had mounted to such an extent that the Subordinate Judge of Sukkur awarded a decree of Rs 1,481.[52] The debts of another zamindar amounted to Rs 1,127 with their interest. His bania incorporated them into a fresh bond, added *panjot* of Rs 498 to bring the total up to Rs 1,725, and after six years he was able to sue for repayment of Rs 7,471.[53]

Small debtors were as badly affected as large ones. In 1873, Gungadin Ramsingh confessed sadly, 'Some ten months ago I had the misfortune of borrowing twelve rupees from a bunia money lender.' He had since repaid sixteen rupees, but with interest running at 32.5 per cent per month, he still owed thirty-five rupees. To recover this, the bania seized all his property 'and I am now ruined.'[54] Gungadin was, of course, a Hindu, confirming that it was not just Muslims who suffered at the hands of banias. In 1894, there was a report of a hari being sued for Rs 110, of which the principal accounted for only Rs 30, the remainder being interest which had accumulated at 75 per cent per year.[55]

These high rates were justified on the grounds of the lack of security offered by agriculturists. Certainly, anyone lending money to landless haris and the smallest zamindars was taking a considerable risk. Experience of the Punjab led Malcolm Darling to conclude that it was probably easier to recover a *lakh* of rupees from a reputable merchant than a hundred from an improvident cultivator.[56] Some banias of Mirpur Sakro asserted in 1894 that if they lent money to Muslims at low rates, 'there seems very little chance of getting the money back.'[57]

This explanation, however, is unsatisfactory. Land was the safest possible security. There was no question of banias losing all their money if their debtors held land. Moreover, the interest was so heavy as to make repayment virtually impossible. That is to say, it looks as if banias did not actually want their money back. In fact, they seem to have gone to a great deal of trouble to ensure that it would not be repaid. The object of the exercise was, rather, to secure a regular income from the capital outlay. If the capital was paid back, the income would be lost. This was the crux of the banias' system, and their activities only make sense in this context.

The accounts in Table 15 illustrate the point. The account of Shah Nawaz Jatoi opened with a debt of Rs 160. Over the next seven years, he borrowed another Rs 93–8. Shah Nawaz made his first repayment, of Rs 200, four years after taking out the loan, but this did not even cover the interest which, at 24 per cent, had built up to Rs 208–8. Altogether, after seven years, he paid back Rs 234–3, less than Rs 20 short of the principal debt, but little more than half of the interest which by then had accumulated to Rs 457–8.

Three points stand out in this account. The first is that the total borrowed by Shah Nawaz was not, for a big zamindar, a large amount. The second is that, even so, the bania still had not recovered it after seven years and had actually gone for four years without seeing any money at all. The third point is that, partly as a result of the irregular repayments, the principal debts dwindle into insignificance when set against the interest charged.

The other accounts show a similar pattern. The bania recovered barely half of his capital from Chakar Khan Suhrani after seven years,

Table 15 Debtors' accounts

	Rs	*as*	*p*	*Rs*	*as*	*p*	*Rs*	*as*	*p*
Chakar Khan Suhrani									
12 July 1877	1,694	1	0	22	0		722	10	0
26 July 1878	1,046	2	6	379	8	0	123	12	0
20 October 1879	930	13	6	820	8	0	1,012	8	0
20 January 1880	294	12	6	202	0	0	–	–	–
28 June 1880	603	10	0	410	0	6	97	0	0
10 April 1881	1,004	8	9	635	8	0	530	14	0
11 May 1883	2,424	15	9	3,109	0	0	1,531	6	6
20 March 1885	116	4	6	–	–	–	12	0	0
	8,115	4	6	5,578	8	6	4,030	3	6
Angan Nabi Bakhsh Gachal									
15 June 1886	183	15	6	32	15	6	45	0	0
27 June 1886	33	6	6	65	4	6	62	8	0
21 July 1890	26	8	0	77	0	0	61	8	0
10 July 1892	–	–	–	59	12	0	117	4	0
8 April 1895	1	0	0	56	12	0	24	8	0
	244	14	0	291	12	0	310	12	0
Shah Nawaz Khan Jatoi									
14 May 1887	160	0	0	–	–	–	–	–	–
1 November 1888	–	–	–	80	0	0	–	–	–
22 March 1891	–	–	–	128	8	0	200	0	0
28 March 1891	1	8	0	–	–	–	–	–	–
21 December 1892	–	–	–	74	13	0	2	0	0
7 April 1893	80	0	0	–	–	–	–	–	–
11 April 1894	–	–	–	89	6	0	2	3	0
16 March 1895	12	0	0	104	2	0	30	0	0
	253	8	0	476	2	0	234	3	0
Chuto Khan Panah									
2 November 1888	30	0	0	10	12	0	23	0	0
17 August 1891	38	0	0	35	0	0	–	–	–
17 July 1894	80	0	0	141	4	0	1	2	6
	148	0	0	187	0	0	24	2	6

Source: Sind Encumbered Estates Annual Administration Report, 1899–1900, 9, 125–6

while the repayments did not even cover the interest. The bania sued Chakar Khan for debt, and on 24 October 1886 was awarded Rs 14,000 – rather more than one would have expected, considering that it had stood at only Rs 9,663 the previous March. On 28 March 1898, the bania put in a new, and similarly inflated, claim for Rs

60,233–3–2.[58] It is hard to believe that he seriously expected Chakar Khan to repay such vast sums. In fact, by inflating the debt, he seems to have gone to some trouble to keep repayment continually out of the debtor's reach.

In one of the other cases, the debtor, Angan Gachal, was relatively conscientious. After ten years he had covered all the interest, but he still owed Rs 226, nearly as much as he had borrowed in the first place.

These examples suggest that, whatever their reasons for borrowing, debtors had little chance of repaying their debts. By the same token, banias had little chance of recovering their loans, and this leads to a reappraisal of their place in the rural economy. In the literature of the nineteenth century, they are habitually referred to as 'moneylenders,' but if that were so, they were singularly unsuccessful. It is a sorry moneylender who cannot get his or her money back after ten years. In fact, banias could usually recover their principal if they wished to, but were in no hurry because discharging the debt killed the goose that laid the golden egg: for the interest, taken in kind, fuelled their activities as traders.

If one thinks of the banias as shareholders, then their activities make more sense. Their loans represented investments, and the interest was their dividend. Naturally, they would not want their clients to pay back the loan, just as stockholders do not recover their investments except to change them. Capital has no value if it is lying idle. The banias' system, therefore, was more sophisticated than Victorian commentators were prepared to allow. They were not the equivalent of pawnbrokers in a London slum, who appear to be the image uppermost in the minds of British officials. On the contrary, the bania was a shrewd financial operator who 'looks upon money as the means of acquiring more money.'[59]

It is doubly misleading to think of the nineteenth century banias as moneylenders for the simple reason that most of their transactions were carried out in kind, agriculturists seldom having any need for cash. The currency of the countryside was grain. Even if a farmer did require cash (to buy land, pay assessment or put on a wedding), the loan was repaid in grain. The banias attributed cash values to these transactions to maintain a consistent record, and also for their own convenience as traders. Banias were merchants, and moneylending provided a means of acquiring grain cheaply. Much of the produce which village banias traded in the market centres had been obtained as interest.

To create opportunities for investment and maintain the supply of interest, banias offered easy credit. The accounts discussed above demonstrate that no banks or co-operative societies could hope to replace the bania as a source of credit, so long as zamindars were accustomed to unlimited credit facilities and did not expect their creditors to ask for their money back. Late twentieth century observers may be better able to appreciate the imperatives of the bania's world than their thrifty Victorian ancestors. Anyone who has used a credit card is familiar with interest rates considered usurious by nineteenth century standards, easy unsecured credit, minimal repayments which barely cover interest, capital and interest compounding until they are virtually indistinguishable. Neil Charlesworth has remarked on 'the personally more sanguine view of borrowing and debt required of the heavily mortgaged late twentieth century historian.'[60]

Generous credit and punitive interest tied the agriculturist to the bania, just as the stalwarts of the contemporary consumer economy are tied to their plastic cards. Nineteenth century Sindhi agriculturists, though, had even less choice than dedicated twentieth century consumers. For, however prudent they might be, there was one obligation Sindhi farmers could not avoid, and that was the government assessment.

The land revenue system of British India must provide one of the best proofs of Benjamin Franklin's dictum that death and taxes are the only certain things in this world. Death might be inevitable, but its date is hidden in the book of fate. The demand for land revenue, by contrast, fell due, relentlessly, on prescribed days of the year. There was no escaping it and the government, like the angel of death, would accept no credit or deals in kind. The assessment had to be paid, on the due date, in cash, on the nail. And there was only one source of cash in the rural economy of nineteenth century Sind, and that was the bania. To pay their debt to the government, farmers had to raise debts with banias. There was no way out of it.

What made matters worse was that they all had to strike their deals with the banias together: with so many people anxious to sell at once, the price of grain always fell as the instalments of revenue became due. Lewis Mountford, the Manager of Encumbered Estates, had personal experience of the problem. In good seasons, when the market was glutted, the zamindar often 'simply could not sell grain to pay off the assessment except at ruinous rates.' The Encumbered Estates Department had the resources to pay the assessment while keeping back the bulk of its produce until prices rose again, but most ordinary landholders were not so fortunate. They had to dispose of some of their produce hastily at uneconomic rates, merely to raise the cash required by government. Few could afford to hold on until prices went back up again.[61] The first instalment of *kharif* revenue was due on 1 January every year, the second on 15 February and the third on 1 April. The first instalment was particularly badly timed, since the rice harvest was not always over by then. Throughout the first four months of the year, prices were low: and if the harvest was especially good, it might be impossible to sell at any price.[62] In 1902, the Bombay government agreed to drop the first instalment and postpone the third by two weeks. Similar changes were made for collection of *rabi* revenue, which had been due on 15 May, 15 June and 15 July – the May instalment was abandoned.[63] These concessions were intended to make life easier for agriculturists, but they came late in the day and the effect was marginal. Prices still fell when the assessment became due.

However thrifty agriculturists might be, then, they were bound to resort to banias every year to pay their revenue, and they were obliged to do so under unfavourable circumstances. There was no way round this unless farmers had large reserves of capital and could afford to play the market. That is to say, only a large zamindar could pay the government assessment and be confident of selling surplus produce at a profit.

In consequence, rather than negotiate when they had no bargaining power, many agriculturists simply left the whole business to their banias. In 1883, Colonel Anderson, Superintendent of the Sind Revenue Survey, commented that agriculturists could seldom tell him how much revenue they paid, without reference to their banias.[64] Twenty years later, the Collector of Shikarpur recalled that when he first came to Sind as an Assistant Collector, he had tried to inspect the agriculturists' receipt books, in line with Presidency practice, to ensure that junior revenue officials were not defrauding them over the assessment – but it was a vain quest:

> Village after village would be visited without a single receipt book being forthcoming, owing to their being all deposited with the local Bania, who was generally on his rounds.

An Assistant Collector, he remarked, had more important things to do than 'wasting his time knocking at the doors of petty Banias.'[65] Even in progressive Larkana Division, only five per cent of the zamindars paid their assessment themselves at the turn of the century, the banias acting on behalf of the others.[66] If the burden of debt was increasing in the nineteenth century, one important factor may have been as simple as the change-over from a *batai* to a cash assessment, which forced zamindars to find ready money from the banias.

This analysis of the bania's system shows that the vexed question of whether agricultural debt in India was contracted for productive or non-productive purposes was almost of secondary importance. Agriculturists were bound to turn to the bania to pay their land revenue. And, whatever their reason for borrowing, much of their profit was drained away as interest, preventing them from getting the full benefit even of productive investments.

No doubt, thriftless habits aggravated the problem. Waderos' tendency to enhance their prestige by taking up huge amounts of wasteland undermined their solvency. Large and sloppily cultivated estates could be liabilities at the best of times, but when their owners borrowed money to acquire yet more uneconomic tracts, they were in danger of indebting themselves twice over. Waderos' incomes were further eroded by their need to impress their neighbours by surrounding themselves with an entourage of retainers and servants, and by displaying lavish hospitality. Isa Khan Junejo of taluqa Khipro was unable to pay his assessment in 1905–06 and had debts to a total of Rs 6,767, yet he prided himself on spending Rs 125 per month to feed beggars and *faqirs*, and 'a crowd of loafers' would gather round at the time of batai.[67]

In addition, agriculturists of all classes were obliged to host expensive receptions to mark marriages, funerals, circumcisions, births, etc. Malcolm Darling believed such festivals were at the root of indebtedness, backing his conclusion with the assertion that this was also 'the opinion of the countryside.'[68] However, the 'opinion of the countryside' may not have counted for much. If 'the countryside' had understood the causes of debt, the problem would not have been so acute. J.C. Jack, in his *Economic Life of a Bengal District*, found that on average domestic festivals and entertainments accounted for only six per cent of the annual expenditure of a 'family in comfort' and four per cent of the expenditure of a 'family in extreme indigence.'[69] This is by no means excessive, unless one begrudges agriculturists any form of non-productive spending. Jack also found that the 'family in comfort' devoted eleven per cent of its expenditure to rent and local tax, which took up four per cent of the expenditure of the indigent family. No equivalent study was ever carried out in Sind, but these figures reinforce the supposition that domestic festivals may not have been so heavy a burden as was sometimes believed. The cost of weddings, at least, was mitigated in Sind by the custom that guests should bring cash as presents.[70]

The crux of the banias' system, then, was that, because there was no restriction on the interest charged, they were able to acquire much of their grain at virtually no cost. If they had been prevented from levying such high rates, they would still have had to buy the zamindars' grain, but with a more modest profit margin. This process at the same time reduced agriculturists' return on their crops. Agriculturists who considered extending or improving their cultivation may have been discouraged by the knowledge that so much of the profits would revert to their financiers.

With easy credit and heavy interest, banias kept their clients on a loose rein, while giving them enough rope to hang themselves with, should the need arise. Once indebted to a bania, if was difficult for a farmer to avoid sinking further into debt – and debtors who objected to the arrangements had the threat of a civil suit hanging over their heads. Once taken to court, clients became aware of the negative aspects of the easygoing credit facilities they had been enjoying. They had to pay back the impossible debts, together with any other items the bania could bring into the picture to strengthen the case – such as advances to haris for which zamindars had stood surety. Having won their cases, the banias called the tune. If they demanded, as a compromise, that the clients should sell them some land, the debtors had little choice but to comply.

III

Inevitably, banias' commanding economic position, and the use some of them made of it, made them objects of envy and resentment. This was intensified in Sind by communal bitterness. It went against the grain for Muslims – especially those belonging to respected families – to see Hindus not only flourishing, but also exercising power in the civil courts and even depriving Muslims of their land.

Hindus occupied an ambiguous place in Sindhi society. Before the British conquest, they enjoyed such respect as traders and civil servants that they were excused payment of the *jeziat-al-hunud*, the tax paid by non-Muslims living under the protection of Islam. Great merchants and civil servants were exempt from all taxation, while smaller merchants had to donate an annual *peshkash* of five to ten rupees per head.[71] Even James Burnes, who took a jaundiced view of Muslim religious tolerance, had to admit after visiting Sind in 1827 that Hindus had considerable influence at the Court of the Mirs.[72] His brother, Alexander, confirmed this more enthusiastically a few years later. In his opinion, Hindus in Sind were tolerated and powerful.[73]

Despite their importance, though, Hindus were never in any doubt that they depended on the good will of the majority. They could not pass through the countryside without paying a fee to each local Wadero for protection.[74] Consequently, they could not hold land in villages, but restricted themselves to cultivation around the towns, or else managed estates for powerful families.[75] In addition, there was before the British conquest a constant threat of forcible conversion to Islam. Any Hindu who defrauded a Muslim had to forfeit property to ten times the value of the fraud and at the same time embrace Islam.[76] James Burnes was so shocked by the treatment endured by Hindus in Sind that he could not understand why any of them stayed there, unless it was because of 'that attachment, which man shares with the vegetable, to the soil in which he was reared.'[77] Thomas Postans and Charles Masson, who also visited Sind before the British conquest, recognized a more practical reason. There was nothing to prevent Hindus emigrating if they felt persecuted. Their reluctance to take the opportunity indicated that their profits compensated for other disadvantages.[78]

In the end, though, these disadvantages may have proved the undoing of Muslim government in Sind. Seth Naomal Hotchand, one of the greatest merchants of Sind, provided such valuable assistance to the British before, during and after the conquest, that he was rewarded with a 5,000 acre first-class jagir. He provided British forces with food, transport and other necessities between 1837–43, gathered intelligence, arranged the safe delivery of Napier's correspondence during the campaign of 1843, and helped to reconcile the defeated Baluchi jagirdars to British rule.[79] His antagonism towards the Talpur government dated from 1832 when his father, Seth Hotchand, discovered after a communal riot in Hyderabad that his friendship with Mir Ali Khan Talpur did not prevent him from being arrested and threatened with circumcision. Naomal declared later:

> my family felt aggrieved by the wrongs inflicted upon them by the later Amirs in their blind zeal for their faith, and my principal object in being thus useful to the British Government at such personal sacrifice was simply to secure their interest and regard for future good.[80]

The conquest freed Hindus from their dependence on the majority community, putting them under the patronage of the British. They could move about the countryside freely and they could practise their religion openly. Commerce and the bureaucracy expanded under British rule and both continued to be dominated by banias and

Amils. Nor would Hindu moneylenders have dared to defraud their clients as blatantly under Talpur rule as some appear to have done under the British. That Hindus appreciated their good fortune long after British rule was well established was confirmed by Jethmal Parsram, a well-known Hindu literary figure. In 1924, he wrote that old people still spoke of 'the terror which hung over them' during the days of Talpur government.'[81]

Evan James gave an interesting account of what the Hindus' improved circumstances meant in day-to-day terms. When he first served in Sind in the 1870s, Hindus still had an inherent fear of Muslims, not even venturing to ride horses which, it was generally agreed, were noble animals fit only for the superior community. When he returned to Sind as Commissioner in the 1890s, he noticed that the Hindus who two decades previously 'never dreamed of riding aught but a camel, now bestride as good horses as their former Beluch masters, and never think of alighting to "salam" whoever it be that passes.' Idols and religious pictures, he remarked, were now openly displayed in shops and temples, something that would have been unthinkable during his earlier time in Sind.[82]

The old order was changing to the advantage of Hindus. Lewis Mountford, the Manager of Encumbered Estates, accused Hindus of deliberately enforcing their power, as a community, through the civil courts. Most of the Subordinate Judges were Hindus. Mountford claimed that, with banias as friends and relations, they took a warped view of what constituted reasonable interest charges, tending to be overly sympathetic towards the claims of creditors.[83] In other words, the courts were run by Hindus, for Hindus.

This charge was made by many Muslims. Karam Ali, a zamindar from taluqa Moro, insisted in 1902 that it was impossible for Muslims to obtain justice from civil courts because all the pleaders were Hindus:

> They combine with the mofussil [country] banias and help them in concocting false accounts against us poor creditors. After the filing of false suits, these very pleaders represent the bania plaintiffs. The claims are easily proved against us. We poor men have no means to engage pleaders and altho we made vehement protests against the plaintiffs' claims and bring forward Mahomedan witnesses in proof of the falsity of their claims, we are not heard.[84]

Whether his accusations were justified or were merely an exclamation of frustration at being outmanoeuvred by sharp lawyers, Karam Ali voiced an opinion shared by large numbers of Muslims. Khan Saheb Ali Muhammad Akhund, the only Muslim Subordinate Judge in Sind, apparently made some misguided attempts to turn the balance against Hindus in his court. In 1894 he disallowed the interest demanded by a Hindu from a Muslim on the ground that, 'Formerly you Hindus used to ride on donkeys, and the interest you have extorted from Mahomedans has made you ride horses.'[85] In a reversal of Mountford's criticism of Hindu judges, some Hindus whose cases had been heard by Ali Muhammad alleged that he was in league with the local Waderos. He entertained them in his chambers and visited them in their villages. Debtors boasted that, with a Muslim Judge, they would no longer have to repay their debts.[86]

These accusations and counter accusations were indicative of communal antagonisms which sporadically erupted into violence. The occasional conversion of Hindus to Islam was a common trigger for public disturbance since it would provoke angry claims from representatives of the Hindu community that force had been used. This was in itself a measure of their increased security since they would hardly have dared an open challenge on so sensitive an issue if the British had not been there to intervene. Muslim representatives would angrily refute the charges: and the debate would be taken to the streets. Disputes over conversions provoked riots in Sukkur in 1872, in the Sehwan area in 1884, in Hyderabad in 1892 and 1893 and in Matiari in 1901.[87] Communal riots also flared up over other issues. In 1882, Baluch soldiers attacked Hindus in the Hyderabad bazaar, for no apparent reason beyond boredom, while a dispute over the playing of music in a temple in Thatta provoked violence in 1891.[88] In 1893, a Mohurram procession in Sukkur turned into an anti-Hindu riot during which the Town Inspector of Police, a Hindu, was badly beaten.[89]

These constituted evidence of friction between the two communities, but there were no specifically anti-bania riots in Sind along the lines of the riots which took place in the Deccan in 1875. When, in 1892 and 1896, Evan James, the Commissioner in Sind, asked his district officers to provide details about attacks against moneylenders, the consensus was that the situation was not serious in the province as a whole.[90]

A disturbing picture, though, emerged in the Hyderabad Collectorate, where the proportion of Hindus was relatively high. Attacks were not frequent – three murders and eleven dacoities between 1886–95[91] – but when they did occur a conspiracy of silence thwarted police investigations. This implied that the attacks were tolerated, if not actively instigated, by the local Waderos. It underlined that any power exercised by Hindus was more apparent than real. They were in practice as vulnerable as they had ever been under the Talpurs, and were entirely dependent on the protection of the British government. The final proof of this was to come in 1947, when the majority of Hindus fled Sind in the wake of the departing British.

Even power obtained through the civil courts was precarious, for enforcing a decree could be difficult, even dangerous, in country areas. As one administrator commented wryly, 'foreclosures are tempered by assassination.'[92] If a debtor decided to take the law into his own hands, there was little the police could do about it, for the sympathies of the countryside were with the criminal. In 1888, Muslims in Tando Jam took up the cause of a Saiyid accused of murdering two banias. They succeeded in scaring off all the Hindu witnesses and intimidating the District Public Prosecutor, a Hindu. The Collector of Hyderabad had to ask for the case to be taken up by the Public Prosecutor in Sind who, being English, would not be targeted.[93]

This was not an isolated example. Two interesting cases illustrate the issues. The first shows how the relationship between bania and client could break down, leading to argument, litigation and, in this instance, death. Saiyid Ahmed Shah, of taluqa Naushahro, shared three fields with a bania named Daya. One day, he cut a nim tree from one of the fields and presented it to his Pir, Nasirdin. Unfortunately, he did not first discuss his gift with Daya. Daya therefore filed a suit against him for Rs 75, claiming that in addition to the nim, Ahmed Shah had previously cut down two babul trees. The Saiyid was naturally anxious to avoid a civil suit which would surely have gone against him. He appealed to Pir Nasirdin to intervene and persuade Daya to compromise, but the reconciliation meeting turned into a slanging match. Daya called Ahmed Shah a liar, and the Saiyid responded with derogatory remarks about the bania's sister. Daya now filed a second suit, for libel, claiming damages of Rs 1,000. He ignored several appeals from influential people to withdraw the cases. A couple of months later, Daya was killed in broad daylight, while riding along the high road. It was almost certain that Ahmed Shah was responsible, and he and some relations were arrested, but the case was dropped because no-one could be found to testify against them.[94] Both men appear on this occasion to have had recourse to the respective weapons of their communities. The Hindu turned to the courts. The Muslim appealed to influential men and then, when this failed, allegedly resorted to violence.

The second case gives an exceptionally vivid insight into the shelter provided by the Muslim community for those who attacked banias. In 1881, Gopaldas, a wealthy bania of taluqa Moro, disappeared. He was a notoriously extortionate moneylender and it was common knowledge that some of his debtors had taken their revenge. They murdered him and threw his body into the river. There was no secret about that. His fate became a byword, children taunting each other with it.

Gathering evidence was another matter. It seemed that nobody knew anything. The Superintendent of Police was certain the local people were deliberately obstructing his investigations, and he quartered punitive police on the villages from which the perpetrators were believed to come, but to no avail. No charges were ever brought. Indeed, the Superintendent himself sympathized with the villagers, remarking that, 'If only one half of the misdeeds of the murdered man . . . are based on facts, I scarcely wonder at the tenacity with which the secret of this murder is guarded.'[95]

A few years later, Gopaldas' brother, Jairamdas, was badly wounded and much of his property stolen. Again, it proved impossible to identify the culprits.[96] As Evan James remarked, 'the murderers of Hindu moneylenders are rarely convicted in Sind.'[97]

Cases of dacoities committed against banias shed further light on the vulnerability of village banias. A bania named Ladho, of taluqa Moro, had filed many suits against his fellow villagers and had acquired large store of their ornaments, which they had pawned to him. When dacoits broke into his home in 1892, his neighbours were in no mood to help him. On the contrary, they let the thieves go ahead with their business of stealing over twenty thousand rupees-worth of property. It may have been by way of return for this favour that the dacoits took the opportunity, while they were on the premises, to burn all of Ladho's books and accounts. Once the dacoits had gone the villagers, far from assisting the police to identify the criminals, 'openly . . . rejoiced at the damage done to him.'[98] Around the same time, in 1889, another bania, Mangho, of taluqa Tando Allahyar, was thrown out of his house with his family after being beaten up. The dacoits locked themselves in and spent the next two hours coolly going through his possessions and destroying his accounts. Meanwhile, about 150 village men surrounded the house, but they did not help Mangho. In fact, it is hard to avoid the suspicion that they came specifically to prevent help from being given. The police found it impossible to get any information out of the vast number of witnesses, and were unable to bring charges against the two men they suspected.[99]

In neither of these two cases did the police suggest that the villagers as a whole had instigated the dacoities, but the suspects were all local. What one can say is that the villagers considered the banias fair game and cheered the dacoits on. It is also clear that the dacoits sympathized with the villagers since they destroyed the banias' accounts. Moreover, Waderos almost certainly connived at the incidents even if they did not inspire them. The District Superintendent of Police, Hyderabad, believed the local Waderos had deliberately obstructed the police investigations into the two dacoities just mentioned and in similar incidents, while a couple of years later the Collector of Shikarpur accused Waderos in taluqa Nasirabad of conspiring to murder a bania and intimidate prosecution witnesses.[100] Earlier, the Hindu community of Sehwan had accused the local Saiyids of organizing attacks on Hindus.[101] It was of course extremely difficult to prove charges against Waderos.

When it came to crimes against banias, there is little doubt that Waderos were interested parties who were, at the very least, unwilling to assist the British authorities to enforce justice. Since British rule depended on the influence of the Waderos, anything which reduced their willingness to collaborate was, potentially, a threat to that rule. The problem was most acute in the Hyderabad region but Evan James warned in the 1890s that good relations between Hindus and Muslims were beginning to break down all over the province. This was a result of the improved social position of Hindus and Muslim resentment at the working of the Civil Code.[102]

It was in this context that the problem of indebtedness was tackled by the Government of Sind. At worst, it seemed that banias were depriving indebted Waderos of their land and therefore of their power. At best, indebtedness created bad feeling among Waderos and a sense of disenchantment with British rule. The Sind authorities accordingly devoted themselves to relieving the debts of the Muslim landed magnates, the jagirdars and great zamindars.

Chapter 6

Class Legislation[1]

I

British officials saw debt as a political rather than an economic problem. It was not their primary concern that the bania creamed off the profits of agriculture, nor were they generally disquieted by the predicament of the smallholder. Administrators were preoccupied with the consequences indebtedness might have for the traditional leaders of rural society. Victorian officers stationed in Sind believed that power was slipping from Waderos to Hindu merchants. Sometimes the process was legally sanctioned as land, the basis of power, passed from Muslim debtors to Hindu creditors. Less visible, but more common, was the insidious ruin of zamindars who virtually became tenants on their own mortgaged estates. Local administration without the Waderos was unthinkable. Banias could not replace them because they did not possess the influence, respect or status of Waderos: they had no *izzat*. Nor could government expect serious help from petty zamindars who were accustomed to depending on their powerful neighbours. Debt interfered with the smooth running of the colonial system and eroded the foundation of imperial rule.

The Sind government therefore concentrated its sympathy on the Waderos, to reinforce the old order and preserve the balance of power. It introduced no less than four Encumbered Estates Acts to rescue them, in 1876, 1881, 1884 and 1896.

No action was taken to help the mass of agriculturists in the nineteenth century. The Deccan Agriculturists Relief Act, which was brought into operation elsewhere in the Bombay Presidency in 1879, provided support for all classes of indebted agriculturists. However, in 1882, the Commissioner in Sind ruled out this, or any similar Act, for Sind. There was, he advised, no need to assist people 'whose position in the social scale gave them no special claims to consideration.' On the contrary, he felt that the Encumbered Estates Act itself had embraced too wide a social spectrum.[2] Petty holders were just as indebted as big ones, if not more so, but they had to fend for themselves until 1901, when the Deccan Agriculturists Relief Act was at last extended to Sind.

II

Colonel Dunsterville, a Karachi Settlement Officer, was the first person officially to draw government's attention to the problem of debt among largeholders. In 1859, he found that all the cultivable land in taluqa Sehwan had been mortgaged. Not a single estate was free of debt. All the Waderos had mortgaged their property to banias, who were duly milking their profits. One of the leading proprietors was 'troubled for his actual subsistence.'[3]

Bartle Frere, the Commissioner in Sind, recognized the significance of Dunsterville's report, and reacted with characteristic vigour. He introduced a modified version of the Irish Encumbered Estates Act. The Deputy Collector of Sehwan took over management of the most important estates, with powers to negotiate compromises with the creditors. In some cases, he sold off parts of the estates to pay their liabilities.

There was no suggestion at this time that debt was a general problem, so Frere did not ask for investigations into conditions elsewhere. In 1861 Dunsterville reported that the crisis was over. The Deputy Collector had cleared most of the debts.[4]

A decade later, however, it seemed that Dunsterville's confidence was premature. The new Deputy Collector was Evan James, on his first tour in Sind, and in 1872 he raised the issue of debt in Sehwan again, but with more urgency. He believed that unsuitable raiyatwari settlements had attacked the economic foundations of Waderos' power and that inflexible civil courts were delivering the coup de grâce. Banias now had a stranglehold over the big zamindars. Government, urged James, must act swiftly to restore the natural social order. It was a political issue of the highest importance, which had implications for the very survival of British rule in Sind.

In the first place Waderos might, quite simply, be indebted out of existence. The 'genuine aristocracy of the country,' James alleged, was being replaced by 'a race of rack-renting usurers, who grind the agricultural classes, exhaust the land, and who, apart from their being of an idolatrous faith and therefore despised by the bulk of the population, can never in an emergency be of service to the government.' He feared the destruction of the whole system of local administration through Waderos.

But he raised a more frightening spectre – the possibility of a rebellion like the Mutiny of 1857: 'One of the chief causes of the mutiny was the general ruin of the upper classes of native society in some Provinces.' If British rule appeared to be destructive, those Waderos who survived the onslaught of indebtedness would become disenchanted and bitter. With their desperate, dispossessed neighbours to goad them on, they might turn to rebellion as a last resort to save themselves and their families. James admitted that Sindhis were 'more loyal than any other race in India,' but loyalty has its limits and he believed he could see signs that the British were starting to lose their popularity. And this 'cannot but be a source of political danger.'[5]

James realized that his arguments might not find favour with his colleagues. Many disliked Waderos. They wanted the land to be held by small proprietors and James caricatured their approach as a belief that it would be 'a good thing for Sind to get rid of such cumberers of the earth' as the great zamindars. He conceded that in an ideal world this might be the best solution but since Waderos did exist, for good or ill, it would be 'absolutely immoral' to allow them to be deprived of their property by unjust laws. James suspected that 'the unworthy Zemindars of Bengal' had given big zamindars in general a bad name, but this should not be held against the Sindhis. There was, he pointed out, no general government prejudice against Indian zamindars. The taluqdars of Gujarat, Oudh and Broach had been helped by Encumbered Estates legislation, so there was no reason why the zamindars of Sehwan should be denied similar aid. The solution would be once again to empower the Deputy Collector of Sehwan to take over the management of the estates of indebted zamindars.[6]

Despite his apocalyptic language, James did not advocate action for the whole province. He seems to have had in mind nothing more far-reaching than a revival of Bartle Frere's rescue-bid. The current Commissioner in Sind, Sir William Merewether, however, believed James' analysis had greater significance. He doubted whether Sehwan was isolated. Help was needed for all the landed magnates of Sind.[7]

Merewether knew, though, that Bombay would not act on the unsubstantiated assertions of himself and James. Four years earlier, when he had requested an Act to relieve the debts of Sindhi jagirdars, his proposal had been dismissed out of hand. W.R.S.V. Fitzgerald, the Governor of Bombay, had refused to contemplate 'class legislation.'[8] Merewether did not make this mistake twice. To obtain evidence of the magnitude of the problem in Sind, he ordered his district officers to investigate the debts of all hereditary jagirdars and zamindars paying over Rs 500 per year as land revenue assessment.

The figures, compiled in 1874, confirmed Merewether's suspicions. The debts of the Sehwan zamindars (or, rather, those around Lake Manchar, including some from taluqa Johi) amounted to Rs 166,243: but the total debt of 659 of Sind's greatest magnates came to nearly Rs 30 *lakhs*, giving an average debt per debtor of Rs 4,447 (see Table 16). In most cases, the debts amounted to more than twice the net yearly income of the debtor. Nearly two-thirds of the hereditary jagirdars' total debt was owed by the four great Talpur families alone. Merewether described the jagirdars as 'a class steeped in debt, they live in a chronic state of difficulty, and they die so, leaving their debts to embarrass and weigh down their heirs.'[9]

The figures were impressive. Backed by James' report, they reinforced Merewether's concern over the gravity of the crisis facing the Waderos. Moreover, the timing of his submission to government was right. James had been appointed Under-Secretary to the Government of Bombay the previous year, so was in a position to support Merewether from within the Presidency capital. In addition, Fitzgerald had left Bombay and his successor, Sir Philip Woodhouse, proved more sympathetic to Merewether's ideas. When Merewether demanded an Encumbered Estates Act which embraced, not just jagirdars, but big zamindars as well, Woodhouse promptly agreed. Referring to Fitzgerald's qualms, Woodhouse specifically rejected 'the objection that so-called "class legislation" is objectionable.' There

Table 16 Debt in Sind, 1876

Debts of jagirdars and zamindars paying over Rs 500 p.a. as revenue assessment

Collectorate	*No of debtors*	*Value of Debts* *Zamindars Rs*	*Jagirdars Rs*	*Total Rs*	*Average debt per debtor Rs*
Karachi	291	520,120	93,640	613,760	2,109
Hyderabad	77	278,015	844,093	1,122,108	14,573
Shikarpur	98	692,750	41,100	733,850	7,488
Upper Sind Frontier	93	364,605	17,650	382,255	4,110
Thar & Parkar	100	123,681	–	123,681	1,237
TOTAL	**659**	**1,979,171**	**996,483**	**2,975,654**	**4,515**

Source: Bombay Govt. Resn. no. 7628, 2 Dec. 1876 (P.G.B., R.D.L., 1876, 1005)

could be no objection in principle to applying to Sind legislation which had been introduced elsewhere. In fact, Woodhouse considered such measures to be even more urgent in a frontier province. This was an oblique reference to the civil war in Kalat and the risk that it might spread to discontented Baluchis in Sind. The Bombay government submitted its proposals to the Government of India for approval in stirring language which would have struck a chord in the heart of Evan James – who may indeed have had a hand in drafting the letter:

> The Jagirdars and Zemindars, the nobles, gentry, and yeomen of that province are overwhelmed with debt, and there is absolutely no hope of relieving them unless special action be taken. If matters are allowed to drift on as they have done hitherto, the result can but be a social revolution of a grave character. The land will pass out of the hands of the hereditary owners, who . . . will thus feel they have a distinct grievance against the British government.[10]

The Government of India was impressed and the Sind Encumbered Estates Act was passed in 1876. This enabled government to restore the fortunes of indebted zamindars. Those who wished to take advantage of it applied to the Manager of Encumbered Estates. If he approved their applications, then he took complete responsibility for their holdings, managing their cultivation and accounts and using the surplus to discharge their debts. Estates remained in the Manager's charge until all their liabilities had been cleared. They were then returned, solvent and financially secure, to their owners.[11]

The Act included two provisions on which Woodhouse had insisted as a result of experience in Oudh. No creditor could sue for recovery of any debt incurred by the owner while the estate was under management. This would prevent new debts from accumulating while the Manager was busy with the old ones. Anyone lending money to someone whose estate was under management must do so on the understanding that the money might never be recovered. The other provision was that an estate could not be taken under management until the debts had been investigated, lest it were found to be hopelessly involved, becoming a burden on the time and resources of the Encumbered Estates Department. As well as satisfying himself that an estate was sufficiently encumbered to warrant his protection, the Manager therefore had to ensure that it was not so bankrupt as to leave no hope of reviving it.[12]

The Sind Encumbered Estates Act was intended as a temporary

measure, to meet the specific crisis. Applications had to be made within six months of it coming into force.[13] However, it proved so successful that it was extended in 1881, a further six-month period being assigned for receiving applications.[14] The Encumbered Estates Department remained in existence for eleven years. It was set up in 1876 under Colonel Boulton. He was succeeded as Manager of Encumbered Estates by Thomas Hart-Davies in 1879 and the Department was wound up in 1887. During that period, it dealt with 772 estates and paid off debts worth Rs 3,807,602.[15]

The operation was conducted as cheaply as possible. It was self-financing, the salaries of the Manager and other employees of the Encumbered Estates Department being paid out of the profits of the estates. The Manager aimed to keep the costs of management at around ten per cent of the gross receipts. The requirement that the estates must pay for the officials who managed them undoubtedly prolonged proceedings in some cases. In 1884, when his work was drawing to its conclusion, Hart-Davies explained that several estates – principally large jagirs – were solvent but that he could not discharge them because the costs of management would fall too heavily on the remaining, smaller estates. Indeed, 'the costs of management on these unfortunate estates would be more than doubled.'[16]

Such relatively small estates were a burden on the Encumbered Estates Department and, consequently, on the estates of other, more substantial zamindars. They had come into the Manager's charge as a result of the terms in which the Act had been framed. An Encumbered Estates Act had to be restricted to a particular class or area. By definition, it merely aimed to extricate certain individuals from their difficulties. It had no claim to eradicate the underlying causes of indebtedness, and so the number of estates involved had to be kept to the minimum. The benefits of the Sind Act were limited to hereditary jagirdars and to zamindars paying over Rs 300 per year as land revenue. Government regarded this as 'the line which should separate the landed gentry from the mere peasant proprietor,'[17] but it was a surprisingly generous definition which embraced the pettiest of largeholders. Estates as small as a couple of hundred acres were eligible. It may have found its way into the drafting as a result of lingering resistance to 'class legislation' within the Bombay government, but officials soon concluded that the line had been drawn too low. Colonel Boulton, the first Manager, interpreted his terms of reference liberally in 1876 and admitted to his protection all zamindars who were eligible. Many held small estates which could not be supervised successfully without enlarging the Encumbered Estates Department. These zamindars were not politically significant, so they were regarded as a drain on the Manager's resources. What was worse, it turned out that some had exaggerated their debts, giving a false picture of insolvency in order to qualify for management. When he heard of this, the Commissioner declared sternly that the Act was not intended to enable petty zamindars to evade their liabilities, but to free the estates of jagirdars and large zamindars from debts which they could not repay without help.[18] In the Commissioner's mind, then, small debts constituted evasion, large ones misfortune – an interesting illustration of the propensity for vice to become more tolerable as the perpetrator moves up the social scale.

When the Act was extended in 1881 and fresh applications were made, Hart-Davies showed that he had learned from his predecessor's mistakes. He assured the Commissioner that he would not keep any small fry in his net: 'as the Act is essentially a political measure, I should be careful to recommend only those for relief who were really influential men of considerable property.'[19] In the event, he accepted no more than a third of the applicants, weeding out those of no importance.[20] He was even more discriminating in 1884. A third Encumbered Estates Act had been introduced to cover the heirs of jagirdars whose jagirs had lapsed at their death, provided they had a zamindari interest assessed at over Rs 300 per year.[21] They had previously been excluded on a technicality relating to the interpretation of the word 'zamindar.' Hart-Davies' vigilance ensured that this Act, though equitable in spirit, remained negligible in effect. It prompted fifteen applications, of which he accepted one.[22]

The Sind Encumbered Estates Acts, therefore, despite the nominal inclusion of lesser zamindars, was intended to benefit only the leaders of society, the Waderos and hereditary jagirdars. These were the people who must not be left to the perils of the unregulated market place. It was a remarkable operation which provided practical insight into the way in which zamindars and banias managed their business. The implementation of the Acts accordingly needs to be considered in some detail before their wider implications can be assessed.

III

The Manager's first task, on receiving an application for protection and confirming the estate's eligibility, was to establish whether its financial condition warranted his intervention. This was easier said than done. In 1879, the Commissioner in Sind suggested that an estate should not be regarded as encumbered unless its debts amounted to at least five years' income.[23] However, it is not recorded whether this criterion had actually been adopted by the Manager when he accepted applications three years previously. The likelihood is that discretion played a larger part in his decision, if only because it was so difficult to make an accurate estimate of the estate's income in the first place. There were seldom any books to work from, while the Manager had to contend with the perennial problem of valuing the harvest and seed at different times of the year and, often, in different areas. Dodo Khan Bhutto and his two sons, for example, stated their joint income at Rs 20,000 per year and estimated their debts at Rs 134,644. With their debts standing at nearly seven years' income, they seemed well qualified for protection. After three years experience of managing the estate, the Manager concluded that the annual income of Dodo Khan alone, leaving aside his sons, was actually Rs 52,798, putting quite a different complexion on matters.[24] It is impossible to say which figure was correct but such a vast discrepancy emphasizes the difficulty of deciding which applicants could afford to service their debts and which could not. Moreover, with so much land held by cosharers, there must have been quite an art to deciding in which part of an estate an applicant's interest should be deemed to lie. In 1881, some banias accused their debtors of transferring solvent fields into the names of their relatives, so that only mortgaged fields were included in the estate to be put under management. They added that the debtors had concealed movable assets, such as jewellery, camels and horses, to give a false impression of poverty.[25] Whatever the truth of it, such deception must have been temptingly easy to practise.

After completing the preliminary enquiries, the Manager forwarded his recommendation to the Commissioner in Sind. If the latter agreed that the estate needed relief, he issued an Order of Management. This made the Manager, legally, the estate owner.[26]

The applicant was put on a monthly pension. It must have felt similar to being given an allowance by a bania, but without the risk of a civil suit. Against this advantage, though, should be set the loss of flexibility which must have resulted from dependence on the Manager's bureaucracy. Instead of the bania, ever ready to trickle out more credit if times were hard, the zamindar had to appeal to government clerks, with their forms, their interminable procedures and their need to refer decisions back to higher authority.

There is no record of how the Manager calculated zamindars'

allowances. Latif Allah Kalhoro, who held a large estate of 13,938 acres, received Rs 100 per month, while Diwan Parsram, whose estate was almost the same size (13,227 acres) received only Rs 50; Fateh Khan Subayo, with only 3,094 acres, received Rs 15 per month.[27] Presumably the decision took account of the number of dependants the zamindar was obliged to maintain, and it would be surprising if weight was not also given to the zamindar's status. After all, the object of the exercise was to preserve the authority of the Waderos, which would not survive the loss of izzat, so it would have made no sense to undermine them by diminishing the figure they could cut in the countryside. One would expect a correlation between the allowances approved and the Manager's assessment of the applicant's social standing. The Manager's working papers do not appear to have been preserved but, if they are ever discovered, they will provide a fascinating insight into the caste values of Victorian administrators.

With the zamindar pensioned off, the most urgent task confronting the Manager was, as the estate's new owner, to secure its income. If possible, he leased it out. In a few cases, Hart-Davies leased parts of the estates back to the owners themselves, provided they could find someone to stand surety for them.[28]

More commonly, the Manager rented the land to the highest bidder. Sometimes this was enough, almost at the stroke of a pen, to restore solvency. Many zamindars had leased their estates to their creditors at miserable rates to pay off their mortgages. Under threat of a civil suit or with a decree already issued against them, they were in no position to bargain. They had to accept whatever terms their banias extorted from them. The Manager laboured under no such disadvantage. If he judged the rent too low and the creditor refused to pay more, the Manager could disregard the mortgage bond. He could turn the mortgagee off the land and give a new lease at the highest rate the market would bear. Mir Ghulam Shah Nizamani, had leased parts of his estate to three creditors in consideration of mortgage bonds. Bachumal's bond was for Rs 4,000 so he had taken up a lease for sixteen years at Rs 250 per year; the Manager leased the same area for five years at Rs 1,825 per year, sufficient to yield more than double the value of the bond. Tursiomal had taken some land for twelve years, at Rs 208 per year, to recover a debt of Rs 2,500; the Manager leased it for Rs 700 per year. A third part of the estate, which Asumal had leased for ten years, at Rs 160 per year, for a bond worth Rs 1,600, was leased by the Manager for Rs 1,556 per year. That is to say, the Manager had arranged to clear debts to the value of

Rs 8,100 within five years and, on top, generate Rs 12,300 of income. Similarly, Mir Bijar Khan, who owed Wadhumal and Basarmal Rs 60,000, had leased part of his estate for ten years at Rs 6,000 per year, but the Manager was able to negotiate a lease of Rs 13,000, sufficient to pay off the debt within five years.[29] The gainers from these leases had been the creditors, who had the benefit of cheap land and were able to keep all the surplus income to themselves. With more favourable terms, the debts were paid and the profits diverted from the creditors to the original owners.

This could only happen, of course, on estates where the land itself was good. Some estates could not be leased profitably because their condition was too poor. They had to be run directly by the staff of the Encumbered Estates Department. Since the Manager was unable to exercise close supervision over all his officers, these estates were vulnerable to peculation. Both the zamindars, living on small allowances, and the low-paid subordinate officers had every incentive and opportunity to appropriate some of the produce for themselves at batai, keeping it out of the Departmental accounts. Occasionally, they also succeeded in taking advantage of the Manager's inexperience of Sindhi farming. *Karbi*, for example, the straw remaining after rice had been threshed, was valuable cattle fodder, but Hart-Davies did not discover this until 1885, at the tail end of his tenure. Until then, he had dismissed *karbi* as just 'a little grass.' Meanwhile, it had been left out of his receipts to the benefit, presumably, of his staff and various zamindars.[30]

In the same year, Hart-Davies realized he was being cheated by Dodo Khan Bhutto and his two sons. As a result of their 'persistently dishonest behaviour,' the financial condition of their estate had actually deteriorated since being taken over. The zamindars had 'thrown every obstacle in the way of the Manager instead of aiding him' and their debts, both to the government and private creditors, had increased. Hart-Davies did not specify their sins, but they had probably been taking produce away before it was credited to their income, making it appear that the estate was operating at a loss. In the end, Hart-Davies forcibly seized the government debt by selling off part of the estate.[31] Around the same time, Robert Giles, the Deputy Commissioner of Upper Sind Frontier, discovered that some other zamindars were cultivating land surreptitiously on their own account, to raise money independent of the estate which was being managed for them. Their fraud was exposed when they refused to pay land revenue on it – naturally, they would not have wanted their names recorded as registered occupants, since that would have given the game away. Giles, complaining that they were 'playing fast and loose with Government and the Manager,' urged that it was 'time to check them.' The Commissioner in Sind agreed, ordering that Hart-Davies should 'in future exercise stricter supervision' over them.[32]

This advice was easier to give than to implement. Hart-Davies had 270 estates on his books, most divided between several cosharers. He could not monitor the activities of every zamindar. While he was sorting out this problem, he discovered that yet another pair of zamindars had been carrying off part of their harvest before the crops had been inspected. He added the value of the lost produce to the rest of their government debts.[33] These cases all took place towards the end of the life of the Encumbered Estates Department, and it may be that they reflect Hart-Davies' increasing familiarity with the various wiles of the debtors. It had however been a perennial problem. A couple of years previously, Hart-Davies had commented sadly: 'It is a discouraging fact that zamindars in whose interest so much trouble is being taken cannot be prevented from misappropriating produce.'[34] Hart-Davies must have found this especially aggravating since it diverted him from his primary task of clearing debt. Once he had organized an estate's finances, either by leasing it or managing it departmentally, he needed to be free to deal with the creditors.

The moment an Order of Management was issued, the Manager became responsible for the estate's debts. All proceedings against the owner had to stop and the creditors had to present their claims to the Manager. Unlike a civil judge, he could use his discretion in investigating any abuses banias might have perpetrated. Far from being bound by the bond like a civil court, he was not permitted to allow any interest at all unless he was satisfied that the accounts were in order: while if a creditor failed to prove that the entire principal debt was genuine, the Manager would automatically halve whatever sum had actually been proved.[35] If no accounts were produced to back up a bond, the Manager took it for granted that the claim was fraudulent and disallowed it unless the debtor was prepared to acknowledge that he had received the amount in cash. However, if the debtor asserted that the bond contained interest, then the whole claim was forfeit, for interest could not be included in the principal.[36] Since it was standard practice for banias to mix old interest and principal together when writing up bonds, this jeopardized much of the amount owing to them. Even civil court decrees were not inviolate. In 1878, the Commissioner ruled that the Manager could set decrees aside and investigate accounts according to his own harsh procedures, as if no previous adjudication had taken place.[37]

Even when a bania succeeded in proving the legitimacy of his claim, he was unlikely to receive what he was asking for. Interest could not exceed the principal and the Manager would not allow more than ten per cent per year – simple, not compound – interest.[38] This was a severe blow to the bania's system, but worse could follow. If an estate's assets were insufficient to meet the claims which the Manager had admitted, then the interest, which had already been drastically curtailed, was arbitrarily reduced until the debts were within the means of the estate.[39]

These were draconian powers. Between 1876–79, debts of Rs 3,077,693 were claimed against 313 estates, but the Manager admitted only Rs 1,660,693.[40] That is to say, he disallowed nearly half.

When he had decided how much he was prepared to allow against an estate, the Manager submitted a liquidation scheme to the Commissioner in Sind. In this, he discussed the estate's finances and, most important, explained how he proposed to liquidate the debts. Usually, this involved a compromise in which he persuaded the creditors to accept less than he had awarded. They were more willing to go along with this than one might imagine. It was a cardinal principal of the Encumbered Estates Department that any creditors who refused to compromise must be kept waiting until the estate had paid off all its debts to government. During this time, they would receive nothing at all – neither principal nor interest. Colonel Boulton, the first Manager of Encumbered Estates, had been unwilling to enforce this because it penalized those who had stood firm.[41] No less an authority than the Government of India itself assured him that penalizing was precisely the object of the exercise. Creditors should be forced to accept whatever terms the government considered to be just.[42] When Hart-Davies became Manager, he reported that this was essential to the smooth working of the Act. Creditors who had already seen their claims curtailed by the Manager knew that they would have to wait an indefinite period for whatever money he had allowed them. They were usually prepared to cut their losses and take what they could get. They preferred cash in hand to vague hopes of a fuller settlement in the distant future.[43] When the Manager awarded Rs 4,939 to the creditors of Qazi Muhammad Khaliq in 1887, they agreed to knock off twenty-five per cent if they were paid within a month. On other occasions, creditors leased parts of the estates in consideration of their claims, and even the government was sometimes willing to compromise by writing off outstanding balances of assessment on estates which were particularly badly favoured.[44]

Nevertheless, Hart-Davies seems to have had occasional qualms of conscience. Like Boulton, he believed the compromises were often unfair on the creditors. Not only had their original claims been cut down but they had been kept out of their money, perhaps for years. When the creditors had dealt honourably with the debtors and had co-operated with himself, he felt it was preferable to sell part of the estate so that he could pay them in full.[45] The Commissioner in Sind, however, objected that liquidation schemes along these lines violated the spirit of an Act designed to preserve estates, not break them up. He agreed that creditors who had 'behaved fairly by the debtor' deserved consideration, but many had 'charged the most exorbitant rates of interest.' The priority must be to keep the estates intact.[46]

Most liquidation schemes, therefore, were reasonably straightforward. After investigating the debts, the Manager made an award and cajoled the creditors into compromising on it. If the Commissioner supported the Manager's proposals, he sanctioned the scheme. The Manager then borrowed money from the government Treasury and discharged the private debts. The estate was now unencumbered and saved from the attentions of banias who had refused to compromise. All that remained was to repay the government loan out of the profits over the next few years. Once that had been done it was released from management and restored, solvent, to the owner.

Few banias refused to cooperate. In theory, if they were dissatisfied with the sums awarded by the Manager, they did not have to accept them. They could file civil suits. In practice, the small number who did this gained little from it. Even when a case was decided in their favour, they could not attach any land or demand any money so long as the estate was under management. They had to wait their turn like any other creditors who had refused to compromise. The main effect was merely to delay implementation of the liquidation scheme.[47]

In some cases, the Manager found that an estate was so hopelessly insolvent that he could not prepare a liquidation scheme. The only option was to relinquish management. About ten per cent of estates were forlorn hopes of this sort. Out of the 772 estates taken under management between 1876–87, 76 were relinquished uncleared.[48] Almost every one of these suffered from insurmountable natural disadvantages. The estate of Dost Muhammad Karmani was situated on low ground and the soil deteriorated as a result of constant flooding. It was given up as 'quite hopeless' in 1886, the Manager explaining that 'It could not be sold at any price nor could it be leased.' Dost Muhammad owed the government Rs 131 which had been lent to him to assist his cultivation, but the Manager saw no prospect of recovering it and it was written off. Budho Khan Talpur's estate was relinquished in the same year, after repeated disasters to the crops. He owed the Manager Rs 429 for cultivation expenses but, again, the amount was written off as irrecoverable.[49] Estates abandoned in this way were left to the mercy of their creditors, but it is doubtful whether they were worth much to them.

This brief sketch of the Manager's operations makes it clear that the Encumbered Estates Acts loaded the dice heavily against creditors. The Acts were an open offensive against the bania's system. The objective of a liquidation scheme was to force banias to take back their principal. Since they were primarily grain dealers, rather than 'moneylenders,' they were reluctant to do this. The principal was an investment which entitled them to a steady share of the harvest as interest. It was like compelling shareholders to give up their stock. The moment the principal was paid back, they lost their dividend. In fact, unless the creditors were very lucky, they had already lost it because the Manager usually stopped all interest payments while he was investigating the debts. Under the circumstances, banias had little choice but to accept whatever cash the Manager offered in a compromise since it was their only chance to recover their capital quickly and free it for investment elsewhere. From the bania's point of view, it was a thoroughly unsatisfactory arrangement. In 1881, some banias accused their debtors of applying to the Manager for protection 'only with a view to cause us loss.' Deprived of their interest, and unable to withdraw their capital until the Manager had completed his investigations, the banias complained that they could no longer maintain themselves.[50]

Many banias, anticipating how weak their position would become once their debtors were under management, did their best to prevent zamindars from obtaining protection in the first place. Although a civil court decree could be overruled by the Manager after an Order of Management had been issued, nothing could be done if it had already been executed while he was still deciding whether to take over management of the estate. The Manager could not take back land seized by order of a civil court. Once creditors realized that one of their clients had applied for sanctuary with the Manager, therefore, they often made desperate attempts to foreclose on their mortgages before the Manager could intervene. The fact was, they had nothing to lose. They anticipated punitive treatment from the Manager in any case, with no reward for good behaviour, so if they failed to foreclose in time it was unlikely that he could deal with them more harshly than he would have done anyway. On the other hand, the threat of court action might frighten their clients into dropping their applications for protection, while if they obtained an order they could recover their investments before they fell into the hands of the Manager. However, the government was usually able to outmanoeuvre banias when it heard of such cases. When Ghulam Haider Khan Khatian and Kadir Bakhsh Khan Laghari were threatened with imprisonment by their creditors after applying for protection in 1876, the Commissioner appointed the Deputy Collector as manager, pending the enquiries of the substantive Manager of Encumbered Estates.[51] In other cases, the Sadar Court ordered stays of execution against zamindars who had applied for protection.[52] What cannot be estimated, of course, is the number of zamindars who were successfully intimidated without the Manager even hearing of their intentions.

When the Act was extended in 1881, all of these difficulties recurred. Many banias set about harassing any debtors they suspected of applying for protection. Colonel Boulton, the original Manager, who was now Collector of Karachi, warned the Commissioner that some zamindars were in serious danger: 'there is every possibility of their estates passing out of their hands before the relief comes.'[53] Creditors were helped by the fact that the current Judge of the Sadar Court, unlike his predecessor, refused to intervene by ordering stays of execution.[54] After some urgent correspondence, the Bill was rushed into law and the Commissioner notified by telegraph, so that the problem could be bypassed and the estates taken under management more quickly.[55] To prevent a repetition of these ugly incidents, the Commissioner was given authority, when the Act was again extended in 1884, to suspend all proceedings pending in civil courts while the Manager conducted his preliminary enquiries.[56] Since only one estate was taken under management as a result of the Act, this turned out to be a striking case of the stable door being slammed after the horse had bolted.

Some creditors adopted another ploy to frustrate the Manager. After the Order of Management had been issued, they did not prefer any claims against the estate, or sometimes only a couple of the smaller creditors would come forward to allay the Manager's suspicions. Since the debts apparently did not exist, they could not be liquidated. The estates would then be relinquished and left prey to the creditors who were now free to pursue their claims at leisure in the civil courts.[57] This gambit successfully undermined the Act for several years. The solution was discovered in 1879, when a formula was devised allowing the Commissioner to sanction a liquidation scheme even if there were no debts to liquidate, with the proviso that any claims not brought forward to the Manager were 'deemed . . . to have been duly discharged.' This took the rug from under the feet of any creditors who had been playing this trick, since it prevented them from reviving the debts in civil suits.[58]

The more unpopular the Encumbered Estates Acts proved with creditors, the more popular they became with debtors. Many Waderos held back in 1876 because they felt it would be beneath their dignity to seek protection from the Manager, and they were wary of how the Act would work in practice. As they grew to appreciate its advantages, their inhibitions wore off. By 1880, Hart-Davies had been approached by over a hundred influential zamindars, and he was anxious to assist. It was his representations on their behalf which prompted the Bombay government to pass the second Sind Encumbered Estates Act in 1881. This enabled him to add 143 estates to his books and, since he focused on the people of real substance, cutting out the petty holders, it greatly increased the significance of the Act.[59]

Three years later, he began to consider winding up his operations. At this time, 155 estates remained under management, but liquidation schemes had been prepared for only 55 of them.[60] The Commissioner in Sind, growing impatient, tried to hurry Hart-Davies along. Liquidation schemes must be prepared quickly, some estates having been under management since 1876 without any schemes being submitted. He ordered that the disposal of these estates should take precedence over everything else.[61]

Over the next year, Hart-Davies was able to clear a third of the estates, and he reported in 1885 that no more than a hundred remained. Success generated its own problems, however. As the total number of estates decreased, the costs of management for each one increased proportionately. These costs would have to be severely cut to ease the burden on the remaining estates. Hart-Davies advised that the overall size of the Department should be reduced, the retrenchment starting with himself: he should be relieved by a less highly paid officer. His recommendation was accepted and Hart-Davies was replaced by J.L. Jenkins, who was on a more junior grade. This reduced the annual cost of management by over Rs 20,000, from Rs 64,547 to Rs 44,270.[62] At the same time, the smoothest running estates were handed over to the various Collectors for management. Within two years, all the estates had either been released or put in the charge of the Collectors and so, in 1887, the Sind Encumbered Estates Department ceased to exist.[63]

IV

The preceding account of the working of the Encumbered Estates Acts has given an indication of the labour and resources that the Sind government put into extricating estates from their liabilities, and the difficulties that were encountered. The Manager had to investigate the zamindars' debts and uncover any irregularities. He had to bargain with the creditors, decide how much to pay them, and devise an appropriate method of payment. Discharging the debts, though, was only a means to an end. The ultimate objective was to put Waderos as a class onto a sound financial footing, to keep them out of debt in the future. The success of the operation must be measured not in the number of estates discharged, but the number that remained solvent afterwards. Accordingly, it is now necessary to consider the long-term impact of the Encumbered Estates Department.

At the most fundamental level, some of the zamindars taken under management may have been saved from total ruin. This not quantifiable, but the fate of Khalifa Muhammad Panah of Larkana supports the contention, since he was someone for whom the Act came too late. In 1866, he was hailed by government as an 'influential and enterprising Zemindar' and singled out for praise for improving his lands to such an extent that his assessment had risen from Rs 301 to Rs 10,985 in fourteen years. The increase was an index to the mounting value of his property. The annual profits of the Khalifa and his nephew were estimated at no less than Rs 21,000, after deducting assessment and the costs of cultivation. They also had batai rights in fourteen dehs, and these brought in another Rs 5,500. The family appear to have been conscientious farmers, who invested in their land. They had subscribed Rs 10,000 to the construction of the Fordwah canal and spent Rs 43,000 on excavating canals for their own farms. However, considering the punitive interest rates some banias charged, their very enterprise may have been their undoing, committing them to repayments beyond their means. Whatever the cause, it is certain that, just when the family appeared to be at the peak of prosperity, they found themselves entwined in debts which they could not repay. Their principal creditor, Gokuldas, obtained a decree from a civil court ordering that their entire estate be put to auction. The Collector of Shikarpur tried to avert disaster by getting a stay of execution and managing the estate himself, but his efforts were in vain. There was as yet no procedure for taking over encumbered estates and the Bombay government refused to give the

Collector the money he needed. He had to stand by and watch the estate break up. The ruin of the Khalifa and his nephew was so complete that their names did not even appear on the list of indebted zamindars prepared in 1874.[64] There can be little doubt that, if the Encumbered Estates Department had existed, the Khalifa would have been saved.

The career of Dodo Khan Bhutto, one of the Khalifa's neighbours in Larkana, shows how this could be done. Without the help of the Manager, he might have found himself in Muhammad Panah's position, for his career followed a similar course. Like the Khalifa, he was a large and powerful zamindar. He and his sons held land all over Upper Sind. In 1872, the Commissioner in Sind praised him as 'one of the best and most enterprising Zemindars in the Province.'[65] Nevertheless, four years later, he and his sons were revealed to be heavily indebted and theirs was one of the first estates to be taken over by the Manager of Encumbered Estates. They had estimated their debts at Rs 134,644 but in the event no less than fifty-eight claims were made against them, totalling Rs 203,753. Most of this must have been interest, for the Manager admitted only Rs 98,673, less than half of that demanded.[66] When the Manager brushed aside over a *lakh* of debt in this way, his intervention must have appeared almost providential to the encumbered zamindars.

Such enormous liabilities might eventually have crushed Dodo Khan's family as brutally as Muhammad Panah's, wiping them off the Sindhi map. Instead, they prospered. Their debts were cleared through a government loan in 1879. By 1884, this had been repaid in full and the estate was released from management.[67] Eight years after seeking protection, Dodo Khan had been freed from apparently overwhelming debts and his financial position was so secure that five years later, in 1889, he was able to invest in the construction of a canal across some of his land.[68] The contrast with Muhammad Panah could hardly be more complete.

It is worth pausing to take an extremely long-term view of this case. Dodo Khan was the patriarch of the Bhutto clan. If it was true that he was in danger of being wiped out by debt, then unspectacular administrative decisions taken by Thomas Hart-Davies in the late nineteenth century may have influenced the course of Pakistani, Indian and Bangladeshi history in the late twentieth: for Dodo Khan's great-great-grandson, Zulfiqar Ali Bhutto, and his great-great-great-granddaughter, Benazir, both became Prime Ministers, playing critical roles in the politics of the sub-continent.

There was a danger that such spectacular results as the Manager achieved with Dodo Khan Bhutto might actually militate against the long-term success of the operation. In 1882, H.N.B. Erskine, the Commissioner in Sind, expressed fear that the net impact of the Encumbered Estates Acts could be negative. Zamindars whose estates had been cleared by the Manager might find it hard to obtain credit in the future and he suspected that the Acts, by alarming creditors, were forcing up interest rates for zamindars who did not enjoy protection. In the meantime, suggested Erskine, landholders who were under management were being made less self-reliant and would not be able to cope when thrown back upon their own resources.[69]

Government never systematically followed up the later careers of zamindars who had been under management, but Erskine's comments about creditors appear to underestimate the power of economic reality. Banias' priority was to do business and make money, not to score points off clients who had sought government assistance, however tempting this might be. So long as the estates represented good risks, they were bound to lend money to them. To that extent, restoring estates to solvency should have improved their holders' chances of getting credit. As to the possibly debilitating effects of a spell under management, everything would depend on the personalities of the zamindars concerned. Some, no doubt, grew lazy. Others, by contrast, may have picked up useful management skills from the Manager and gained a better understanding of the economic value of their land. Dodo Khan Bhutto clearly was able to find the credit he needed to cut his canal in 1889, and his family went from strength to strength, despite or even because of being under management. Hart-Davies initially echoed Erskine's concerns. In 1882, he complained that, once zamindars were safe from their creditors, they showed no interest in getting themselves out of debt but were left all responsibility to the Manager.[70] Three years later, though, in 1885, he detected a change in attitude. Zamindars, he reported, 'no longer regard the Manager as a "Deus ex Machina" to clear them of debt with no effort on their behalf.'[71] However, Erskine remained unconvinced. Now that the settlement system was being adapted to suit the interests of the great zamindars, there was no longer any need for 'a class of privileged estates in Sind.' This scepticism, reflecting the old dislike of 'class legislation,' prompted Erskine to goad Hart-Davies into hastening the demise of the Encumbered Estates Department.[72]

Evan James, who was appointed Commissioner in Sind in 1892, just five years after the Department had been closed down, believed

Erskine's policy was wrong. James had helped to frame the 1876 Act and he had not lost faith in its utility. In contrast to Erskine, James maintained that the Manager's activities had helped to teach zamindars to manage their business affairs more prudently: 'One of the indirect effects of the Incumbered Estates Act was . . . that many zemindars who were kept long out of their estates really did become wiser men.'[73] In his opinion, the circumstances which had made the Act necessary still prevailed. Waderos still required special machinery to protect their interests.

James accordingly recommended the establishment of a Court of Wards. This would have an advantage over an Encumbered Estates Department, in that it could take preventative action. Government could intervene whenever it was considered necessary, especially in the case of minors and children, to prevent an estate from becoming insolvent in the first place. What was more, there was no obligation to discharge an estate once its finances were settled, so the profits could be soundly invested before the Ward had a chance to squander them away. The Bombay government chewed over the idea for a few years until, in 1895, Sir Charles Ollivant, as Acting Commissioner, came out into the open with a demand to resuscitate the Encumbered Estates Department. For all the merits of a Court of Wards in forestalling insolvency, the fact remained that it was not geared towards picking up the pieces after the damage had been done. The main issue in Sind continued to be the handling of estates which were already insolvent, and this was where a full-blown Encumbered Estates Act came into its own. A Court of Wards could investigate and compromise debts, but it did not have the power of the Manager of Encumbered Estates arbitrarily to cut them down.[74] An Encumbered Estates Act would enable the government to drag Waderos out of their debts.

When James returned to his post the following year, he supported Ollivant. Personally, he would have preferred a Court of Wards Act provided the Court had the power to compel creditors to accept compromises – in other words, he favoured a Court of Wards beefed up with the powers of the Manager of Encumbered Estates, a most formidable beast. However, he recognized that drafting and passing such an Act would be time-consuming and in the meantime many estates would have disintegrated. Only a few words needed to be altered to revive the Encumbered Estates Act, and bring it into law immediately.[75]

Like Merewether before him, James reinforced his arguments with statistical evidence. There had been no investigation into indebtedness in Sind since Merewether's initiative in 1874 as part of the preparation for the 1876 Encumbered Estates Act, but the Government of India, alarmed by reports of widespread rural debt throughout the Empire, had instructed provincial governments to examine the problems and propose remedies.[76] This provided James with an opportunity to institute a fresh enquiry into indebtedness in Sind. The findings, which became available in 1896, confirmed his worst fears. Hindus held twenty-eight per cent of the occupied area of Sind, while a further fifteen per cent was mortgaged to them.[77] James alleged that most of their progress had been at the expense of Muslim debtors. He did not attempt to estimate the magnitude of debt, but argued that these figures sufficed to show the gravity of the situation.

There was nothing in the report to indicate whether banias were profiting at the expense of largeholders, smallholders or both, but James inferred that the problems of smallholders were relatively minor. The demand for labour was so great that, if they lost their land, they could always stave off starvation by working as haris, which he evidently considered good enough compensation for losing the independence of a peasant proprietor. In any case, plenty of unoccupied land was available if they wished to take up new holdings, though James did not explain why ruined peasants should be in a better position than ruined Waderos to raise the capital which would enable them to take advantage of these wastelands.

In fact, Table 9, which compared the holdings of Hindu and Muslim largeholders, suggests that Waderos were not suffering unduly at the end of the nineteenth century. Any decline in the number of largeholdings was generally matched by a rise in the average size of occupancies, and Muslim fortunes were roughly parallel to those of Hindus. It does not appear, then, that Muslim largeholders were losing their land to Hindus on a substantial scale. Nevertheless, James concluded that it was 'the leaders of the people,' the jagirdars and great zamindars, who were worst hit. He used the same terms as when he had championed the cause of the Manchar zamindars in 1872. Waderos, he said, found it hard to pay the assessment when they had to offer high batai rates to their haris to prevent them from seeking work elsewhere, and at the same time had to bear the costs of canal clearance and the like. As in his report two decades earlier, he raised the spectre of civil discontent, reminding government how dispossessed landlords in Agra and Oudh had taken back their estates during the 1857 Rebellion. In this context, James felt that some observations made by the Government Advocate of the

Punjab about the Punjabi peasant could with equal justice be applied to the Sindhi Wadero:

> What has he to fear from a political cataclysm? What motive has he to aid our Government in its hour of need? None whatsoever. Quite the contrary. And may we hope that help from the Banya which the splendid Panjabi peasant could so well have afforded? A flock of sheep would be of more practical utility to us than every money-lender in the province.[78]

In James' opinion, then, the Waderos were as seriously riddled with debt as ever. The Encumbered Estates Department had rescued individuals but, as a class, they continued to collapse. The political dangers remained. Even if they did not become actively disaffected from government and foment rebellion, Waderos would do nothing to help if a crisis arose, and the government would be left with no-one to turn to for support but the despised and ineffectual bania. The Encumbered Estates Department should never have been disbanded. As an officer was to put it a few years later, the 1876 Encumbered Estates Act had given a brief respite to a few fortunate estates, but constant vigilance must be maintained 'unless we desire to see our zamindars evolved off the face of the Province.'[79]

The Government of India was surprised to find the Sind authorities demanding a new Encumbered Estates Act so soon after the original one had lapsed. The Government had been under the impression that this Act had been passed 'to meet special circumstances which have now ceased to exist,'[80] and it was inclined in the first instance to resist. However, it relented in the face of James' arguments and the new Encumbered Estates Act was passed at the end of 1896. Lewis Mountford took over as Manager in March 1897, just ten years after the old Department had been closed down. The Act proved to be extremely popular among Waderos. 383 estates were taken under management in the first year of operation and by 1900 Mountford had 544 estates on his books.[81]

Unlike its predecessor, the 1896 Sind Encumbered Estates Act was not passed in isolation. Because the legislation already existed, and could be revived speedily, it was merely the first concrete result in Sind of the comprehensive investigation into agricultural indebtedness throughout the Presidency which the Bombay government had initiated in 1895 under the instructions of the Government of India. Collecting the facts, discussing them and drawing conclusions was a lengthy process and the final recommendations were not presented until 1899. They resulted in a spate of legislation, the most important measures in Sind being the 1899 Government Occupants Act, the extension of the Deccan Agriculturists Relief Act to Sind in 1901, the Co-operative Credit Societies Act 1904 and the 1905 Bombay Court of Wards Act.

The one piece of legislation which was not introduced was the one favoured by the majority of officers serving in Sind, including James.[82] They demanded a measure along the lines of the Punjab Alienation of Land Act. Whereas an Encumbered Estates Act was restricted to a particular class, and only applied after the problems had become acute, an Alienation of Land Act could help all landholders, regardless of status, before they fell into debt. Its main purpose was to prevent agriculturists from mortgaging their lands or selling them to satisfy debts. In effect, it would have restored the situation prevailing before the British conquest of Sind, when zamindars could mortgage their produce but not their land. It would have made it difficult for banias even to lease fields, and impossible for estates to break up and pass to creditors. However, Lord Sandhurst, the Governor of Bombay, 'strenuously opposed' any such measure. It had always been a cardinal principle of the Bombay settlement system that landholders should enjoy full proprietorial rights over their land, and Sandhurst was not prepared to compromise on this. Zamindars should have freedom to dispose of their property as they wished. An Alienation of Land Act could result in 'tying to his field a cultivator who desires for perfectly good reasons to part with it.'[83] He did compromise over the lands newly irrigated by the Jamrao Canal system, because this did not affect existing rights, and the Government Occupants Act 1899 made colonists granted plots in the Jamrao Tract liable to eviction if they transferred or sublet their lands.[84] It was a negligible concession at the time, but it became important after the opening of the Sukkur Barrage in 1932. All Barrage lands were granted on restricted tenure under the Government Occupants Act, effectively bringing half the occupied area of Sind under an Alienation of Land Act.[85]

Sandhurst was more responsive to requests for the Deccan Agriculturists Relief Act to be extended to Sind. This was targeted at smallholders, who had not previously received protection in Sind. Since it had long been in operation elsewhere in the Presidency, no points of principle were at stake. James suggested an extension of the Act in 1896, to complement the aid to largeholders under the Encumbered Estates Act, but did not press the point since he did not believe smallholders were in such urgent need of assistance.[86] The Encumbered Estates Act was passed immediately, but consideration of the Deccan Agriculturists Relief Act was deferred until the Government of India had been able to review all the papers relating to debt in the Bombay Presidency. Sandhurst forwarded his report to Calcutta in 1899, repeating his recommendation that the Act should be extended to Sind, and in 1901 the appropriate amendments were passed.[87]

The main provision of the Deccan Agriculturists Relief Act empowered civil courts to investigate the mortgage bonds presented in suits and to establish the circumstances under which they had been drawn up. This meant that, whereas previously any bond acknowledged by a debtor had to be enforced, a Judge could now modify it, or even set it aside altogether, if he suspected that the creditor had used force or fraud to obtain it. Since many debtors, despairing of being able to prove their stories in court, did not trouble to attend hearings but left their creditors to win by default, the Act obliged the Judge to summon all parties in an undefended suit and look into the background. The Act also gave him discretion to reduce interest charges to whatever level he considered reasonable, removing the obligation to enforce whatever rates debtors had agreed to.[88]

The Act was well intentioned, and effective as far as it went, but a civil suit was a last resort and banias did not take all their clients to court. In practice, it did not profoundly affect relations between debtors and creditors. Only the minority of debtors who were actually sued for debt could benefit from it – that is to say, those who were already in considerable difficulty. Debtors who were not taken to court could not be helped unless, being fully aware of their rights under the Act, they stood up to their creditors and refused to sign unfair bonds: but the people most desperately in need of protection were those with the least understanding of business and the law and, consequently, least likely to know about the Act's provisions. Moreover, the courts themselves did not inspire confidence. Protracted investigations into debt could involve debtors in considerable expense. They had to travel – sometimes a long distance – to the town where the court was sitting and maintain themselves in lodgings throughout the proceedings. Apart from the money they were spending, they risked losing some of their agricultural income in the meantime, for smallholders could not afford to leave their lands for long, especially around harvest-time. The problem of travel had been anticipated when the Act was originally introduced in the Deccan. A court had been set up in every taluqa and a system of local conciliation had been devised.[89] There is no record of why similar services were denied to Sind. The issue never appears to have been discussed. Perhaps it was simply overlooked. A small step was taken to remedy the defect in 1903, when four new courts were created in Shikarpur, Larkana, Rohri and Hala, to make the law slightly more accessible.[90]

On top of the inconvenience of travelling to court, debtors remained dubious about the treatment they would receive once they did arrive. Over some forty years, the civil court had established its reputation as a forum in which debtors were brought to judgment, the claims against them ruthlessly enforced and their property attached. The equitable provisions of the Relief Act did nothing to change the balance of power in the courtroom: debtors still had to hold their own against professional lawyers. H.C. Mules, the Collector of Shikarpur, sympathized with zamindars' reluctance to put their trust in the courts:

> At present the ordinary Mahomedan holder looks upon the Civil Court much as the sheep or goat may be imagined to look upon the slaughter house, a place above which he can discern in his mind's eye the inscription "All hope abandon ye who enter here," and he would not readily understand that the Civil Court could ever be a haven of refuge to him.[91]

Their scepticism may have been justified. In a circular to Judges in November 1900, the Judicial Commissioner in Sind advised that, since banks regarded twelve per cent as liberal, they should use this as a guide when determining 'reasonable' interest charges.[92] However, Judges were still allowing rates as high as twenty-four to thirty-seven and a half per cent a few months after the Act had been passed,[93] and the Judicial Commissioner had to jog their memories by reissuing the memorandum in 1904 and again in 1905. A pointer to the attitude of some Judges is provided by the fact that he felt obliged to emphasize in the circular that, while doing justice to lenders, it was usually the *borrowers* who needed more protection. Since the Act was specifically designed for the relief of debtors, not creditors, it is extraordinary that this needed to be said at all.

Zamindars' reluctance to take advantage of the Deccan Agriculturists' Relief Act was compounded by pressure put upon them by banias, who sometimes threatened to withhold credit except on the most rigorous terms if they feared a case might go against them.[94] Many creditors believed the loss of credit facilities outweighed any hope of relief afforded by the court and they refused to defend themselves. Since undefended cases automatically had to be investigated, they sometimes connived with banias to circumvent this awkward rule, by settling out of court, or allowing themselves to be described as non-agriculturists. If all else failed, some banias managed to persuade their clients to sign affidavits in which they admitted all claims against them and asserted that they were aware of their rights under the Act. They were usually aware of no such things but, once they had taken this course, their cases were exempt from investigation even if they were undefended.[95]

Many small zamindars, then, felt the Deccan Agriculturists Relief Act was more trouble than it was worth. They had to make an expensive and time-consuming journey to a court where they could not be sure of a sympathetic hearing. If they did win justice, they might lose their credit rating. For all the defects of its implementation, however, the Relief Act did have intrinsic merits in principle, if only because it stopped creditors from being sure of having everything their own way. They could no longer rely on the civil courts to rubber-stamp their mortgage bonds. While many debtors retained their fears of the courts, those with the courage to resist now had some weapons at their disposal. They could force their banias to deal honourably.

As the Deccan Agriculturists Relief Act, largely designed for the benefit of smallholders, got into its stride, largeholders were given further support by government. A Court of Wards was at last set up in 1905, to supplement the work of the Encumbered Estates Department. It could take over the holdings of minors, widows and people declared by a civil court to be incapable of handling their own affairs. In addition, any other zamindar could be protected if the Governor of Bombay agreed that it was 'in the public interest' to preserve his estate.[96] By 1912, eighty-five estates were under management of the Court of Wards.[97]

The Encumbered Estates Act, the Deccan Agriculturists Relief Act and the Court of Wards Act were all attempts to defend debtors against their creditors. A more positive way of relieving debt was to bypass the bania altogether. Indian governments traditionally gave interest-free *taqavi* loans to landholders to stimulate agricultural development, but for much of the nineteenth century, the Sind authorities had ideological objections to using public money in this way. They believed zamindars would become dependent on the state. They would not learn thrift and self-reliance.[98] Between 1877–82, an average of only Rs 31,367 was given out as *taqavi* per year. Ten years later, between 1887–92, average annual advances had increased slightly to Rs 47,526, but this was still a drop in the ocean. The Manager of Encumbered Estates, dealing with only a few hundred estates, seldom repaid less than a *lakh* of rupees to creditors each year. Only in the closing years of the century did a new generation of administrators appreciate the potential value of *taqavi* advances. Between 1897–1902, no less than Rs 285,000 were disbursed annually as *taqavi*.[99] In the twentieth century, therefore, the state began to compete with the banias, depriving them of their monopoly of rural credit.

The Co-operative Credit Societies Act of 1904 was a more substantial step in the same direction. Not only did a co-operative society provide an alternative source of credit but, with funds subscribed by the members themselves, it fostered a spirit of self-help. The Act was an initiative of the central government. It was applied to the whole of British India and introduced to Sind with little encouragement from local officials. When official opinion had been canvassed in 1901, the Assistant Collector of Larkana was the only officer to concede that such a scheme might work in Sind.[100] His colleagues' disinterest reflected the lack of enthusiasm for co-operatives among officials elsewhere in the Presidency and indeed throughout India. By 1909, there was still just one registered co-operative society in Sind.[101] A society had been started in Kandiaro in 1906 but it proved a memorable failure. Only two leading Muslim zamindars had joined it, one of whom was already insolvent, his estate being under the Manager of Encumbered Estates. The members subscribed a total of Rs 300, but when the Registrar of Co-operative Societies refused to allow them to borrow more than this, they asked for it to be wound up. It had survived no more than a year. A Sind official interpreted the members' attitude as proof that 'they did not intend to do anything for themselves,'[102] but that was not a fair comment. This little incident illustrates the main obstacle which retarded the development of the co-operative movement in India. Agriculturists were accustomed to easy credit. They did not invest money with banias: they simply borrowed from them, repaying the interest sporadically. If they went to the trouble of putting hard cash into a society, then they would naturally expect even better credit facilities than they obtained from banias. Another stumbling-block was a rule preventing loans from exceeding Rs 500. This prevented societies from attracting the great zamindars who had the resources to finance them.[103]

Despite its slow start, however, the co-operative movement began to develop rapidly during its second decade, as agriculturists became more familiar with the advantages. The problem of raising capital was overcome through a 'share-model system,' introduced in 1917 to help petty holders and haris build up a reserve of capital. Members subscribed shares of twenty rupees each, which they paid in annual instalments of two rupees. A review of the scheme ten years later claimed that some smallholders had managed to save as much as Rs 300, with haris sometimes having savings as high as Rs 150.[104] By 1929, there were 913 societies registered in Sind, disposing of a working capital of Rs 19,183,000.[105] Meanwhile, largeholders set up co-operative zamindari banks which could grant loans up to Rs 5,000. There were three such banks in 1929, at Mirpurkhas, Larkana and Shikarpur, their assets totalling Rs 1,215,393.[106]

The growth of the co-operative movement and the increased availability of *taqavi* loans combined to make inroads into the banias' monopoly of rural credit, giving Sindhi agriculturists an opportunity to reduce their dependence on them in the twentieth century. Any agriculturist who did fall deeply into debt could at least hope to be spared the worst consequences of a civil court decree, for the Deccan Agriculturists Relief Act had turned the court into a two-edged weapon which might strike the banias themselves if they attempted to sue their clients. Largeholders were doubly secure, since they could also seek shelter with the Manager of Encumbered Estates or the Court of Wards. Finally, after the completion of the Sukkur Barrage in 1932, half the occupied area of Sind was placed on restricted tenure under the 1899 Government Occupants Act and could no longer be sold or mortgaged.

That is not to say that the problem of agricultural indebtedness was solved. The bania's system depended on easy credit and leisurely repayments, but government and co-operative societies were less free with their credit and stricter about repayments. It was also more convenient to borrow from a person who lived locally and to whom one habitually sold one's grain. The Bombay Provincial Banking Enquiry of 1929–30 came to the conclusion that debt was still a serious drain on the resources of Sindhi agriculture, and it was sceptical about the impact of the co-operative movement on the agricultural economy.[107] Perhaps the best that can be said is that serious attempts had been made to provide alternative sources of credit and to improve the bargaining position of borrowers. And, at least, some assistance was now available to smallholders, who had been denied any form of state assistance before 1901.

V

If the Encumbered Estates Acts were intended to resolve the problem of indebtedness among Waderos, then they appear not to have been outstandingly successful. The 1876 Act had to be revived nine years after it had lapsed, while the 1896 Act remained in full vigour until after the British had left India. In 1950, there were still sixty-three estates under the Manager of Encumbered Estates and 359 under the Court of Wards.[108] Whatever the Encumbered Estates Department may have done to help individuals, there was never any shortage of insolvent estates waiting to replace those cleared of their liabilities. This was inevitable when one reflects that debt was a natural part of the cycle of agricultural investment. Exorbitant interest rates, poor business sense on the part of some Waderos and unwise borrowing for non-productive purposes – all these factors increased the burden of debt, but there was no escaping the necessity to raise capital. As soon as the old debts were cleared, new loans must be taken out if the process of cultivation was to continue. There could be no end to it, and though British officials frequently spoke as though indebtedness was a finite problem which could be, in some final sense, 'cleared,' they knew this was not true in practice. Accordingly, the Encumbered Estates Act did nothing to combat the causes of debt, and it was not designed to do so. It was a palliative.

A palliative, though, may have been all that was needed. It has been stressed throughout this study that officials saw Waderos' indebtedness primarily as a political problem. The arguments put forward by Evan James, had the sub-theme of impending insurrection. The Encumbered Estates Act was a piece of political legislation. It was not an economic measure. It could save individual estates but if Waderos, as a class, were unable to survive in the financial climate created by British rule, then government action could do no more than postpone the inevitable.

In fact, the situation was not as serious as British officers commonly appeared to fear. A few estates did break up, but many Waderos actually extended their holdings in the latter part of the nineteenth century and the majority simply muddled through. People like James may actually have been aware of the general trend. It is doubtful that they genuinely feared that a presence as solid as the Wadero was in real danger of vanishing from the Sindhi scene. The alarming statistics were a means to a political end and, as in all political debates, perceptions carried more weight than facts. Whatever the truth of it, if Waderos *felt* under threat, that was enough. Action had to be taken to give them a sense of security: to confirm that government was on their side: to encourage them to continue to turn out their haris to repair *bunds* and chase *dacoits*. In other words, to oil the machinery of local administration.

The Encumbered Estates Department therefore reinforced, rather than saved, the Wadero class. It revived the fortunes of those who had difficulty in meeting their liabilities. More importantly, their recovery in turn boosted the morale of neighbours who, while not so seriously encumbered, nevertheless felt threatened by the increasing prosperity of the Hindu banias. The existence of the Encumbered Estates Department reassured them that they were not alone in their struggle to maintain their status. The state was behind them and had provided a safety net if their situation became precarious. In this context, the Manager hardly needed to root out indebtedness, so long as he succeeded in building up his image as a manifestation of government's determination to preserve the status quo, with the Waderos in their mansions, the banias in their counting houses and the haris tilling the soil.

Conclusion

The Governors Govern

By the start of the twentieth century, the Government of Sind had done all it reasonably could, if not more, to reinforce the position of the great Muslim landholders. It is on reflection curious that it should have been so preoccupied, for so long, with the welfare of so self-assured a body of men. It reveals considerable insecurity. British officials saw threats to their rule – in the form of threats to the position of the Waderos on whom their rule depended – at every step. If haris ran away, they were cutting the ground from under the Waderos' feet. If smallholders bought land, the competition would put the Waderos out of business. If a conventional legal system was introduced, Waderos would stop co-operating with the police because they could not tolerate the indignity of cross-examination. Courts which relied on evidence rather than the uncorroborated word of a Wadero would produce anarchy because they would leave hardened criminals roaming the country, free and defiant. The land revenue system would tax the Waderos out of existence, while banias bled them to death through debt. Every new development would, it seemed, eradicate the Wadero from the face of the land.

This nervousness reflected administrators' awareness of their dependence upon the Wadero. To adapt Lord Cromer's remark about Egypt, quoted in the Introduction, Waderos were the governors of Sind, through whom the British governed. Which is to admit that, without those governors, they would govern nothing. If the Waderos disappeared, so would the administration which had been superimposed upon the existing social and political structure of Sind. It is demoralizing to put one's destiny into the hands of others. Paranoia was intrinsic to colonial rule. Administrators throughout the European empires glanced over their shoulders, suspicious of every change or hint of change, fearful that their brittle systems, bound up as they were with the status quo, might crack under the strain of evolution.

This anxiety was all the more remarkable in Victorian Sind when one considers that it was manifested during the hey-day of the British empire. At the end of the nineteenth century, there was no significant challenge to British supremacy in India, either external or internal. France was an earlier generation's problem, transformed since Waterloo into an uneasy ally. Russia, consolidating its position in Central Asia, was close at hand but hardly an immediate threat. Germany was a European rival, not an Asian one. The 1857 Rebellion was a distant memory. The Indian National Congress was a debating society which occasionally ventured a loyal resolution of the mildest criticism. Sind itself was regularly hailed as a model of political tranquillity.

On the face of it, there should have been little in Sind to raise alarm. The province was sufficiently affluent to avoid the destabilizing poverty and famine elsewhere in the Bombay Presidency, yet not prosperous enough to sustain in significant numbers an educated middle class with far-reaching and frustrated ambitions like the Bengali *bhadralog*. Sind was relatively comfortable, and so quiescent.

What is more, the status quo flourished. Sind remained rural, with no manufacturing industry. Although Karachi developed into a major seaport, it never became an emporium of central Asian trade as had once been hoped. It got on with its own business, without disturbing the traditional patterns of trade in its hinterland. Sind's economic life continued to depend on processing and exporting agricultural produce, which is to say, as ever, it depended on the Indus river and its canal system. With desert covering nearly half the province, irrigational facilities were unreliable even on the reclaimed lands. Land could lie parched for years on end: and then be swamped as a result of a shift in the set of the river or the working of a canal. Consequently, Sind still could not support a large population. Sindhis remained in small, isolated villages, scattered wherever water was available. Many cultivators led semi-nomadic lives, shifting their homes as sources of water dried up or flowed again. There were few permanent villages and no established village institutions. Only the Waderos, with their large, well-built *autaqs*, provided secure havens in the shifting landscape and the poorer agriculturists looked to them for security, protection and leadership.

In effect, therefore, in 1900 as in 1843, Waderos, in partnership with a handful of hereditary jagirdars, ruled the Sindhi countryside. Both owed little to the British.

Jagirdars could in theory be threatened with the confiscation of their grants if they misbehaved, but they were not obliged to perform services for the government and their titles had in any case been awarded in recognition of their political importance. Depriving them of their jagirs would be self-defeating and perhaps dangerous.

As to the Waderos, their power came from the land and, so long as they paid land revenue, they could not be dispossessed. Attempts in the 1850s to buy their loyalty through *seri* grants were futile. The government could not afford to alienate land on a sufficiently grand scale to tempt Waderos to sacrifice their independence. The Sind government, like other colonial regimes, had to collaborate with the local magnates on their own terms. Fortunately, most Waderos were happy to co-operate. They had no incentive to oppose a regime which so zealously championed their interests and favoured them with 'chairs,' lungis and other trinkets. By the turn of the century, Waderos were an integral feature of the local administration.

To put it another way, the local administration revolved around the Waderos. It could barely have functioned without them, and the British officials knew it. This led them down some strange alleyways. They had to be sure the Wadero prospered, even if it meant setting aside their own principles. Throughout the empire, the rule of law was regularly cited as one of the main blessings of British rule. Even at the end of the twentieth century, when decolonization itself is a remote memory, the survival of British legal traditions is occasionally hailed as one of the positive legacies of empire. The preservation of vital legal principles was regularly cited in the first half of the twentieth century to justify the denial of independence to India and other territories. Yet district officers in nineteenth century Sind argued passionately against the maintenance of their own Bombay Criminal Code on the ground that it subverted the status of Waderos. They preferred arbitrary justice, based on hearsay, prior knowledge and all the inadmissible circumstantial evidence which it is the function of a strong court system to exclude. Similarly, despite being products of a mercantile empire dedicated to free trade, they implacably opposed the one representative of the entrepreneurial spirit in Sind – the bania. What, after all, did middle class Englishmen, schooled in the disciplines of laissez-faire utilitarianism, preaching prudence and thrift, have in common with the profligate extravagance of feudal barons? The answer of course was power, and that was where the empire started to unravel.

If the accommodation with the Waderos produced some strange contortions in the principles upon which the British claimed to govern the empire, it also took the British into conflict with the dynamics of their own rule. Their alliance was with the one set of people who had nothing to gain from them. The Waderos were self-sufficient and, while appreciative of honours and suchlike baubles, really had no use for the British. The banias, by contrast, owed almost everything to the British. It was British law which gave them the right to unlimited interest and the acquisition of land; it was the framework of security enforced by the British police which enabled them to move relatively freely about the countryside. The truth of bania reliance upon Britain was put to the test when the British left in 1947: the Hindus fled from Pakistan en masse, to live in exile in Bombay. Virtually none now remain Sind. If Britain had a natural ally in Sind, it was the bania. But their accommodation with the Wadero inevitably built up an antipathy among British officials towards the banias and, by extension, towards the Hindu population of the country.

Therefore, a contradiction developed within the imperial power structure. The administration identified itself with the Waderos, who had little to gain from the perpetuation of British rule, and alienated the banias, who had most to lose if British power collapsed. That is to say, the British spurned their natural allies and cultivated their natural enemies. The fact that they had no choice highlights the long term weakness of their position and of the imperial world order in general.

The basic problem recurred throughout the European empires. If a colonial regime was to co-exist with the local power structure, which was the only way to survive short of genocide to replace natives with settlers, then it had to form an alliance with whichever grandees or elites were capable of bringing the rest of the population with them. They had to identify the governors and persuade them to co-operate. In Sind, that meant gaining the trust of the Waderos and jagirdars but in every colony without a substantial settler community it involved a commitment to preserve the status quo, almost at any cost. An alliance with the wrong people – that is, with people who did not have the necessary local authority – would be self-destructive. It would antagonize the people of influence who might then employ their formidable resources to claim back their rights. There were of course variations on the theme. A small elite like a ruling family might be isolated by an appeal to a wider aristocracy; and in some areas, such as the Deccan, the appropriate elite might be a numerous body of relatively minor headmen rather than a more compact grouping of magnates like the Waderos. The principle was however the same. A threat to the regime's allies was a threat to the regime itself. Whatever help their allies needed had to be provided to prevent the system from being undermined.

Unfortunately, the converse did not hold true. A threat to the regime was not necessarily a threat to the local elite. By definition, the local grandees were powerful in their own right. They had survived the overthrow of the previous administration, and would no doubt survive the passing of the new order. If the colonial government was attacked, that was no concern of theirs. It could not rely on its allies to risk their lives and property in its defence.

The only groups who would be prepared to take such risks would be those who had a great deal to lose from the demise of the colonial government. But – again, almost by definition – these were not heavyweight social leaders who could bring the bulk of the people with them. They were either marginal groups or, like the Sindhi banias, aspirant classes who were potential rivals to the existing elites. Attempts to collaborate with them would offend or alarm the regime's powerful allies, or else provoke a social revolution which undermined the stability on which the government depended. It was 'Catch 22.' If the colonial administration failed to ally itself with people who wielded real power, it would never establish itself. If it did ally with such people, it would be left to sink or swim on its own. That is why, when the crisis in imperial confidence came to a head in the mid-twentieth century, the European colonial powers had no option but to go home – they went with better or worse grace, sooner or later, after more or less bloodshed: but go, eventually, they must, for they lacked the dependable power-base to perpetuate their rule.

The practical implications of this can be seen in Sind. In effect, the colonial government had been secured as a by-product of the Waderos' own system. Its survival depended upon convincing the Waderos that it should figure in their plans for the future. To borrow a piece of political jargon from the 1990s, the British promoted a 'feel-good' factor among the Waderos. They projected a positive image of their government through the honours system, the Encumbered Estates Acts, changes to the land revenue system and the rest, so that Waderos would feel that life would be better with the British than without them. Any politician accustomed to cultivating a crucial section of the electorate would recognize the general principles involved. Of course, nineteenth century colonial administrators did not think of their business in these terms. They were not politicians. They were brought up in a more heroic mould. They were custodians of an empire which had been won by the sword and which they believed would be held or lost by the sword. They thought in more stirring language – of loyalty and treachery, of rebellion and insurrection. To the extent that the challenge to British rule might come from the Waderos themselves, dispossessed by debt and resentful, their dramatic view of the world was justified. There was every reason to keep the Waderos content. They would have been a formidable enemy.

However, a general mood of contentment would not inspire Waderos to lay down their lives in defence of the British Raj if their own position was not threatened. That was where the British officials misjudged the situation. Waderos and the like certainly enjoyed receiving lungis and attending darbars, and after the British left some undoubtedly regretted the glamour which passed with the empire. But glamour was not central to their lives. It was not a fundamental issue. Survival was. When, in the 1930s, the progress of nationalist politics under the leadership of the Indian National Congress raised the prospect of a Hindu-dominated independent Indian state, the Muslim grandees in Sind, the Punjab, the United Provinces and Bengal did not rally round the British flag. They concluded that the days of the Raj were numbered. The British were no longer a force to be reckoned with. They fought Congress on its own terms, by rallying to the Muslim League. By the time India obtained independence in 1947, Britain was little more than a complicating factor, struggling to extricate itself before the empire fell apart in its hands.

The long cultivated alliance with the Waderos was accordingly of limited value once the empire found itself on the defensive in the second quarter of the twentieth century. The Waderos were prepared to assist the colonial regime so long as it was able to deliver practical support to enhance and reinforce their izzat, but they were willing to go no further. It was not so much that they actively opposed the British government, although several Waderos did in the 1920s, 1930s and 1940s. It was simply that the majority of them simply did not help it. They left it to its own devices.

Accordingly, in 1947, Britain quit India, to the mild regret of those Waderos who had enjoyed the honours system, and Sind joined Pakistan. A new rivalry entered its life. The ancient Hindu communities fled, to be replaced by Muslim refugees, or *muhajirs*, from the truncated Dominion of India. The *muhajirs* replaced Hindus in the most literal sense. In some cases, they physically took over abandoned property but, more generally, they slipped into their commercial and administrative roles as well. Just as, at the end of the nineteenth century, the religion of the countryside was predominantly Muslim, that of the towns predominantly Hindu, so, at the end of the twentieth century, the language of the countryside is Sindhi, while that of the towns is Urdu, the mother-tongue of the *muhajirs*. Karachi, in particular, with its cosmopolitan trading culture, located in an especially barren corner of Sind, is a city largely divorced from its Sindhi hinterland, to the extent that there have even been *muhajir* demands for its separation from the province. The dividing line is linguistic, not religious, but Sind maintains a pattern of conflict which would be readily recognized by the ghost of an officer from the old Sind Commission.

He would also, of course, recognize the Waderos, flourishing as ever and probably even more powerful now that elections have provided them with provincial and national assembly seats, ministerships and all the influence that accompanies a well developed system of political patronage. If the police were nervous in dealing with Waderos in the nineteenth century, they have even more reason for caution now that the Wadero himself, or his cousin, may be a minister with his hands on the levers of state power – or an equally dangerous enemy of a minister. Sindhi politics largely revolves around rivalries between Waderos. Attempts to build political organizations among haris have never prospered. They have been stifled at birth. The position of the hari is no stronger now than it was a hundred or perhaps two hundred years ago. The waxing and waning of British rule, and the dawn of Pakistan, have had virtually no impact on the Sindhi cultivator, either for good or ill. Even Zulfiqar Ali Bhutto, the most politically and intellectually formidable of Pakistan's leaders, who undoubtedly struck a chord with the country's poor, came from a prominent Wadero family and displayed many of the strengths and weaknesses of his background.

The triumphant success of the Waderos in contemporary Sind gives the lie to any suggestion that they formed some sort of a comprador class or were a creation of the British. They were and are independent and self-sufficient. British rule was an episode in their history. The instincts of the British officials in Sind were entirely correct. Though they exaggerated the extent of the threat to the Wadero's survival, which was never seriously at risk, they were right to identify his prosperity as the key to their own survival. Like their fellow administrators in British, French, Russian, Belgian, Dutch and other colonies around the world, they found the source of local power and clung to it for dear life: for in Sind, the Waderos were everything; the British were nothing. It was the Waderos who effectively governed Sind, as they still do.

Notes

Abbreviations

Actg.	Acting
Admin.	Administration
Agri.	Agriculture
App.	Appendix
Asst.	Assistant
B.N.S.	*Selections from the Records of the Government of Bombay, New Series*
Bombay Admin.	*Reports on the Administration of the Bombay Presidency*
Cattle-lifting in Sind	*Report of the Committee appointed to enquire into the question of Cattle-lifting in Sind* (Karachi, 1926)
Collr.	Collector
Coln.	Colonization
Commr.	Commissioner
Compn.	Compilation
Confl.	Confidential
Co-op Report	*Annual Report relating to the establishment of Co-operative Societies in the Bombay Presidency*
Cttee.	Committee
'Debtors & Creditors'	L.J. Mountford, Manager, Encd. Estates, Sind, 'Relations Between Debtors and Creditors in Sind' (P.G.B., R.D.L., 1902 (Aug.–Dec.)
Dept.	Department
Depy.	Deputy
Educ.	Educational
Encd.	Encumbered
Encd. Estates Report	*Sind Encumbered Estates Annual Administration Reports*
Encl.	Enclosure
Fallow Rules Cttee.	*Report of the Members of the Fallow Rules Committee, Sind* (Karachi, 1926)
G.D.	General Department
Govr.	Governor
Govt.	Government

Hbad.	Hyderabad
H.D.	Home Department
History of Alienations	*History of Alienations in the Province of Sind* (Bombay, 1886–88)
Inspr.	Inspector
I.O.R.	India Office Records, London
Irrig.	Irrigational
Jagheer Holdings	*B.N.S.* 66, *Summary of Proceedings relating to the Settlement of Jagheer Holdings in the Province of Sind* (Bombay, 1862)
J.D.	Judicial Department
Jud.	Judicial
Land Revenue Code, 1892	H.V. Sathe, *Annotated Edition of the Land Revenue Code, containing Bombay Act V of 1879 and the rules passed thereunder* (Poona, 1892)
Land Revenue Code, 1919	R.N. Joglekar, *Annotated Edition of the Land Revenue Code, Bombay Act V of 1879* (Bombay, 1919)
Memo.	Memorandum
Misc.	Miscellaneous
Muncher Papers	*Papers relating to the Indebtedness of the Zemindars of the Muncher Lake in Sind* (Madras, 1874)
N.d.	No date
Offg.	Officiating
Offr.	Officer
Para.	Paragraph
P.G.B.	Proceedings of the Government of Bombay, at the India Office Records, London
Pol.	Political
Pr.	Proceeding
pre-Mutiny Records	*Selections from the pre-Mutiny Records of the Commissioner in Sind* (n.d.)
P.S.C.	Proceedings of the Sind Commission, at the Commissioner's Record Office, Karachi
Rasai Cttee. Report	*Committee appointed by Government to enquire into Rasai, Lapo and Chher in Sind* (Karachi, 1919)
R.D.	Revenue Department
R.D.L.	Revenue Department (Lands)
Resn.	Resolution
Rev.	Revenue
Revenue Papers	*Papers relating to the Revenue Settlement in Sind* (Bombay, 1875)
Rough Survey	*Official Correspondence relative to the Introduction of a Rough Survey and Settlement in the Province of Sind*
Secy.	Secretary
Settlt.	Settlement
Shpur.	Shikarpur
S.R.	Settlement Report
Sup.	Superintendent
Tenancy Legislation Cttee.	*Report of the Tenancy Legislation Committee*

Tenures and Survey	*B.N.S.* 278, *Character of Land Tenures and System of Survey and Settlement in the Bombay Presidency* (Bombay, 1908
T. & P.	Thar and Parkar
U.S.F.	Upper Sind Frontier

INTRODUCTION

1 Eastwick, 239.
2 Sorley, *Gazetteer*, 183.
3 Said, 87–8.
4 Lambrick, *Napier*, 36.
5 *Ibid.*, 61.
6 Said, 192.
7 Kaye, vol. II, 435.
8 Mason, 189.
9 A. Conan Doyle, 'Silver Blaze' (*The Memoirs of Sherlock Holmes*: London, 1893).
10 'Il n'y a pas, Monsieur, de colonisation possible sans terre. Il faut donc déposséder les tribus pour mettre les Européens à leur place.' (Quoted in Habart, 50.)
11 Bennoune, 40.
12 Said, 222.
13 Ruedy, 69.
14 Habart, 50.
15 Quoted in Said, 217.
16 Quoted in Ruedy, 73.
17 Sellar and Yeatman, 84.
18 Quoted in Said, 239.
19 Visit to Biskra, January 1974.
20 Wilson and Dalton, 4.

1 THE SCENE OF ROMANTIC ACHIEVEMENTS

1 A. Burnes, vol. I, xxvii.
2 *Ibid.*, 48, 49.
3 Haig, 5.
4 Temple, 483–4.
5 Romer, 10.
6 Pol. Sup., T. & P., 1 May 1870 (P.S.C., J.D., file 1, 1870, vol. II, pt. II, compn. 21).
7 Commr., Sind, to Govr., Bombay, 28 March 1854 (P.G.B., R.D., 10 June 1854, pr. 5706, para. 2).
8 Aitken, *Gazetteer*, 1.
9 Rahman, *Geography*, 12.
10 6.82 miles per hour
11 Snelgrove, 120–1.
12 Rahman, *Geography*, 10.
13 Bombay Govt. Resn. no. 2845, 20 May 1881 (*B.N.S.* 200, *Larkana S.R.*); Haig, 4–5.

14 A. Burnes, vol. III, 265; Sup. Engineer, Sind, to Commr., Sind, 20 Dec. 1883 (P.S.C., R.D., file 86, 1884, vol. II, compn. 18, 626).
15 Lambrick, *General Introduction*, ix–x, 80–7, 91–2; *Sind Before the Muslim Conquest*, 46–9.
16 Commr., Sind, to Govr., Bombay, 28 March 1854 (P.G.B., R.D., 10 June 1854, pr. 5706, para. 4).
17 Settlt. Offr. to Collr., Shpur., 1 Aug. 1872 (*B.N.S.* 201, *Shpur. S.R.*, 3); Commr., Sind, to Govr., Bombay, 25 July 1893 (*B.N.S.* 322, *Kashmore S.R.*, 2); Depy. Collr., U.S.F., to Commr., Sind, 18 July 1904 (*B.N.S.* 305, *Kashmore S.R.*, 3); Govt. of Sind, *Bund Manual*, 186.
18 Actg. Commr., Sind, to Govr., Bombay, 17 Feb. 1898 (*B.N.S.* 318, *Shpur. S.R.*, 2).
19 Settlt. Offr. to Actg. Collr., Shpur., 31 Aug. 1867 (*B.N.S.* 202, *Ghotki S.R.*, 3); Commr., Sind, to Govr., Bombay, 7 Aug. 1893 (*B.N.S.* 456, *Kambar S.R.*, 2); Settlt. Offr., 2 July 1877 (*B.N.S.* 202, *Rohri S.R.*, 31); Settlt. Offr., 22 June 1872 (*B.N.S.* 201, *Naushahro Abro S.R.*, 12); Depy. Collr., Shpur., to Collr., 21 Nov. 1872 (*ibid.*, 30).
20 Pithawalla, *Geography*, 42; Snelgrove, 11.
21 Settlt. Offr., 10 Jan. 1876 and 13 Dec. 1878 (I.O.R. no. (9)2015, *Sehwan S.R.*, 2, 84); Actg. Sup., Sind Rev. Survey, to Commr., Sind, 19 Sept. 1889 (*B.N.S.* 455, *Sehwan S.R.*, 11–2).
22 Sorley, *Gazetteer*, 458–63, 468–512; Rahman, 91–8, Pithawalla, *Geography*, 196–210.
23 *Economic Condition of Sind: State of Roads, Canals and Forests in 1846* (Selections from the Records of the Commissioner in Sind, compn. 7 of 1844–7), 54; Burton, *Sindh*, 41.
24 Commr., Sind, to Govr., Bombay, 28 March 1854 (P.G.B., R.D., 10 June 1854, pr. 5706, para. 9).
25 Settlt. Offr. to Collr., Karachi, 13 Aug. 1869 (*B.N.S.* 308, *Mirpurkhas S.R.*, 2).
26 Sup. Engineer, Sind, 23 Nov. 1883 (P.S.C., R.D., file 86, 1884, vol. I, pt. II, compn. 2, para. 5).
27 Actg. Settlt. Offr. to Collr., Shpur., 6 Apr. 1867 (*B.N.S.* 199, *Kakar S.R.*, 4).
28 Actg. Sup., Sind Revenue Survey, to Commr., Sind, 8 July 1892 (*B.N.S.* 454, *Dadu S.R.*, 7); Sup., Sind Rev. Survey, 27 Apr. 1882 (*B.N.S.* 199, *Nasirabad S.R.*, 32); Aitken, *Gazetteer*, 259–62.
29 Aitken, *Gazetteer*, 259.
30 *Economic Condition of Sind*, 10, 53.
31 Commr., Sind, to Govr., Bombay, 19 Apr. 1852, 29 June 1853 (P.G.B., R.D., May 1852, pr. 6179A, para. 9, & June 1853, pr. 7252, paras 2–6).
32 Bombay Govt. Resn. no. 5163, 26 Sept. 1874 (P.G.B., R.D.L., 1874, 647).
33 Offg. Chief Secy., Govt. of Bombay, to Secy., Govt. of India, 4 Nov. 1863 (P.G.B., R.D., 1863, 915).
34 Asst. Settlt. Offr. to Collr., T & P, 15 June 1915 (*B.N.S.* 500, *Umarkot S.R.*, 4).
35 *Ibid.*
36 Visit to Umarkot, Apr. 1977.
37 *Economic Condition of Sind*, 10.
38 Aitken, *Gazetteer*, 312.

39 Commr., Sind, memo., 12 Feb. 1855 (P.G.B., R.D., 16 May 1855, pr. 4221–6, paras 2–13, 37–45); Rev. Surveyor, 31 Oct. 1861 (*ibid.*, Jan. 1862, 107–10); Actg. Commr., Sind, to Govr., Bombay, 4 July 1892 (*B.N.S.* 307, *Nara Valley S.R.*, 1–2); Aitken, *Gazetteer*, 322–5.
40 Aitken, *Gazetteer*, 326.
41 Commr., Sind, 12 Apr. 1899 (P.G.B., R.D.L., 1899 (July–Dec.), 812; *Annual Administration Reports* of Coln. Offrs., Jamrao Canal, 1898–1904 (*ibid.*, 1901 (July–Dec.), 2183ff.; 1902 (Jan.–July), 56 ff.; 1903 (Aug.–Dec.), 1410 ff.; 1904 (July–Dec.), 2477 ff.
42 Commr., Sind, 21 Aug. 1897 (P.S.C., R.D., file 69A, 1896–9, vol. I, 195); Coln. Offr., Jamrao Canal, *Admin. Report*, 1898–1901, 2186–7. For details of the Punjab canal colonies, see I. Ali, 8–58.
43 Commr., Sind, to Collr., Karachi, 16 Jan. 1899 (P.S.C., R.D., file 69A, 1896–9, vol. III, 922).
44 Asst. Settlt. Offr. to Collr., T. & P., 13 Apr. 1920 (*B.N.S.* 539, *Khipro 'S.R.*, 1–2); Asst. Settlt. Offr., 30 Apr. 1930 (*B.N.S.* 656, *Khipro S.R.*, 1–2).
45 Actg. Director, Land records & Agri., 'Memorandum on the Material Condition of the People of the Bombay Presidency, 1892–1902,' 1 Aug. 1902 (P.G.B., R.D.L., 1902 (Aug.–Dec.), 1267, 1270–1; Depy. Collr., T. & P., to Depy Commr., T. & P.: 31 March 1905 (*B.N.S.* 460, *Pithoro S.R.*, 2, 15); 23 July 1906 (*B.N.S.* 483, *Sanghar S.R.*, 3); 23 July 1906 (*B.N.S.* 469, *Khipro S.R.*, 2).
46 Young, 114, 85, 113; Ali, 32–3; Sorley, *Gazetteer*, 236–9.
47 *Bombay Government Gazette*, 21 Apr. 1904 (cited in P.G.B., R.D.L., 1904 (Jan.–June), 546–7, 556–7). The *Report of the Indian Famine Commission, 1898*, estimated subsistence rations for labourers (49, 260).
48 *Census Reports.*
49 Aitken, *Gazetteer*, 155.
50 Nehru, 49; Wheeler, 5, 110–26.
51 Quoted in Nehru, 47.
52 Sup., Sind Rev. Survey, 10 June 1886 (*B.N.S.* 194, *Kohistan S.R.*, 6–9); 'Notes on the places visited during the Commr's tour to the hills,' n.d. (P.S.C., R.D., file 86, 1888–9, vol. I, comp. 2, 281–305); Aitken, *Gazetteer*, 174–5, 178.
53 Aitken, *Gazetteer*, 174; S. Ali, 54; Postans, 40.
54 Aitken, *Gazetteer*, 177–8; S. Ali, 61–3, 81; Postans, 58–60.
55 See Bhutto, 140–2.
56 Ansari, *Sufi Saints*; especially 22–35.
57 D.K. Thadani, 16.
58 Collr., Hbad., to Commr., Sind, 27 Sept. 1887 (P.S.C., J.D., file 1, 1887, vol. II, pt. II, compn. 74, para. 2).
59 Masson, vol. I, 379.
60 J. Burnes, 81.
61 Ansari, *Sufi Saints*, 32.
62 Note for Commr., Sind, 23 June 1904, signed N.A.C. (P.S.C., J.D., file 1, 1901, vol. IX, compn. 13, 317).
63 Proceedings of *jirga* at Sukkur, 3 Sept. 1901 (P.S.C., J.D., file 1, 1901, vol. III, pt. I, compn. 13, 108).
64 Proceedings of *jirga* at Jacobabad, 24 Dec. 1900 (P.S.C., J.D., file 1, 1901, vol. III, pt. I, compn. 13, 242–3).

65 Depy. Commr., U.S.F., to Commr., Sind, 10 June 1887 (P.S.C., J.D., file 1, 1887, vol. II, pt. II, compn. 41, para. 21).
66 Masson, vol. I, 359; also 350 and vol. II, 155.
67 Quoted in Lambrick, *John Jacob*, 148.
68 Jacob to Commr., Sind, 24 Dec. 1852 (P.G.B., R.D., Apr. 1853, pr. 4237).
69 Depy. Commr., U.S.F., to Commr., Sind, 28 Feb. 1887 (P.S.C., R.D., file 58, 1877–86, compn. 1a, para. 18).
70 Quoted in District Sup. of Police, Karachi, to Commr., Sind, n.d. (P.S.C., J.D., file 1, 1874, vol. I, compn. 7, para. 1).
71 See District Sup. Police, Karachi, 13 May 1874, 1 July 1874, 7 Nov. 1874 (P.S.C., J.D., file 1, 1874, vol. I, compn. 7).
72 Quoted in District Sup., Police, Karachi, 7 Nov. 1874 (P.S.C., J.D., file 1, 1874, vol. I, compn. 2, para. 2).
73 Thornton, 63–9, 80–3, 91–2.
74 Bombay Govt. Resn. no. 3198, 22 May 1882 (P.S.C., J.D., file 2, 1883, vol. V, compn. 45, 59).
75 Depy. Commr., U.S.F., to Commr., Sind, 16 March 1883 (P.S.C., R.D., file 58, 1877–86, compn. 1).
76 Actg. Sup., Sind Rev. Survey, to Commr., Sind, 27 March 1893 (*B.N.S.* 322, *Kashmore S.R.*, 20).
77 Depy. Commr., U.S.F., to Commr., Sind, 4 Aug. 1902 (P.S.C., J.D., file 1, 1902, vol. V, pt. II, compn. 63, 67–71).
78 Commr., Sind, to Govr., Bombay, 12 Feb. 1855 (*B.N.S.* 21, *Umarkot and Nara S.R.*, 3–5).
79 Burton, *Sindh*, 309–13, 323–4; Aitken, *Gazetteer*, 182, 185; Enthoven, *Tribes and Castes*, vol. II, 381–2; T.S. Thadani, 166.
80 See *1881 Census, Bombay, vol. I, 46; 1901 Census, Bombay, vol. IX-B, pt. I, 59.*
81 Mariwalla, 256; Thakur, 129–34; Burton, *Sindh*, 326–33.
82 Enthoven, *Tribes and Castes*, vol. II, 383–4; Gidumal, 25, 29, 43; Parsram, 75–80; Rewachand, 90.
83 Postans, 65.
84 Parsram, 52–4, 338–9, 341; Aitken, *Gazetteer*, 186, 193; Burton, *Sindh*, 149, 335; Collr., Karachi, to Commr., Sind, 16 Aug. 1880 (P.S.C., G.D., file 4, 1880–1, compn. 14, para. 12).
85 Aitken, *Gazetteer*, 193; Burton, *Sindh*, 316–7.
86 Postans, 68.
87 Masson, vol. II, 137–40.
88 Postans, 35.
89 A. Burnes, vol. I, 168–70, 286; vol. II, 424–35.
90 Masson, vol. I, 353–4.
91 Bease, 58.
92 James, *Naomal Hotchand*, 69–71.
93 Bease, 47.
94 1843 – Rs 1,221,600; 1858 – Rs 14,201,879; 1901 – Rs 135,807,107: Aitken, *Gazetteer*, 368–9; *The Sind Kossid*, 26 Jan. 1858.
95 Aitken, *Gazetteer*, 388–9.
96 Bease, 47; Feldman, 5–6; Baillie, 241.
97 Aitken, *Gazetteer*, 376–84.
98 Quoted in Aitken, *Gazetteer*, 261.

2 THE SERFS OF THE SOIL

1 Revenue Queries of R.K. Pringle, Commr., Sind, 1847: reply to Query no. 9 by Collr., Karachi, *pre-Mutiny Records*, 86.
2 See Habib, 136–41.
3 Commr., Sind, to Govr., Bombay, 12 Aug. 1896, Note A (P.G.B., R.D.L., 1899 (July–Dec.), Confl. Pr. 795).
4 M.R. Haig, Settlt. Offr., 6 Jan. 1873 (*B.N.S.* 194, *Kotri S.R.*, 37); Actg. Sup., Sind Rev. Survey, to Commr., Sind, 8 March 1892 (*B.N.S.* 315, *Larkana S.R.*, 36); Depy. Commr., U.S.F., to Commr., Sind, 31 March 1895 (*B.N.S.* 324, *Jacobabad S.R.*, App. XXII, 84).
5 Commr., Sind, to Govr., Bombay, 11 Dec. 1899 (P.G.B., R.D.L., 1900 (Jan.–July), 222; Collr., Larkana to Commr., Sind, 4 May 1902 (P.G.B., R.D.L., 1903 (Jan.–July), 112).
6 Asst. Collr., Sehwan, to Collr., Karachi, 29 March 1892 (P.S.C., R.D., file 1, 1889–6, vol. III, compn. 22a, para. 5).
7 Settlt. Offr. to Collr., Hbad., 2 May 1872 (*B.N.S.* 196, *Hbad. S.R.*, 19).
8 *Land Revenue Code, 1919*, 447.
9 Commr., Sind, to Govr., Bombay, 7 Aug. 1893 (*B.N.S.* 327, *Ratodero S.R.*, App. XXII, 138; Depy. Commr., U.S.F., to Commr., Sind, 31 March 1895 (*B.N.S.* 325, *Jacobabad S.R.*, App. XXII, 138; Depy. Collr., Sukkur, to Actg. Commr., Sind, 9 Feb. 1899 (*B.N.S.* 325, *Naushahro Abro S.R.*, App. XXII, 91); Actg. Sup., Sind Rev. Survey, to Commr., Sind, 8 March 1892 (*B.N.S.* 325, *Larkana S.R.*, 36).
10 Depy. Collr., Sukkur, to Actg. Commr., Sind, 15 Sept. 1902 (*B.N.S.* 316, *Mehar S.R.*, App. XXII, 90); to Commr., Sind, 18 July 1904 (*B.N.S.* 335, *Kashmore S.R.*, App. XXII, 187); *ibid.*, (*Kandhkot S.R.*, App. XXII, 159); to Actg. Commr., Sind, 23 Dec. 1898 (*B.N.S.* 328, *Sukkur S.R.*, App. XXII, 85); Depy. Commr., U.S.F., to Commr., Sind, 31 March 1895 (*B.N.S.* 324, *Jacobabad S.R.*, App. XXII, 84).
11 Actg. Sup., Sind Rev. Survey, to Commr., Sind, 28 Apr. 1892 (*B.N.S.* 408, *Labdarya S.R.*, 14); Actg. Sup., Land records & Agri., to Commr., Sind, 28 Apr. 1892 (*B.N.S.* 318, *Nasirabad S.R.*, 4).
12 Manager, Encd. Estates, Sind, to Commr., Sind, 27 March 1900 (P.G.B., R.D.L., 1900 (July–Dec.), 1235); G.M. Bhurgri, oral evidence (*Rasai Cttee. Report*, vol. IV, pt. VII, 88).
13 Interview with Rukundin, Special Attorney to Saiyid Pir Bakhsh Shah of Sehwan, 21 Nov. 1976.
14 Commr., Sind, to Govr., Bombay, 18 May 1892 (*B.N.S.* 315, *Larkana S.R.*, 4).
15 Actg. Sup., Sind Rev. Survey, to Commr., Sind, 19 Sept. 1899 (*B.N.S.* 455, *Sehwan S.R.*, 15); Sup., Land Records & Agri., to Commr., Sind, 20 Apr. 1899 (*B.N.S.* 326, *Jati S.R.*, 16); Asst. Collr., Larkana, to Commr., Sind, 13 Aug. 1906 (*B.N.S.* 468, *Labdarya S.R.*, 8).
16 Asst. Settlt. Offr. to Collr., T. & P., 15 June 1916 (*B.N.S.* 500, *Umarkot S.R.*, 11).
17 Local batai terms were discussed in all Settlt. Reports, but see especially Sup., Sind Rev. Survey, to Commr., Sind, 5 Dec. 1883 (*B.N.S.* 200, *Larkana S.R.*, 109); Sup., Land Records & Agri., to

Commr., Sind, 4 Apr. 1894 (*B.N.S.* 325, *Naushahro Abro S.R.*, 17); Depy. Commr., U.S.F., to Commr., Sind, 28 March 1905 (*B.N.S.* 448, *Jacobabad S.R.*, 2).

18 Sup., Sind Rev. Survey, 24 July 1886 (I.O.R. (9)2207, *Jati S.R.*, 6).

19 Depy Collr., Sukkur, to Actg. Commr., Sind, 23 Dec. 1898 (*B.N.S.* 328, *Sukkur S.R.*, 23).

20 Settlt. Offr., to Collr., Shpur., – Sept. 1873 (*B.N.S.* 201, *Sukkur S.R.*, 56); *Famine Commission, 1898*, 49, 260.

21 Settlt. Offr., to Commr., Sind, 17 Jan. 1878 (*B.N.S.* 202, *Rohri S.R.*, 64; G.M. Bhurgri, oral evidence, *Rasai Cttee. Report*, vol. IV, pt. VII, 88.

22 Depy. Collr., Nara Valley, to Depy. Commr., T. & P., 23 July 1906 (*B.N.S.* 469, *Khipro S.R.*, 19).

23 Asst. Collr., Tando, to Collr., Hbad., 28 Dec. 1908 (*B.N.S.* 488, *Guni S.R.*, 22).

24 Settlt. Offr. to Commr., Sind, 29 June 1918 (*B.N.S.* 533, *Shpur. S.R.*, 19); *Rasai Cttee. Report*, vol. IV, pt. V, 74, 98).

25 Revenue Queries of R.K. Pringle, Commr., Sind, 1847: reply to Query no. 9 by Collr., Karachi, *pre-Mutiny Records*, 86.

26 A. Young, Depy. Collr., memo. on the batai system, 23 March 1851 (*pre-Mutiny Records*, 486).

27 Young, memo., 23 March 1851 (*pre-Mutiny Records*, 482).

28 Depy. Collr., Mehar, to Commr., Sind, 15 Sept. 1902 (*B.N.S.* 316, *Mehar S.R.*, 31).

29 Young, memo., 23 March 1851 (*pre-Mutiny Records*, 486).

30 A.U. Khan, written evidence, *Rasai Cttee. Report*, vol. IV, pt. V, 73.

31 Shaikh Ibrahimjee, written evidence, *ibid.*, vol. IV, pt. VII, 124.

32 M.K. Pathan, written evidence, *ibid.*, pt. V, 48.

33 Masud, 9.

34 Manager, Encd. Estates, Sind, to Commr., Sind, 27 March 1900 (P.G.B., R.D.L., 1900 (July–Dec.), 1235.

35 Sessions Judge, Shpur., summing up, 20 Nov. 1896 (P.S.C., J.D., file 2, 1896, vol. III, pt. III, compn. 72, 726).

36 Sub-Collr., Mehar, to K. Young (cited in Young, 113).

37 Masud, 10.

38 Sup., Sind Rev. Survey, 24 Apr. 1883 (*B.N.S.* 195, *Guni S.R.*, 8).

39 Commr., Sind, to Govr., Bombay, 5 March 1886 (*B.N.S.* 195, *Guni S.R.*, 42).

40 Asst. Collr., Tando, to Collr., Hbad., 28 Dec. 1908 (*B.N.S.* 488, *Guni S.R.*, 23.

41 Interview with Mir Ghulam Allah Khan Talpur, of Umarkot, 29 Apr. 1977.

42 Asst. Settlt. Offr., Shahbandar, to Commr., Sind, 16 March 1915 (*B.N.S.* 497, *Mirpur Bathoro S.R.*, 21).

43 *Cattle-lifting in Sind*, 1.

44 *Ibid.*, 2.

45 Asst. Collr., Larkana, to Collr., Shpur., 14 Apr. 1883 (P.S.C., R.D., file 86, 1884, vol. I, pt. II, compn. 2, para. 21); Asst. Collr., Tando, to Collr., Hbad., 28 Dec. 1908 (*B.N.S.* 488, *Guni S.R.*, 22).

46 Asst. Collr., Tando, to Collr., Hbad., – 1908 (*B.N.S.* 489, *Dero Mohbat S.R.*, 12); Depy. Collr., Kotri, to Commr., Sind, 14 Feb. 1919 (*B.N.S.*

535, *Manjhand S.R.*, 101); Asst. Sup., Sind Rev. Survey, 14 Apr. 1892 (*B.N.S.* 307, *Sanghar, Khipro, Umarkot S.R.*, 21).

47 Asst. Sup., Sind Rev. Survey, to Collr., Karachi, 20 Jan. 1892 (*B.N.S.* 308, *Mirpurkhas S.R.*, 34); Asst. Collr., Tando, to Commr., Sind, 16 July 1906 (*B.N.S.* 461, *Tando Allahyar S.R.*, 14).

48 Depy. Collr., Kandhkot, to Commr., Sind,, 7 Feb. 1918 (*B.N.S.* 499, *Kandhkot, Kashmore S.R.*, 5).

49 Asst. Collr., Tando, to Commr., Sind, 16 July 1906 (*B.N.S.* 461, *Tando Allahyar S.R.*, 14).

50 Personal Asst. to Collr., Nawabshah, to Collr., 10 Apr. 1919 (*B.N.S.* 537, *Sakrand S.R.*, 13).

51 Settlt. Offr., 6 Jan. 1873 (*B.N.S.* 194, *Kotri S.R.*, 37).

52 Depy. Collr., Kotri, to Commr., Sind, 12 Oct. 1918 (*B.N.S.* 535, *Kotri S.R.*, 23).

53 Asst. Collr., Hala, to Commr., Sind, 15 Apr. 1905 (*B.N.S.* 336, *Hala S.R.*, 26).

54 Depy. Collr., Kandhkot, to Commr., Sind, 7 Feb. 1918 (*B.N.S.* 499, *Kandhkot, Kashmore S.R.*, 6).

55 A. Young, Depy. Collr., Note on Revenue Settlement in Sind (1855) (*B.N.S.* 18, pt. 1, *Rough Survey*, 135.

56 Manager, Encd. Estates, Sind, to Commr., Sind, 1 Sept. 1882 (P.S.C., R.D., file 86, 1881–92, vol. I, compn. no. not marked).

57 *Fallow Rules Cttee.*, 54.

58 Actg. Sup., Sind Rev. Survey, 12 March 1887 (*B.N.S.* 195, *Tando Bago S.R.*, 3).

59 Collr., Shpur., to Commr., Sind, 2 May 1901 (P.G.B., R.D.L., 1901 (Jan.-June), 1174.

60 *Tenancy Legislation Cttee.*, 3.

61 Masud, 2.

62 Quoted in Aitken, *Gazetteer*, 410.

63 Settlt. Offr. to Commr., Sind, 22 June 1904 (*B.N.S.* 332, *Mirpur Sakro S.R.*, 14).

64 Depy. Collr., Nara Valley, to Depy. Commr., T. & P., 23 July 1906 (*B.N.S.* 483, *Sanghar S.R.*, 18.

65 Actg. Coln. Offr., Jamrao Canal, to Commr., Sind, 27 June 1906 (*B.N.S.* 483, *Hbad. S.R.*, 21).

66 Actg. Sup., Sind Rev. Survey, to Commr., Sind, 27 March 1893 (*B.N.S.* 322, *Kashmore S.R.*, 13).

67 Settlt. Offr., Naushahro, to Commr., Sind, 31 May 1909 (*B.N.S.* 493, *Kandiaro S.R.*, 13).

68 Manager, Encd. Estates, Sind, to Commr., Sind, 1 Sept. 1882 (P.S.C., R.D., file 86, 1881–92, vol. I, compn. no. not marked).

69 Coln. Offr., Jamrao Canal, to Commr., Sind, 24 Oct. 1904 (*B.N.S.* 334, *Jamrao Tract S.R.*, 19).

70 Asst. Collr., Hala, to Commr., Sind, 15 Apr. 1905 (*B.N.S.* 336, *Hala S.R.*, 27).

71 Asst. Settlt. Offr. to Commr., Sind, 30 March 1916 (*B.N.S.* 498, *Kandhkot S.R.*, 84).

72 Actg. Depy. Collr., U.S.F., to Pol. Sup., U.S.F., 9 Nov. 1882 (P.S.C., R.D., file 58, 1877–86, compn. 1).

73 Depy. Collr., U.S.F., to Depy. Commr., U.S.F., 14 Feb. 1887 (P.S.C., R.D., file 58, 1877–86, compn. 1a).
74 Depy. Commr., U.S.F., to Commr., Sind, 28 Feb. 1887, Exec. Engineer, Begari Canals, to Depy. Commr., 23 Feb. 1887 (P.S.C., R.D., file 58, 1877–86, compn. 1a).
75 Coln. Offr., Jamrao Canal, Report (pt. III), 31 July 1901 (P.G.B., R.D.L., 1901 (July–Dec.), 2191).
76 Actg. Depy. Commr., T.& P., to Commr., Sind, 13 Aug. 1901 (P.G.B., R.D.L., 1901 (July–Dec.), 2404).
77 Commr., Sind, memo., 3 March 1902 (P.G.B., R.D.L., 1902 (Jan.–July), 381).
78 Settlt. Offr. to Commr., Sind, 22 June 1904 (*B.N.S.* 332, *Mirpur Sakro S.R.*, 14).
79 *Ibid.*
80 Settlt. Offr. to Commr., Sind, 20 June 1904 (*B.N.S.* 331, *Thatta S.R.*, 2, 18).
81 Settlt. Offr. to Commr., Sind, 28 June 1904 (*B.N.S.* 333, *Ghorabari S.R.*, 2, 12); Sup., Land Records & Agri., Sind, to Commr., Sind, 20 Apr. 1899 (*B.N.S.* 326, *Jati S.R.*, 16).
82 See Raj, 81; Metcalf, 176–9.
83 See Philips, 631; Neale, 104.
84 Commr., Sind, memo., 15 May 1902 (P.G.B., R.D.L., 1903 (Jan.–July), 109).
85 Collr., Larkana, to Commr., Sind, 9 May 1902 (P.G.B., R.D.L., 1903 (Jan.–July), 113).
86 *Land Revenue Code, 1892*, 114.
87 Collr., Larkana, to Commr., Sind, 9 May 1902 (P.G.B., R.D.L., 1903 (Jan.–July), 113.
88 *Tenancy Legislation Cttee.*, 3–6.
89 H.E.M. James, Under Secy., Govt. of Bombay, memo., 21 July 1873 (*Papers Relating to the Revenue Settlement in Sind* (Bombay, 1875), 488).
90 Depy. Collr., T. & P., to Depy. Commr., T. & P., (*B.N.S.* 459, *Umarkot S.R.*, 15).
91 Asst. Collr., Tando, to Collr., Hbad., 8 Feb. 1901 (*B.N.S.* 451, *Tando Allahyar S.R.*, 42).
92 *Tenancy Legislation Cttee.*, Minute of Dissent by Dialmal Doulatram, 13.
93 Interview with Depy. Commr., Thatta, 19 Oct. 1976.
94 Govr., Sind, to Govr.-General, India, 5 June 1937 (I.O.R., Pol. & Jud. Dept., *Govrs' Fortnightly Reports: Sind*, 1937.

4 HOLDING BY THE PATERNAL ACRES

1 *Muncher Papers*, 19.
2 *Tenures and Survey*, 19.
3 For account of Settlement Officers' work under raiyatwari settlement, see Mukherjee, 126–38, 150–76.
4 For North-Western Provinces system, see B.H. Baden-Powell, *Land Systems*, vol. II, 30 – 62, 156 – 177; Neale, 56 – 77; Metcalf, 39 – 42. For Punjab system see Baden-Powell, vol. II, 544–5; Metcalf, 43–4; Mathur,

14–5, 143–7. For village lease system in Sind, see Commr., Sind, to Collr., Karachi, n.d. (P.S.C., R.D., file 86, 1857–8, compn. 1, 76).

5 For Deccan system, see Baden-Powell vol. II, 210–22; Kumar, *Western India*, 84 – 127, & in Low (ed.), 25, 30 – 55; Charlesworth, 47–65. For principles behind Deccan & N.W. Provinces systems, see Stokes, *English Utilitarians*, 93–110, *Peasant*, 92–118; Secy., Govt. of India, to Secy., Govt, of Bombay, 30 March 1864, *Revenue Papers*, 107–8).

6 H. James, Depy. Collr., 'Report on the Purguna of Chandookah, in Upper Sind,' 31 Dec. 1847 (*B.N.S.* 17, *Memoirs on Shikarpoor*, pt. 2, 728).

7 *History of Alienations*, vol. I, 62.

8 Baden-Powell, *Land Systems*, vol. III, 337.

9 Commr., Sind, to Govr., Bombay, 12 Jan. 1855 (*Rough Survey*, Pt. 1, 3).

10 Commr., Sind, to Govr., Bombay, 21 Dec. 1854 (P.G.B., R.D., 11 July 1855, pr. 6136, para. 2).

11 Baden-Powell, *Land Systems*, vol. III, 337; Settlt. Offr., Sind, 27 July 1869 (*B.N.S.* 200, *Larkana S.R.*, 10).

12 Collr., Upper Sind, to Commr., Sind, 24 Jan. 1854 (*Rough Survey*, pt. 1, 27).

13 Commr., Sind to Collr., Shpur., 28 March 1854 (*Rough Survey*, pt. 1, 37).

14 Baden-Powell, *Land Systems*, vol. III, 337.

15 Commr., Sind to Collr., Karachi, n.d. (P.S.C., R.D., file 86, 1857–8, compn. l, 73–8).

16 Asst. Commr., Sind, n.d. (*Rough Survey*, pt. 2, 260).

17 Commr., Sind, to Govr., Bombay, 12 Jan. 1855 (*ibid.*, pt. 1, 5) & remarks on Jameson's report on Sahiti (P.G.B., R. D., March 1853, pr. 3034, para. 48).

18 Secy., Govt. of India, to Secy., Govt. of Bombay, 30 March 1864 (*Revenue Papers*, 107); Baden-Powell, *Land Systems*, vol. III, 337–8.

19 Commr., Sind, to Govr., Bombay, 24 Sept. 1862 (P.G.B., R.D., 1863, 846).

20 *Ibid.*, 864.

21 Habib, 111–8, 154; Neale, 55).

22 E. James, report, (*Muncher Papers*, 12).

23 Commr., Sind, to Govr., Bombay, 12 Aug. 1896, Note A (P.G.B., R.D.L., 1899 (July–Dec.), Confl. Pr., 795).

24 *Fallow Rules Cttee.*, 53–4.

25 *Standing Orders of the Revenue Department*, Order 2, Section C.

26 J. Francis Sup., Rev. Survey & Assessment, Thana & Ratnagiri, on Special Duty in Sind, report, 16 March 1863 (P.G.B., R.D., 1863, 873–96; copy also in *Revenue Papers*).

27 Commr., Sind, to Govr., Bombay, 24 Sept. 1862 (P.G.B., R.D., 1863, 864).

28 Francis, report, 16 March 1863, 888.

29 Sup., Sind Rev. Survey, to Commr., Sind, 1 Nov, 1883 (*B.N.S.* 200, *Larkana S.R.*, 101).

30 Commr., Sind, to Govr., Bombay, 8 Apr. 1874 (*Revenue Papers*, 501).

31 Settlt. Offr., to Collr., Hbad., 19 June 1865 (*B.N.S.* 198, *Kandiaro S.R.*, 47).

32 Survey Commr.'s office, memo., 11 March 1880 (1.0.R. no. (9)2016, *Dadu S.R.*, 12); Settlt. Offr., 12 Aug. 1880 (*B.N.S.* 198, *Naushahro Feroze S.R.*, 35).
33 Commr., Sind, to Govr., Bombay, 8 Apr. 1874 (*Revenue Papers*, 501).
34 Bombay Govt. Resn. no. 1438, 10 March 1875, para. 10 (*Revenue Papers*, appended after 525).
35 Sup., Sind Rev. Survey, to Commr., Sind, 1 Nov. 1883 (*B.N.S.* 200, *Larkana S.R.*, 102).
36 *Fallow Rules Cttee.*, 32.
37 Bombay Govt. Resn. No. 1438, 10 March 1875 (*Revenue Papers*, appended after 525).
38 Francis, report, 16 March 1863, 874 875; Commr., Sind, to Govr., Bombay, 20 Aug. 1864 (*Revenue Papers*, 136).
39 Francis, report, 16 March 1863, 876–7.
40 A. Rogers, Minute, 10 Aug. 1872 (*B.N.S.*, 196, *Hbad. S.R.*, 29).
41 Bombay Govt. Resn. no. 750, 10 Feb. 1873 (*B.N.S.* 201, *Naushahro Abro S.R.*, 34).
42 Bombay Govt. Resn. no. 1438, 10 March 1875, para. 15 (*Revenue Papers*, appended after 525).
43 Bombay Govt. Resn. no. 750, 10 Feb. 1873 (*B.N.S.* 201, *Naushahro Abro S.R.*, 34).
44 Settlt. Offr., memo., 4 March 1873 (*B.N.S.* 201, *Naushahro Abro S.R.*, 34a).
45 Sup., Sind Rev. Survey, 9 Feb. 1881 (*B.N.S.* 199, *Tigar S.R.*, 20–2); 10 Feb. 1881 (*B.N.S.* 200, *Labdaria S.R.*, 30–4); 14 Feb. 1881 (*B.N.S.* 199, *Mehar S.R.*, 29–31).
46 Bombay Govt. Resn. no. 3397, 13 June 1881 (cited in Sup., Sind Rev. Survey, 14 June 1882 (*B.N.S.* 200, *Kambar S.R.*, 1).
47 *B.N.S.* 278, *Character of Land Tenures*, 17.
48 *Fallow Rules Cttee.*, 6; Sup., Sind Rev. Survey, to Commr., Sind, 19 Jan. 1885 (P.S.C., R.D., file 86, 1885–92, compn. 1, para. 1).
49 Secy., Govt. of India, to Secy., Govt. of Bombay, 30 March 1864 (*Revenue Papers*, 108–17); Metcalf, 43.
50 Commr., Sind, to Govr., Bombay, 20 Aug. 1864 (*Revenue Papers*, 130–7); Francis to Secy., Govt. of Bombay, 8 Aug., 1864 (*ibid.*, 145–6).
51 Secy., Govt. of India, to Secy., Govt. of Bombay, 14 Feb. 1865 (*ibid.*, 150–5).
52 Bombay Act I of 1865, Survey and Settlement Act, 1865.
53 Metcalf, 166, 189–95; Gopal, 62.
54 Francis, 8 Aug. 1864 (*Revenue Papers*, 145).
55 Francis, report, 16 March 1863, 887.
56 Settlt. Offr., Karachi, to Commr., Sind, 23 March 1863 (P.S.C., R.D., file 86, 1862–3, vol. II, compn. 25, 162).
57 Francis, 8 Aug. 1864 (*Revenue Papers*, 145).
58 *History of Services*, 76.
59 Francis, report, 16 March 1863, 881.
60 *History of Services* (1880), 89; Haig to A.W. Hughes, Compiler, *Sind Gazetteer*, 25 March 1875 (P.S.C., R.D., file 86, 1882, vol. II, pt. II, compn. 31, 301).
61 Hughes, *Gazetteer*, 79 – 81.

62 Aitken, *Gazetteer*, 412–3.
63 I.0.R., Military Dept., Cadet Papers, 1845–6, compn. 225, 157–68.
64 Hughes, *Gazetteer*, 81.
65 Settlt. Offr., Hbad., to Commr., Sind, 6 March 1863 (P.S.C., R.D., file 86, 1863–4, vol. I, compn. 3).
66 *Ibid.*, 886.
67 *Ibid.*, 886.
68 Haig, 6 Jan. 1873 (*B.N.S.* 194, *Kotri S.R.*, 35–6).
69 Haig to Collr., Shpur., – Sept. 1873 (*B.N.S.* 201, *Sukkur S.R.*, 41); 12 Aug. 1880 (*B.N.S.* 198 *Naushahro Feroze S.R.*, 42).
70 Haig, 6 Jan. 1873 (*B.N.S.* 194, *Kotri S.R.*, 35–6).
71 Haig, 10 Jan. 1876 (1.0.R. no. (9)2015, *Sehwan S.R.*, 14).
72 Haig, 6 Jan. 1873 (*B.N.S.* 194, *Kotri S.R.*, 37).
73 Haig, 10 Jan. 1876 (I.O.R. no. (9)2015, *Sehwan S.R.*, 26).
74 H.E.M. James, 'Report on the Zemindars of the Muncher Lake, 1872' (*Muncher Papers*, 1).
75 James, 'Muncher Report' (*ibid.*, 19).
76 James, 'Muncher Report;' Commr., Sind, to Govr., Bombay, 28 Oct. 1872 (*ibid.*, 17, 1).
77 *Who Was Who, 1916 – 1928*, 500.
78 James, 'Muncher Report' (*Muncher Papers.*, 17).
79 Haig, memo., 7 Aug., 1872 (*ibid.*, 158–9).
80 *Ibid.*, 162, 174.
81 Haig, 10 Jan. 1876 (I.O.R. no. (9)2015, *Sehwan S.R.*, 21).
82 *Ibid.*
83 Haig, memo., 6 Jan. 1874 (*Revenue Papers*, 507).
84 Bombay Govt. Resn. no. 2606, 6 May 1875 (P.G.B., R.D.L., 1875, 318).
85 Haig, 7 Aug. 1872 (*Muncher Papers*, 172); 10 Jan. 1876 (1.0.R. no. (9)2015, *Sehwan S.R.*, 4–5).
86 Haig, 10 Jan. 1876 (1.0.R. no. (9)2015, *Sehwan S.R.*, 10).
87 *Ibid.*, 12–3, 17, 21.
88 Bombay Govt. Resn. no. 1438, 10 March 1875, para. 7 (*Revenue Papers*, appended after 525).
89 Sup., Sind Rev. Survey, 24 July 1886 (1.0.R. no. (9)2207, *Jati S.R.*, 4).
90 James, memo., 21 July 1873 (*Revenue Papers*, 488).
91 Commr., Sind, to Govr., Bombay, 8 Apr. 1874 (*Ibid.*, 498).
92 Haig, memo., 6 Jan. 1874 (*Revenue Papers*, 509–10).
93 *Ibid.*, 509.
94 See Actg. Sup., Sind Rev. Survey, 8 March 1892 (*B.N.S.* 315, *Larkana S.R.*, 29–33); Settlt. Offr., to Commr., Sind, 3O Apr. 1907 (*B.N.S.* 482, *Larkana S.R.*, 2–5).
95 Settlt. Offr. to Collr., Shpur., 27 July 1869 (*B.N.S.* 200, *Larkana S.R.*, 8).
96 Francis, memo., 11 Nov. 1869 (*Ibid.*, 26).
97 Depy. Collr., Larkana, to Collr., Upper Sind, 20 Feb. 1855 B.N.S. 306, *Official Correspondence regarding the Ford Wah*, 14).
98 Collr., Shpur., to Commr., Sind, 5 Oct. 1869 (*B.N.S.* 200, *Larkana S.R.*, 23).
99 Sup., Sind Rev. Survey, 5 Feb. 1881 (*Ibid.*, 36–8).

100 Bombay Govt. Resn. no, 6238, 9 Sept. 1882 (P.G.B., R.D.L., 1882, 826).
101 Larkana zamindars, petition to Govr., Bombay, 9 March 1883 (P.S.C., R.D., file 86, 1884, vol. I, pt. II, compn. 2, paras. 6, 8).
102 Asst. Collr., Larkana, to Collr., Shpur., 14 Apr. 1883 (*ibid.*, para. 21).
103 Manager, Encd. Estates, Sind, to Commr., Sind, 18 July 1883 (*B.N.S.* 200, *Larkana S.R.*, 88).
104 Depy. Collr., Shpur., report, 31 Dec. 1847 (*B.N.S.* 17, pt. 2, 728).
105 Collr., Shpur., to Commr., Sind, 9 Oct. 1883 (*B.N.S.* 200, *Larkana S.R.*, 99).
106 Sup., Sind Rev. Survey, to Commr., Sind, 1 Nov. 1883 (*B.N.S.* 200, *Larkana S.R.*, 100).
107 Bombay Govt. Resn. no. 2659, 28 March 1884 (P.G.B., R.D.L., 1884 (Jan.–June), 344–5).
108 Commr., Sind, to Govr., Bombay, 21 Feb. 1884 (*ibid.*, 290–1).
109 See *Larkana S.R.s.*
110 Settlt. Offr. to Commr., Sind, 30 Apr. 1907 (*B.N.S.* No. 482, *Larkana S.R.*, 6, 42).
111 Collr., Shpur., to Survey & Settlt. Commr., 5 Oct. 1869; Sup., Sind Rev. Survey, 5 Feb. 1881 (*B.N.S.* 200, *Larkana S.R.*, 23, 38).
112 Sup., Sind Rev. Survey, 1 Nov. 1883 (*ibid.*, 100).
113 *Ibid.*, and Commr.'s pencil note on the Sup.'s letter in P.S.C., R.D., file 86, 1884, vol. I, pt. II, compn. 2.
114 The journey took me about fifteen minutes in a tonga in 1976.
115 Sup., Sind Rev. Survey, 5 Feb. 1881 (*B.N.S.* 200, *Larkana S.R.*, 38).
116 Commr., Sind, to Govr., Bombay, 18 May 1892 (*B.N.S.* 315, *Larkana S.R.*, 5–7).
117 Commr., Sind, memo., 7 Nov. 1903 (P.G.B., R.D.L., 1903 (Aug.–Dec.), 1455).
118 Settlt. Offr., to Commr., Sind, 30 Apr. 1907 (*B.N.S.* 482, *Larkana S.R.*, 11).
119 Depy. Collr., Sukkur, to Actg. Commr., Sind, 23 Dec. 1898 (*B.N.S.* 328, *Sukkur S.R.*, 26).
120 Commr., Sind, to Govr., Bombay, 4 Apr. 1899 (*ibid.*, ii).
121 Bombay Govt. Resn. no. 4718, 7 July 1899 (*ibid.*, par. 2).
122 Settlt. Offr., to Commr., Sind, 22 June 1904 (*B.N.S.* 332, *Mirpur Sakro S.R.*, 16).
123 Actg. Asst. Commr., Sind, – 1897 (*B.N.S.* 306, *Sujawal S.R.*, 9).
124 Mountford, 'Debtors & Creditors', 1697.
125 Haig, Settlt. Offr., to Collr., Shpur., – Sept., 1873 (*Revenue Papers*, 206–9).
126 *Ibid.*, 240.
127 Commr., Sind, to Govr., Bombay, 12 Aug. 1896, App: comments by Collr., Shpur., & Depy. Commrs., U.S.F., T. & P. (P.G.B., R.D.L., 1899 (July–Dec,), Confl. Pr., 840, 841, 844).
128 Commr., Sind, memo., 21 Aug. 1897 (P.S.C., R.D., file 69A, 1896–9, vol. 1, 205).
129 James to Collr., Shpur., 4 Feb. 1873 (*B.N.S.* 194, *Kotri S.R.*, 52).
130 Collr., Karachi, memo., 22 March 1873 (*B.N.S.* 194, *Kotri S.R.*, 61).
131 Collr., Sukkur, to Commr., Sind, 4 May 1902 (P.G.B., R.D.L., 1903 (Jan.–July), 112).

132 Commr., Sind, to Govr., Bombay, 12 Aug., 1896 ((P.G.B., R.D.L., 1899 (July–Dec.), Confl. Pr., 801).
133 'The Agricultural Geography of the Lower Indus Valley,' 106; unpublished work held in the Institute of Sindhology, University of Sind.
134 Depy. Collr., Sehwan, to Collr., Karachi, 29 Aug. 1872 (P.S.C., R.D., file 86, 1872, vol. I, compn. 30).
135 Mountford, 'Debtors and Creditors,' 1698–9.
136 Collr., Sukkur, to Commr., Sind, 4 May 1902 (P.G.B., R.D.L., 1903 (Jan.–July), 112).
137 See Actg. Sup., Sind Rev. Survey, to Commr., Sind, 19 Sept. 1889 (*B.N.S.* 455, *Sehwan S.R.*, 13).
138 Haig, Settlt. Offr., 6 Jan. 1873 (*B.N.S.* 194, *Kotri S.R.*, 36, 37).
139 Commr., Sind, to Govr., Bombay, 12 Aug. 1896, Note A (P.G.B., R.D.L., 1899 (July–Dec.), Confl. Pr., 796).
140 Collr., Shpur., to Commr., Sind, 4 May 1902 (P.G.B., R.D.L., 1903 (Jan.–July), 112).

5 THE OMNIPRESENT BANIA

1 Sup., Sind Rev. Survey, 10 June 1886 (*B.N.S.* 194, *Kotri S.R.*, 4).
2 Burton, *Sind Revisited*, vol. I, 299.
3 Commr., Sind, to Govr., Bombay, 12 Aug. 1896, Note A (P.G.B., R.D.L., 1899 (Jul.-Dec.), Confl. Pr., 801).
4 Regulation V of 1827, Chapter V, Section 15 (*The Bombay Code*, 7.
5 Commr., Sind, to Govr., Bombay, 12 Aug. 1896, Note A (P.G.B., R.D.L., 1899 (July–Dec.), Confl. Pr., 798–9.
6 *Ibid.*, 802.
7 *Ibid.*, 803, 825.
8 Settlt. Offr. to Collr., Shpur., 27 July 1869 (*B.N.S.* 200, *Larkana S.R.*, 10).
9 Asst. Collr., Hala, to Commr., Sind, 15 Apr. 1905 (*B.N.S.* 336, *Hala S.R.*, 28).
10 Asst. Collr., Tando, 8 Feb. 1901 (*B.N.S.* 467, *Tando Allahyar S.R.*, 11).
11 Sup., Land Records & Agri., Sind, to Commr., Sind, 7 Feb. 1894 (*B.N.S.* 309, *Hala S.R.*, App. XX, 70) & 30 May 1899 (*B.N.S.* 470, *Kotri S.R.*, 37); Abbasi, 96–7.
12 Bombay Govt. Resn. no. 8761, 26 Oct. 1885 (P.G.B., R.D.L., 1885 (July–Dec.), 1174); pr. 450 (*ibid.*, 1886, 228); Asst. Collr., Sehwan, to Commr., Sind, 30 Apr. 1895 (*B.N.S.* 321, *Manjhand S.R.*, App. XXI, 52).
13 Dodo Khan Burdi, taluqa Jacobabad, petition to Commr., Sind, n.d. (P.S.C., J.D., file 1, 1897, vol. IV, pt. II, compn. 54, 838); District Sup., Police, Hbad., to Commr., 11 Feb. 1892 (P.S.C., J.D., file 1, 1892, vol. III, pt. II, compn. 80, 560–3).
14 Settlt. Offr., 10 Jan. 1876 (I.O.R. (9)2015, *Sehwan S.R.*, 6).
15 Asst. Collr., Tando, 8 Feb. 1901 (*B.N.S.* 467, *Tando Allahyar S.R.*, 11).
16 Sup., Sind Rev. Survey, 10 June 1886 (*B.N.S.* 194, *Kohistan S.R.*, 4).
17 Asst. Collr., Tando, to Collr., Hbad., 8 Feb. 1901 (*B.N.S.* 457, *Tando Allahyar S.R.*, 8).

18 See Asst. Rev. Offr., Lloyd Barrage & Canals Scheme, n.d. (1929) (*B.N.S.* 599, *Larkana, Kambar, Warah, Mehar S.R.s*, 1, 18, 26, 39); Asst. Settlt. Offr., 30 Apr. 1930 (*B.N.S.* 656, *Khipro, Samaro, Sanghar, Umarkot S.R.s*, 2, 56, 99, 134).
19 Settlt. Offr., 6 Jan. 1873 (*B.N.S.* 194, *Kotri S.R.*, 38).
20 Depy. Collr., U.S.F., to Commr., Sind, 18 July 1904 (*B.N.S.* 335, *Thul, Kandhkot, Kashmore S.R.s*, 8); Asst. Collr., Tando, to Commr., Sind, 16 July 1906 (*B.N.S.* 461, *Tando Allahyar S.R.*, 13).
21 Mountford, 'Debtors & Creditors,' 1759.
22 Asst. Collr., Larkana, Admin. Report, 1899–1900 (P.S.C., G.D., file 4, 1901, vol. III compn. 15).
23 Mountford, 'Debtors & Creditors,' 1759.
24 *Ibid.*, 1765.
25 Actg. Sup., Sind Rev. Survey, 24 May 1892 (*B.N.S.* 316, *Mehar S.R.*, 17).
26 Mountford, 'Debtors & Creditors,' 1766. For specimens of bonds issued by Indian bankers, see Jain, 55–61.
27 Sathe, 104.
28 Mountford, 'Debtors & Creditors,' 1766.
29 *Ibid.*, 1768.
30 *Ibid.*, 1766.
31 Interview with Mir Ahmed Khan Talpur, zamindar, 4 Apr. 1977.
32 Settlt. Offr., Nawabshah, 10 Apr. 1919 (*B.N.S.* 537, *Sakrand S.R.*, 12).
33 Mountford, 'Debtors & Creditors,' 1784.
34 Settlt. Offr., Sehwan, to Commr., Sind, 23 Apr. 1909 (*B.N.S.* 487, *Sehwan S.R.*, 10).
35 Burton, *Sindh*, 46.
36 Quoted in Note to Commr., Sind, 29 Oct. 1899 (P.S.C., J.D., file 1, 1899, vol. III, pt. I, compn. 12, 69).
37 Manager, Encd. Estates, Sind, to Commr., Sind, 23 Jan. 1898 (P.S.C., J.D., file 1, 1899, vol. III, pt. I, compn. 12, 112).
38 Collr., Shpur., to Commr., Sind, 30 Sept. 1880 (P.S.C., R.D., file 86, 1888, vol. I, pt. I, compn. 1, 35).
39 Settlt. Offr., Karachi, to Collr., Karachi, 3 May 1859 (P.G.B., R.D., 31 Dec. 1859, pr. 9640, para. 10).
40 James, 'Muncher Zemindars, 1872' (*Muncher Papers*, 41).
41 Mountford, 'Debtors & Creditors,' 1777.
42 Commr., Sind, to Secy., Govt. of Bombay, 20 June 1900 (P.G.B., R.D.L., 1902 (July–Dec.), 1557).
43 Akhund Sayed Khan & others of Raj Mahajan, taluqa Naushahro, petition to Commr., Sind, 4 Dec. 1869 (P.S.C., J.D., file 1, 1870, pt. I, vol. II, compn. 1).
44 Quoted in James, 'Muncher Zemindars, 1872,' 41.
45 Depy. Collr., U.S.F., to Depy. Commr., U.S.F., 18 Dec. 1882 (P.S.C., J.D., file 1, 1880–93, vol. II, pt. I, compn. 4, 270–1).
46 Hindu community of Mirpur Sakro, petition to Commr., Sind, 2 Apr. 1873 (P.S.C., J.D., file 1, 1874, vol. II, pt. I, compn. 11).
47 Panchayat of Kandiaro & Halani, petition to Commr., Sind, March 1870 (P.S.C., J.D., file 1, 1870, vol. II, pt. I, compn. 1).
48 Depy. Collr., U.S.F., to Depy. Commr., U.S.F., 18 Dec. 1882 (P.S.C., J.D., file 1, 1880–93, pt. I, vol. II, compn. 4, 270–1).

49 Asst. Collr., Naushahro, to Collr., Hbad., 10 Jan. 1895; Collr., to Commr., Sind, 7 March & 18 July 1896; Mir Ghulam Muhammad Khan Talpur, petition to Collr., Hbad., 4 July 1896; Commr., note, n.d.; Commr., Order no. 1763, 5 Aug. 1896 (P.S.C., J.D., file 1, 1896, vol. III, compn. 13, 55, 133, 183, 189–92, 200). Actg. Commr. to Mir Ghulam Muhammad, 18 Jan. 1899; Note for Commr., Sind, 29 Oct. 1899 (P.S.C., J.D., file 1, 1899, vol. III, pt. I, compn. 12, 68, 162).
50 Commr., Sind, 14 Nov. 1900 (P.G.B., R.D.L., 1901 (Jan.–June), 689.
51 Mir Ghulam Muhammad Khan Talpur, petition to Commr., Sind, 3 June 1899 (P.S.C., J.D., file 1, 1899, vol. III, pt. I, compn. 12, 159).
52 Mountford, 'Debtors & Creditors,' 1778.
53 *Ibid.*, 1765.
54 Gungadin Ramsingh, petition to Commr., Sind, 26 July 1873 (P.S.C., J.D., file 1, 1873, vol. II, compn. 1).
55 Subordinate Judge, Kotri, to District Judge, Karachi, 13 Oct. 1894 (P.S.C., J.D., file 1, 1895, vol. VIII, compn. 29, 657).
56 Darling, *Rusticus Loquitur*, 328.
57 Inhabitants of Mirpur Bathoro, petition to Commr., Sind, 23 June 1894 (P.S.C., J.D., file 1, 1895, vol. II, pt. II, compn. 29, 631).
58 Manager, Encd. Estates, Sind, 22 Oct. 1900 (*Encd. Estates Report 1899–1900*, App. A, 125).
59 M.S. Gore, 'India,' in Lambert & Hoselitz (eds), 187–8.
60 Charlesworth, 85.
61 Mountford, 'Debtors & Creditors,' 1746, 1752.
62 Commr., Sind, memo., 8 Jan. 1902 (P.G.B., R.D.L., 1902 (Jan.–July), 427); Manager, Encd. Estates, Sind, to Commr., 27 March 1900 (*ibid.*, 1900 (July–Dec.), 1233); Collr., Karachi, to Commr., 1 Oct. 1901 (*ibid.*, 1902 (Aug.–Dec.), 1707.
63 Commr., Sind, memo., 8 Jan. 1902 (P.G.B., R.D.L., 1902 (Jan.–July), 427.
64 Sup., Sind Rev. Survey, to Commr., Sind, 30 July 1883 (*B.N.S.* 200, *Larkana S.R.*, 92).
65 Collr., Shpur., to Commr., Sind, 13 Oct. 1901 (P.G.B., R.D.L., 1902 (Aug.-Dec.), 1712.
66 Commr., Sind, memo., 14 Nov. 1900 (P.G.B., R.D.L., 1901 (Jan.–June), 689).
67 Depy. Collr., Nara Valley, to Depy. Commr., T. & P., 23 July 1906 (*B.N.S.* 469, *Khipro S.R.*, 21).
68 Darling, *Punjab Peasant*, 32–3.
69 Jack, 59–61
70 Actg. Director, Land records & Agri., Bombay, 'Memorandum on the Material Condition of the People of the Bombay Presidency, 1892–1902' (P.G.B., R.D.L., 1902 (Aug.–Dec.), 1281).
71 Burton, *Sindh*, 50.
72 J. Burnes, 12.
73 A. Burnes, vol. III, 226.
74 Masson, vol. I, 379.
75 Mountford, 'Debtors & Creditors,' 1783.
76 Masson, vol. II, 139; J. Burnes, 84, 86.
77 J. Burnes, 83.

78 Masson, vol. I, 287, 389; Postans, 65, 68, 397.
79 Collr., Karachi, 14 Jan. 1848; Secy., Govt. of India, to Secy., Govt. of Bombay., 13 Nov. 1849 (*pre-Mutiny Records*, 397–401, 462).
80 Hotchand, 69–71.
81 Parsram, 56.
82 Commr., Sind, note, n.d. (P.S.C., J.D., file 1, 1894, vol. II, pt. I, compn. 23, para. 3).
83 Mountford, 'Debtors & Creditors,' 1763.
84 Karam Ali & others of taluqa Moro, petition to Commr., Sind, 16 Oct. 1902 (P.S.C., J.D., file 1, 1902, vol. II, pt. II, compn. 6).
85 Inhabitants of Mirpur Bathoro, petition to Commr., Sind, 23 June 1894; Ali Muhammad to District Judge, Karachi, 13 Oct. 1894 (P.S.C., J.D., file 1, 1895, vol. VIII, compn. 24, 632–4, 657–8).
86 Inhabitants of Mirpur Bathoro, petition to Commr., Sind, 23 June 1894 (P.S.C., J.D., file 1, 1895, vol. VIII, compn. 24, 635).
87 See correspondence in P.S.C., J.D.: file 1, 1875, vol. II, compn. 23; file 1, 1884, vol. II, pt. II, compns 67, 448; file 2, 1884, vol. II, compn. 26A; file 1, 1893, vol. II, pt. II, compn. 56, and vol. III, pt. I, compn. 105; file 1, 1901, vol. III, pt. II, compn. 24.
88 District Sup., Police, to Collr., Hbad., 26 Aug. 1882 (P.S.C., J.D., file 1, 1882, vol. II, pt. II, compn. 47, 78–84); Commr., Sind, note, n.d. (*ibid.*, 1894, vol. II, pt. I, compn. 23.
89 Actg. Collr., Shpur., to Commr., Sind, 4 June 1894 (P.S.C., J.D., file 1, 1894, vol. I, pt. I, compn. 9, 334).
90 Commr., Sind, memo., 13 Jan. 1892 (P.S.C., J.D., file 1, 1892, vol. III, pt. II, compn. 80) and correspondence in *ibid.*, 1896, vol. IV, pt. II, compn. 31.
91 District Sup., Police, Hbad., to Collr., Hbad., 17 Feb. 1896; Collr. to Commr., Sind, 26 March 1896 (P.S.C., J.D., file 1, 1896, vol. IV, pt. II, compn. 31, 271, 284).
92 Quoted in Commr., Sind, to Govr., Bombay, 12 Aug. 1896, Note C (P.G.B., R.D.L., 1899 (July–Dec.), Confl. Pr., 835).
93 Collr., Hbad., to Commr., Sind, 9 May 1888 (P.S.C., J.D., file 1, 1888, vol. II, pt. I, compn. 36, 271–3).
94 Depy. Collr., Naushahro, note, 7 Apr. 1892 (P.S.C., J.D., file 1, 1892, vol. III, pt. II, compn. 80, 602–5).
95 District Sup., Police, Hbad., to Commr., Sind, 17 Jan. 1882. See also his letters of 3 Aug. 1881, 28 Jan. & 3 Feb. 1882, and Jairamdas of taluqa Moro, petition to Commr., 15 July 1881 (P.S.C., J.D., file 2, 1882, vol. II, compn. 31(3)).
96 District Sup., Police, Hbad., to Commr., Sind, 18 Jan. 1892 (P.S.C., J.D., file 1, 1892, vol. III, pt. II, compn. 80, 534).
97 Commr., Sind, to Govr., Bombay, 11 Feb. 1892 – rough copy: these remarks were deleted from the final draft (P.S.C., J.D., file 1, 1892, vol. III, pt. II, compn. 80, 562).
98 District Sup., Police, Hbad., to Commr., Sind, 11 Feb. 1892 (P.S.C., J.D., file 1, 1892, vol. III, pt. II, compn. 80, 562).
99 District Sup., Police, Hbad., to Commr., Sind, 11 Feb. 1892 (P.S.C., J.D., file 1, 1892, vol. III, pt. II, compn. 80, 561–2).
100 District Sup., Police, Hbad., to Commr., Sind, 18 Jan. 1892 (P.S.C.,

J.D., file 1, 1892, vol. III, pt. II, compn. 80, 534); Collr., Shpur., 15 March 1892 (*ibid.*, vol. III, pt. I, compn. 53, 169–71).

101 Hindu Panchayats of Lalti, Bhan, Karampur, Mohi, Dari Dero, Otekimen, Labadia: petition to Commr., Sind, n.d. (P.S.C., J.D., file 2, 1884, vol. II, compn. 26A).

102 Commr., Sind, note, n.d. (P.S.C., J.D., file 1, 1894, vol. II, pt. I, compn. 23).

6 CLASS LEGISLATION

1 Bombay Govt. Resn. no. 2606, 6 May 1875 (P.G.B., R.D.L., 1875, 320).

2 Commr., Sind, to Secy., Govt. of Bombay, 25 Nov. 1882 (P.S.C., R.D., file 1, 1880–2, vol. III, compn. 40, 39).

3 Settlt. Offr., Karachi, to Collr., Karachi, 3 May 1859 (P.G.B., R.D., 31 Dec. 1859, pr. 9640, paras 2, 9).

4 Settlt. Offr., Karachi, to Commr., Sind, 12 March 1861 (P.G.B., R.D., Apr. 1861, 779–92).

5 James, 'Muncher Zemindars, 1872' (*Muncher Papers*, 70).

6 *Ibid.*, 71.

7 Commr., Sind, to Govr., Bombay, 28 Oct. 1872 (*ibid.*, 2).

8 Bombay Govt. Resn. no. 2606, 6 May 1875 (P.G.B., R.D.L., 1875, 320).

9 Quoted in Bombay Govt. Resn. no. 2606, 6 May 1875 (P.G.B., R.D.L., 1875, 320).

10 *Ibid.*, 321.

11 Bombay Act XIV of 1876, Sindh Incumbered Estates Act 1876, Chapter III, sections 9–10; Chapter IV; Chapter V, section 25.

12 Sindh Incumbered Estates Act 1876, chapter III, section 8; chapter IV, section 11; Bombay Govt. Resn. no. 2606, 6 May 1875 (P.G.B., R.D.L., 1875, 322).

13 Sindh Incumbered Estates Act 1876, chapter II, section 3.

14 Bombay Act XX of 1881, Sindh Incumbered Estates Act 1881, section 1.

15 *Encd. Estates Reports*, 1879–87.

16 Manager, Encd. Estates, Sind, 11 Sept. 1884 (P.S.C., R.D., file 1, 1885–6, vol. IV, compn. 54, 9–11).

17 Actg. Commr., Sind, to Govr., Bombay, 2 Aug. 1878 (P.G.B., R.D.L., 1878, 579).

18 Commr., Sind, to Govr., Bombay, 15 July 1879 (P.G.B., R.D.L., 1879–80, compn. 6, 10).

19 Manager, Encd. Estates, Sind, to Commr., Sind, 23 Nov. 1880 (P.G.B., R.D.L., 1880–2, vol. II, compn. 20, 2).

20 Bombay Govt. Resn. no. 1572, 26 Feb. 1883 (P.G.B., R.D.L., 1883 (Jan.–June), 180; Resn. no. 1008, 1 Feb. 1884 (P.G.B., R.D.L., 1884 (Jan.–June), 145).

21 Bombay Act XI of 1884, Sindh Incumbered Estates Act 1884, section 1.

22 Bombay Govt. Resn. no. 353, 16 Jan. 1886 (P.G.B., R.D.L., 1886, 46).

23 Commr., Sind, to Manager, Encd. Estates, Sind, 30 June 1879 (P.S.C., R.D., file 1, 1879–80, compn. 6, 3).

24 See lists of estates under management in *Encd. Estates Reports*, 1879–87: estates nos 222, 281, 282, Shpur. Collectorate; Manager, Encd. Estates,

Sind, to Commr., Sind, 5 Dec. 1879 (P.S.C., R.D., file 1, 1879–80, compn. 14).

25 Mulchand & others, petition, 6 Oct. 1881 (P.S.C., R.D., file 1, 1880–2, vol. II, compn. 18, 7–9).

26 Manager, Encd. Estates, Sind, to Commr., Sind, 1 Dec. 1879 (P.S.C., R.D., file 1, 1880–2, vol. II, compn. 19, 61).

27 Manager to Commr., 15 July, 23 July, 6 Aug. 1884 (P.S.C., R.D., file 1, 1883–6, vol. III, compn. 36, 232–4, 241–4).

28 See Manager to Commr., 14 Jan. 1884 (P.S.C., R.D., file 1, 1883–6, vol. II, compn. 16, 9, 15).

29 Actg. Commr., Sind, to Govr., Bombay, 8 Sept. 1900 (P.G.B., R.D.L., 1904 (July–Dec.), 1612.

30 Manager, Encd. Estates, Sind, to Commr., Sind, 18 July 1883; Sup., Sind Rev. Survey, to Commr., 30 July 1883 (*B.N.S.* 200, *Larkana S.R.*, 87, 91).

31 Bombay Govt. Resn. no. 8116, 3 Nov. 1883 (P.G.B., R.D.L., 1883 (July–Dec.), 1112.

32 Depy. Commr., U.S.F., to Commr., Sind, 12 Aug. 1885; Commr., memo., 29 Aug. 1885; see also Manager, Encd. Estates, Sind, to Commr., 14 Apr. 1885 (P.S.C., R.D., file 1, 1883–6, vol. IV, compn. 55, 8, 19, 1–5).

33 Depy. Commr., U.S.F., to Commr., Sind, 4 Apr. 1886 (P.S.C., R.D., file 1, 1883–6, vol. V, compn. 66, 76–8).

34 Bombay Govt. Resn. no. 1572, 26 Feb. 1883 (P.G.B., R.D.L., 1883 (Jan.–June), 181).

35 'Rules made by the Commissioner in Sind under Section 30 of Act XIV of 1876, with the previous sanction of the Honourable the Governor of Bombay in Council,' Rules 4(IV) & 4(V) (P.G.B., R.D.L. 1877, 27–9).

36 Rules under s 30 of Act XIV of 1876: Rule 4(VI), and ruling of Jud. Commr., Sind, 3 July 1883 (P.S.C., R.D., file 1, 1883–6 (vol. no. not marked) compn. 8, 13).

37 Commr., Sind, note, n.d.; Remembrancer of Legal Affairs, memo., 6 Feb. 1878 (P.S.C., R.D., file 1, 1878–9, compn. 8, 13, 3).

38 Rules Under s 30 of Act XIV of 1876: Rules 4 & 4(I).

39 *Ibid.*: Rule 8.

40 Bombay Govt. Resn. no. 6702, 16 Dec. 1879 (P.G.B., R.D.L., 1879, 719).

41 Manager, Encd. Estates, Sind, to Commr., Sind, 10 Apr. 1878 (P.S.C., R.D., file 1, 1880–2, vol. II, compn. 19, 9–12).

42 Secy., Govt. of India, to Secy., Govt. of Bombay, 16 Jan. 1879 (P.S.C., R.D., file 1, 1880–2, vol. II, compn. 19, 49).

43 Manager, Encd. Estates, Sind, to Commr., Sind, 21 Apr. 1880 (P.S.C., R.D., file 1, 1880–2, vol. II, compn. 19, 90).

44 See Manager to Commr., 14 Jan. 1884 (P.S.C., R.D., file 1, 1883–6, vol. II, compn. 16, 10); Depy Commr., U.S.F., 4 Apr. 1886 (*ibid.*, vol. V, compn. 66, 73, 78, 88); Commr., Sind, memo., 16 May 1886 (*ibid.*, 98).

45 Manager to Commr., 17 & 29 Aug. 1882 (P.S.C., R.D., file 1, 1880–2, vol. III, compn. 45, 2, 7).

46 Commr. to Manager, 22 Aug. 1882, and see also 6 Sept. 1882 (P.S.C., R.D., file 1, 1880–2, vol. III, compn. 45, 6, 8).

47 Manager to Commr., 14 March 1882 (P.S.C., R.D., file 1, 1880–2, vol. I, compn. 3, 31).
48 *Encd. Estates Reports*, 1878–87.
49 Manager, Encd. Estates, Sind, to Commr., Sind, 8 May 1886 (P.S.C., R.D., file 1, 1887–8, vol. III, compn. 17, 122–7).
50 Mulchand & others, petition, 6 Oct. 1881 (P.S.C., R.D., file 1, 1880–2, vol. II, compn. 18, 9).
51 Commr., Sind, to Secy., Govt. of Bombay, 31 Jan. 1877 (P.G.B., R.D.L., 1877, 120).
52 Actg. Collr., Karachi, to Commr., Sind, 9 Aug. 1881 (P.S.C., R.D., file 1, 1880–2, vol. II, compn. 22, 2).
53 *Ibid.*, 1, 3.
54 Judge, Sadar Court, Sind, to Commr., Sind, 12 Nov. 1881 (P.S.C., R.D., file 1, 1880–2, vol. III, compn. 26, 5).
55 Bombay Govt., telegraph to Commr., Sind, 8 Sept. 1881 (P.S.C., R.D., file 1, 1880–2, vol. II, compn. 22, 16).
56 Act XI of 1884, Sindh Incumbered Estates Act 1884, section 5A.
57 Commr., Sind, to Secy., Govt. of Bombay, 15 July 1879 (P.S.C., R.D., file 1, 1879–80, compn. 6, 15–9).
58 Remembrancer of Legal Affairs, memo., 26 July 1879 (P.S.C., R.D., file 1, 1879–80, compn. 6, 22).
59 Manager, Encd. Estates, Sind, to Commr., Sind, 23 Nov. 1880; Bombay Govt. Resn. no. 1340, 5 March 1881 (P.S.C., R.D., file 1, 1880–2, vol. II, compn. 20, 1–3, 13); Bombay Govt. Resns no. 1572, 26 Feb. 1883, & 1008, 1 Feb. 1884 (P.G.B., R.D.L., 1883 (Jan.–June), 180; 1884 (Jan.–June), 145).
60 Manager, Encd. Estates, Sind, to Commr., Sind, 21 June & 7 Nov. 1884 (P.S.C., R.D., file 1, 1883–6, vol. IV, compn. 54, 8–11).
61 Commr. to Manager, 21 June, 4 Nov., 29 Nov. 1884 (P.S.C., R.D., file 1, 1883–6, vol. IV, compn. 54, 1–2, 15, 19).
2 Manager to Commr., 15 June 1885; Bombay Govt. Resn. no. 6597, 12 Aug. 1885 (P.S.C., R.D., file 1, 1883–6, vol. IV, compn. 58, 1–2, 15); Bombay Govt. Resn. no. 1248, 26 Feb. 1887 (P.G.B., R.D.L., 1887, 137).
63 Manager to Commr., 7 Sept. 1887 (P.S.C., R.D., file 1, 1887–8, vol. II, compn. 11, 78–85).
64 Bombay Govt. Resn. no. 2606, 6 May 1875; Collr., Shpur., 4 Aug. 1875 (P.G.B., R.D.L., 1875, 323, 545); Commr., Sind, to Govr., Bombay, 18 May 1892 (*B.N.S.* 315, *Larkana S.R.*, 4).
65 Quoted in Bombay Govt. Resn. no. 3771, 29 Aug. 1872 (P.G.B., R.D.L., 1872, 500).
66 See lists of estates under management in *Encd. Estates Reports*, 1879–87 (estates nos 222, 281, 282, Shpur. Collectorate).
67 Commr., Sind, memo., 10 Apr. 1884 (P.G.B., R.D.L., 1884 (Jan.-June), 550).
68 Collr., Shpur., to Commr., Sind, 10 Apr. 1889 (P.G.B., R.D.L., 1889, 381).
69 Commr., Sind, to Secy., Govt. of Bombay, 25 Nov. 1882 (P.S.C., R.D., file 1, 1880–2, vol. III, compn. 40, 39).
70 Quoted in Bombay Govt. Resn. no. 1572, 26 Feb. 1883 (P.G.B., R.D.L., 1883 (Jan.–June), 180).

71 Manager, Encd. Estates, Sind, to Commr., Sind, 26 Aug. 1885 (*Encd. Estates Report*, 1884–5, para. 16).
72 Commr., Sind, memo., 1 Aug. 1884 (P.G.B., R.D.L., 1884 (July–Dec.), 929).
73 Commr., Sind, to Govr., Bombay, 2 July 1892 (*B.N.S.* 316, *Mehar S.R.*, 2).
74 Discussion reviewed in Commr., Sind, memo., 14 Nov. 1900.
75 Commr., Sind, to Govr., Bombay, 6 July 1897 (P.G.B., R.D.L., 1904 (Jan.–June), 967).
76 See Secy., Govt. of Bombay, to Secy., Govt. of India, 7 Oct. 1899 (P.G.B., R.D.L., 1899 (July–Dec.), Confl. Pr., 21).
77 Commr., Sind, to Govr., Bombay, 12 Aug. 1896, Note A (P.G.B., R.D.L., 1899 (July–Dec.), Confl. Pr., 798–9).
78 Commr. to Govr., 12 Aug. 1896, Notes A & B (P.G.B., R.D.L., 1899 (July–Dec.), Confl. Pr., 801, 813).
79 Mountford, 'Debtors and Creditors,' 1745.
80 Offg. Secy., Govt. of India, to Secy., Govt. of Bombay, 30 Apr. 1896 (P.G.B., R.D.L., 1896, 529).
81 Bombay Act XX of 1896, Sind Incumbered Estates Act 1896; *Encd. Estates Reports*, 1897–1900; Commr., Sind, memo., 2 Dec. 1896 (P.G.B., R.D.L., 1897, 206).
82 Commr., Sind, to Govr., Bombay, 12 Aug. 1896, Note B (P.G.B., R.D.L., 1899 (July–Dec.), Confl. Pr., 813–9).
83 Secy., Govt. of Bombay, to Secy., Govt. of India, 7 Oct. 1899 (P.G.B., R.D.L., 1899 (July–Dec.), Confl. Pr., 33).
84 Bombay Act III of 1899, Government Occupants Act (Sind), 1899, section 8. See also Commr., Sind, to Govr., Bombay, 11 Dec. 1899 (P.G.B., R.D.L., 1900 (Jan.–June), 224).
85 *Standing Orders of the Revenue Department*, Order no. 10 (Land Grant), pt. 1, sections B(5), B(9).
86 Commr., Sind, to Govr., Bombay, 12 Aug. 1896 (P.G.B., R.D.L., 1899 (July–Dec.), Confl. Pr., 801).
87 Secy., Govt. of Bombay, to Secy., Govt. of India, 7 Oct. 1899 (P.G.B., R.D.L., 1899 (July–Dec.), Confl. Pr., 55).
88 Bombay Act XVII of 1879, Dekhan Agriculturists Relief Act 1879, chapter III.
89 Jud. Commr., Sind, 22 Nov. 1902 (P.S.C., R.D., file 1, pt. II, 1901–5, vol. I, compn. 1, 166).
90 Bombay Govt. Resn. no. 1971, 11 Apr. 1903 (P.S.C., R.D., file 1, pt. II, 1901–5, vol. I, compn. 1, 243).
91 Collr., Shpur., to Commr., Sind, 4 May 1902 (P.G.B., R.D.L., 1903 (Jan.–July), 113).
92 Jud. Commr., Sind, memo., 13 Nov. 1900, reissued 11 Aug. 1905 (P.S.C., J.D., file 1, 1905, vol. V, compn. 31, 233, 265).
93 Mountford, 'Debtors & Creditors,' 1763.
94 H.S. Lawrence, 'Memorandum on the Material Condition of the Bombay Presidency, 1892–1902 (P.G.B., R.D.L., 1902 (Aug.-Dec.), 1282); Depy. Commr., Mehar, to Commr., Sind, 15 Sept. 1902 (*B.N.S.* 316, *Mehar S.R.*, 32); Actg. Coln. Offr., Jamrao Canal, to Commr., Sind, 27 June 1906 (*B.N.S.* 462, *Hbad. S.R.*, 21).

95 Jud. Commr., Sind, to Commr., 23 Dec. 1901, with App. B: Report of Subordinate Judge, Sehwan; to Secy., Govt. Of Bombay, 22 Nov. 1902, with Apps A, C, D, G: reports of District Judges, Karachi and Hbad., and Subordinate Judges, Mehar and Larkana); note, unsigned, for Commr., Sind, n.d. (P.S.C., R.D., file 1, pt. II, 1901–5, vol. I, compn. 1, 54–6, 73, 163–6, 177, 181, 183, 191, 97–8).

96 Bombay Act I of 1905, Bombay Court of Wards Act 1905, sections 4(I), 5(I), 9(I).

97 Court of Wards, Sind, to Commr., Sind, 22 Sept. 1912 (*Report of the Estates under the Management of the Court of Wards in the Northern, Central and Southern Divisions and Sind, 1911–2*, 17).

98 Commr., Sind, memo., 4 March 1870 (P.G.B., R.D.L., 1870, 190).

99 *Reports on the Administration of the Bombay Presidency, 1877–82, 1887–92, 1897–1902.*

100 Asst. Collr.,, Larkana, to Collr., Shpur., 11 Feb. 1901 (P.G.B., R.D.L., 1901 (Jan.–June), 1176).

101 Bombay Govt. Resn. no. 572, 20 Jan. 1911 (P.G.B., R.D.L., 1911 (Jan.–Apr.), 104).

102 Settlt. Offr., Kandiaro, to Commr., Sind, 31 May 1909 (*B.N.S.* 493, *Kandiaro S.R.*, 14).

103 Registrar, Co-operative Societies, Bombay, to Secy., Govt. of Bombay, 27 Sept. 1926 (*Co-op Report*, 1925–6, 17); Collr., Shpur., to Commr., Sind, 2 May 1901 (P.G.B., R.D.L., 1901 (Jan.–June), 1174).

104 Registrar, Co-ops, 26 Sept. 1927 (*Co-op Report*, 1926–7, 20); see also Jain, 201.

105 Registrar, 3 Sept. 1929 (*Co-op Report*, 1928–9, 21).

106 Registrar, 27 Sept. 1926, 3 Sept. 1929 (*Co-op Report*, 1925–6, 17, 1928–9, 21).

107 *Report of the Bombay Provincial Banking Enquiry Committee, 1929–1930* (Calcutta, 1930), vol. I, 77.

108 Sorley, *Gazetteer*, 552.

Bibliography

A. GOVERNMENT RECORDS

1. Proceedings of the Sind Commission, Commissioner's Record Office, Karachi

General Department

File 4: 'Schools, General Questions,' 1857–93.
File 4, pt. I: 'Educational – Miscellaneous,' 1894–1909.

Judicial Department

File 1: 'Judicial – Miscellaneous,' 1859–1909.
File 1, pt. II: 'Reform of Judicial Courts in Sind and Re-organisation of Judicial Establishment,' 1880–1909.
File 2: 'Police – Miscellaneous,' 1859–1909.

Revenue Department

File 1: 'Financial – Miscellaneous,' 1858–1909.
File 58: 'Frontier Settlement,' 1877–86.
File 69A: 'Jamrao Colonisation,' 1896–1909.
File 86: 'Rough Survey and Settlement,' 1858–1909.

2. India Office Records, London Proceedings of the Government of India

Military Department

'Cadet Papers,' 1845–1846.

Political and Judicial Department

Sind Governor's Fortnightly Reports to Governor-General, 1936–37

Proceedings of the Government of Bombay

Judicial Department, 1848–1917.
Judicial and Home Department, 1918–31.

456. —— *Kambar Taluka of the Larkana District* (Karachi, 1907).
457. —— *Tando Allahyar Taluka of the Hyderabad District* (Karachi, 1908).
458. —— *Hyderabad Taluka of the Hyderabad District* (Karachi, 1908).
459. —— *Umarkot Taluka of the Thar and Parkar District* (Karachi, 1908).
460. —— *Pithoro Taluka of the Thar and Parkar District* (Karachi, 1908).
461. —— *Tando Allahyar Taluka of the Hyderabad District* (Karachi, 1908).
462. —— *Hyderabad Taluka of the Hyderabad District* (Karachi, 1909).
463. —— *Nasrat Taluka of the Hyderabad District* (Karachi, 1909).
464. —— *non-Jamrao Dehs of the Mirpur Khas Taluka of the Thar and Parkar District* (Karachi, 1909).
465. —— *non-Jamrao Dehs of the Sinjhoro Taluka of the Thar and Parkar District* (Karachi, 1909).
466. —— *Shahdadpur Taluka of the Hyderabad District* (Karachi, 1909).
467. —— *Kakar Taluka of the Larkana District* (Karachi, 1909).
468. —— *Labdaria Taluka of the Larkana District* (Karachi, 1909).
469. —— *Khipro Taluka of the Thar and Parkar District* (Karachi, 1911).
470. —— *Kambar Taluka of the Larkana District* (Karachi, 1911).
482. —— *Larkana Taluka of the Larkana District* (Karachi, 1911).
483. —— *Sanghar Taluka of the Thar and Parkar District* (Karachi, 1911).
484. —— *Ratodero Taluka of the Larkana District* (Karachi, 1911).
485. —— *Malir, Mal and Thana Tapas in the Karachi Taluka of the Karachi District* (Karachi, 1912).
487. —— *Dadu, Sehwan and Johi Talukas of the Larkana District* (Karachi, 1913).
488. —— *Guni, Badin and Tando Bago Talukas of the Hyderabad District* (Karachi, 1913).
489. —— *Dero Mohbat Taluka of the Hyderabad District* (Karachi, 1914).
490. —— *Sukkur Taluka of the Sukkur District* (Karachi, 1914).
491. —— *Naushahro Abro (now Garhi Yasin) Taluka of the Sukkur District* (Karachi, 1914).
492. —— *Nasirabad Taluka of the Larkana District* (Karachi, 1914).
493. —— *Kandiaro Taluka of the Hyderabad District* (Karachi, 1915).
494. —— *Moro Taluka of the Hyderabad District* (Karachi, 1915).
495. —— *Naushahro Taluka of the Hyderabad District* (Karachi, 1915).
496. —— *Mehar Taluka of the Larkana District* (Karachi, 1916).
497. —— *Mirpur Bathoro, Sujawal, Shahbandar and Jati Talukas of the Karachi District* (Karachi, 1917).
498. —— *Thul, Kandhkot and Kashmore Talukas of the Upper Sind Frontier District* (Karachi, 1918).
499. —— *Kacha Dehs in the Kandhkot and Kashmore Talukas of the Upper Sind Frontier District* (Karachi, 1918).
500. —— *Umarkot Taluka of the Thar and Parkar District* (Karachi, 1921).
533. —— *Shikarpur Taluka of the Sukkur District* (Karachi, 1921).
534. —— *Mirpurkhas, Jamesabad and Digri Talukas and Dehs Sanghar and Chamaro of Taluka Sanghar of the Thar and Parkar District and Jamrao Dehs of Sinjhoro Taluka in the Nawabshah District* (Karachi, 1921).
535. —— *Kotri Taluka and Manjhand Mahal of the Karachi District* (Karachi, 1922).
536. —— *Hiral Tract in Pithoro Taluka of the Thar and Parkar District* (Karachi, 1922).

537. —— *Sakrand Taluka of the Nawabshah District* (Karachi, 1922).
538. —— *Jacobabad Taluka of the Upper Sind Frontier District* (Karachi, 1922).
539. —— *Khipro, Pithoro (Samaro) and Sanghar Talukas of the Thar and Parkar District* (Karachi, 1922).
649. —— *Larkana, Kambar, Warah, Labdarya, Mehar, Kakar, Dadu, Johi and Sehwan Talukas of the Larkana and Dadu Districts* (Karachi, 1934).
650. —— *Sukkur, Garhi Yasin, Shikarpur, Ratodero, Mirokhan, Garhi Khairo and Shahdadkot Talukas of the Sukkur, Larkana and Upper Sind Frontier Districts* (Karachi, 1934).
651. —— *Rohri Taluka of the Sukkur District* (Karachi, 1934).
652. —— *Hyderabad, Tando Allahyar, Hala, Shahdadpur and Nawabshah Talukas of the Hyderabad and Nawabshah Districts* (Karachi, 1934).
653. —— *Kandiaro, Naushahro, Moro and Sakrand Talukas of the Nawabshah District* (Karachi, 1934).
654. —— *Dero Mohbat and Tando Bago Talukas of the Hyderabad District* (Karachi, 1934).
655. —— *Mirpurkhas, Jamesabad, Digri and Sinjhoro Talukas and two Dehs of the Sanghar Taluka of the Thar Parkar and Nawabshah Districts* (Karachi, 1934).
656. —— *Khipro, Samaro, Sanghar and Umarkot Talukas and eight Dehs of Mithi and Diplo Talukas of the Thar Parkar District* (Karachi, 1934).

2. *Other Official Publications*
(In alphabetical order of titles)

Annual Reports relating to the Establishment of Co-operative Credit Societies in the Bombay Presidency (Bombay, 1905–30).

The Bombay Code (Calcutta, 1880).

Government of Sind, *Bund Manual* (Karachi, 1954).

Census Reports

Census of the Bombay Presidency, 1872 (Bombay, 1875), pts II & III.

J.A. Baines, *Imperial Census of 1881: Operations and results in the Bombay Presidency, including Sind* (Bombay, 1882), vols I & II.

W.W. Drew, *Census of India, 1891: Bombay and its Feudatories* (Bombay, 1892, vol. VII, pt. I & vol. VIII, pt. II.

R.E. Enthoven, *Census of India, 1901: Bombay* (Bombay, 1902), vol. IX-B, pt. III.

P.J. Mead & G. Laird MacGregor, *Census of India, 1911: Bombay* (Bombay, 1912), vol. VII, pts I & II.

Economic Condition of Sind. State of Roads, Canals and Forests in 1846 (Selections from the Records of the Commissioner in Sind, compilation 7 of 1844–47).

Gazetteers

A.W. Hughes, *Gazetteer of the Province of Sind* (London, 1878).

E.H. Aitken, *Gazetteer of the Province of Sind* (London, 1907).

J.W. Smyth, *Gazetteer of the Province of Sind*, B vols –
I. *Karachi District* (Bombay, 1919).

II. *Hyderabad District* (Bombay, 1920).
III. *Sukkur District* (Bombay, 1919).
IV. *Larkana District* (Bombay, 1919).
V. *Thar and Parkar District* (Bombay, 1919).
VI. *Upper Sind Frontier District* (Bombay, 1919).

Gazetteer of the Province of Sind, B vol V: *Nawabshah District* (Bombay, 1926).

H.T. Sorley, *The Gazetteer of West Pakistan, The Former Province of Sind* (c1960).

History of Alienations in the Province of Sind (Bombay, vol. I, 1886; vol. II, 1888).

The History of Services of Gazetted Officers in the Civil Department serving in the Bombay Presidency (Bombay, published every year from 1876).

Papers relating to the Indebtedness of the Zemindars of the Muncher Lake in Sind (Madras, 1874).

Papers relating to the Revenue Settlement in Sind and to the Settlements of Sukkur, Kotri, and Guni Talukas (Bombay, 1875).

Report of the Bombay Provincial Banking Enquiry Committee, 1929–1930 (Calcutta, 1930), vols I & IV.

Report of the Committee appointed by Government to enquire into Rasai, Lapo and Chher in Sind (Karachi, 1919), 4 vols.

Report of the Committee appointed to enquire into the question of Cattle-lifting in Sind (Karachi, 1926).

Report of the Indian Famine Commission, 1898 (London, 1898: Cmd 9178).

Report of the Members of the Fallow Rules Committee, Sind (Karachi, 1926).

Report of the Tenancy Legislation Committee (Karachi, 1945).

Report on the Famine in the Bombay Presidency, 1899–1902 (Bombay, 1903), 2 vols.

Reports of the Estates under the Management of the Court of Wards in the Northern, Central and Southern Division and Sind (Bombay, 1908–30).

Reports on the Administration of the Bombay Presidency (Bombay, 1862–1902).

Reports on the Revenue Assessment of Dadu Taluka, Karachi Collectorate (1878, India Office Record call no. (9)2016).

Revenue Regulations of Sir Charles Napier, Governor of Sind (Selected Records of the Deputy Commissioner, Upper Sind Frontier, compilation 1 of Revenue Miscellaneous file, 1850–1852).

Revised Settlement of the Sehwan Taluka of the Kurrachee Collectorate (1876, India Office Record call no. (9)2015).

Selections from the pre-Mutiny Records of the Commissioner in Sind (n.d.).

Sind Encumbered Estates Annual Administration Reports (Karachi, 1879–1887, 1898–1930).

Standing Orders of the Revenue Department (Karachi 1960).

C. SECONDARY WORKS

M.U. Abbasi (ed.), *The Colourful Personalities of Sind and Famous Firms and Factories* (Karachi, 1944).

J. Abbott, *Sind: A Reinterpretation of the Unhappy Valley* (Karachi, 1977; 1st ed. Bombay, 1924).

Qazi Shakeel Ahmed, 'A Geographical Analysis of the Site of Hyderabad City,' *The Sind University Research Journal (Arts Series): Humanities and Social Sciences*, vol. IX (Oct. 1970).

Imran Ali, *The Punjab under Imperialism, 1895–1947* (Princeton, 1988).

Sadik Ali, *A Short Sketch Historical and Traditional of the Musulman Races found in Sind, Baluchistan and Afghanistan* (Karachi, 1954; 1st ed. Karachi, 1901).

Sarah F.D. Ansari, 'The Pirs of Sind and their Relationship with the British, 1843–1947' (University of London PhD thesis, 1987).

——, *Sufi Saints and State Power: the Pirs of Sind, 1843–1947* (Cambridge, 1992).

B.H. Baden-Powell, *The Land Systems of British India* (London, 1892), 3 vols.

——, *A Short Account of the Land Revenue and its Administration in British India; with a Sketch of the Land Tenures* (Oxford, 1894).

Mahmud Baig, 'A Select List of Articles on Sind, other Provinces of Pakistan and Adjoining Areas – published in the Journal and Proceedings of the Royal Geographical Society of Great Britain during the Years 1838–1962,' *Sind Quarterly*, vol. III, no. 2 (1976).

Alexander F. Baillie, *Kurrachee: Past: Present: and Future* (Calcutta, 1890).

George Bease (compiler), *The Sind Directory* (Bombay, 1862).

Mahfoud Bennoune, *The Making of Contemporary Algeria, 1830–1987: Colonial Upheavals and Post-Independence Development* (Cambridge, 1988).

Benazir Bhutto, *Daughter of the East* (London, 1988).

Alexander Burnes, *Travels into Bokhara together with a Narrative of a Voyage on the Indus* (Karachi, 1973; 1st ed. London, 1834), 3 vols.

James Burnes, *Narrative of a Visit to the Court of Sind* (Karachi, 1974; 1st ed. London, 1829).

R. F. Burton, *Sindh and the Races that Inhabit the Valley of the Indus* (Karachi, 1974; 1st ed. London, 1851).

——, *Sind Revisited* (London, 1877), 3 vols.

I.J. Catanach, *Rural Credit in Western India, 1875–1930: Rural Credit and the Co-operative Movement in the Bombay Presidency* (University of California, 1970).

Neil Charlesworth, *Peasants and Imperial Rule: Agriculture and Agrarian Society in the Bombay Presidency, 1850–1935* (Cambridge, 1985).

K.N. Chaudhuri and C.J. Dewey (eds) *Economy and Society: Essays in Indian Economic and Social History* (Delhi, 1979).

David Cheesman, 'Local Power and Colonial Authority: The Pax Britannica in Nineteenth Century Sind,' *History Today* (July 1981).

——, '"The Omnipresent Bania": Rural Moneylenders in Nineteenth Century Sind,' *Modern Asian Studies* (July 1982).

——, 'Power in Rural Sind in the Late Nineteenth Century,' *Asian Affairs*, vol XII Pt 1 (Feb 1981).

——, 'Rural Power and Debt in Sind in the Late Nineteenth Century, 1865–1901' (University of London PhD thesis, 1980).

Malcolm Darling, *The Punjab Peasant in Prosperity and Debt* (Oxford, 1947; 1st ed. London, 1925).

——, *Rusticus Loquitur* (Oxford, 1930).

Clive J. Dewey and A.G. Hopkins (eds.), *The Imperial Impact: Studies in the Economic History of Africa and India* (London, 1978).

Adrian Duarte, *A History of British Relations with Sind, 1613–1843* (Karachi, 1976).

P.H.M. van den Dungen, *The Punjab Tradition: Influence and Authority in Nineteenth-Century India* (London, 1972).

E.B. Eastwick ('An Ex-Political'), *Dry Leaves from Young Egypt* (reprinted Karachi, 1973, as *A Glance at Sind before Napier*; 1st ed. London, 1849).
R.E. Enthoven, *Tribes and Castes of Bombay* (Bombay, 1920).
Dayaram Gidumal, *Hiranand – The Soul of Sindh* (1903; revised and enlarged 1932).
S. Gopal, *British Policy in India, 1858–1905* (Cambridge, 1965).
David Gilmartin, *Empire and Islam: Punjab and the Making of Pakistan* (1988).
Luther Gulick, 'An Agricultural Geography of the Lower Indus Valley, West Pakistan, with special reference to Hyderabad District' (n.d.; mss in Library of Institute of Sindhology, University of Sind).
Michel Habart, *Histoire d'un Parjure* (Paris, 1960).
Irfan Habib, *The Agrarian System of Mughal India (1556–1707)* (Aligarh, 1963).
M.R. Haig, *The Indus Delta Country* (Karachi, 1972; 1st ed. London, 1894).
P. Harnetty, '"A Curious Exercise of Political Economy:" Some implications of British Land Revenue Policy in the Central Provinces of India, 1861–c1900,' *South Asia*, no. 6 (Dec. 1976).
Naomal Hotchand, *A Forgotten Chapter of Indian History as described in the memoirs of Seth Naomal Hotchand, C.S.I., of Karachi*, ed. by H.E.M. James (Exeter, 1915).
A.W. Hughes, *The Country of Balochistan* (Karachi, 1977; 1st ed. London, 1877).
Robert A. Huttenback, *British Relations with Sind, 1799–1843: An Anatomy of Imperialism* (University of California, 1962).
Sirajul Islam, 'The Bengal Tenantry in Debt, 1904–1945,' *The Dacca University Studies*, vol. XXII, pt. A (1974).
J.C. Jack, *The Economic Life of a Bengal District* (Oxford, 1916).
L.C. Jain, *Indigenous Banking in India* .(London, 1929).
J.W. Kaye, T.R.E. Holmes, *Lives of Indian Officers* (London, 1895, 3rd ed.), 3 vols.
G.H. Khaskhelly, M.A.A. Beg, A.A. Qureshi, *Economy of Sind* (Hyderabad, 1976).
Hamida Khuhro, 'The British Administration of Sind between 1843 and 1865: A Study in Social and Economic Development' (University of London PhD thesis, 1965).
——, *The Making of Modern Sind: British Policy and Social Change in the Nineteenth Century* (Karachi, 1978).
—— (ed.), *Sind Through the Centuries: Proceedings of an International Seminar held in Karachi in Spring 1975 by the Department of Culture, Government of Sind* (Karachi, 1981).
Ravinder Kumar, *Western India in the Nineteenth Century: A Study in the Social History of Maharashtra* (London & Toronto, 1968).
R.D. Lambert & B.F. Hoselitz (eds), *The Role of Savings and Wealth in Southern Asia and the West* (Unesco, 1953).
H.T. Lambrick, *John Jacob of Jacobabad* (London, 1960).
——, *Sind: A General Introduction* (Hyderabad, 1964).
——, *Sind before the Muslim Conquest* (Hyderabad, 1973).
——, *Sir Charles Napier and Sind* (Oxford, 1952).
——, *The Terrorist* (London, 1972).
D.A. Low (ed.), *Soundings in Modern South Asian History* (London, 1968).

C.L. Mariwalla, 'Sehwan Through the Centuries,' *Sindhian World*, vol. I, no. 5 (1940).
Charles Masson, *Narrative of Various Journeys in Baluchistan, Afghanistan, and the Punjab* (Karachi, 1974; 1st ed. London, 1842), 3 vols.
M. Masud, *Hari Committee Note of Dissent* (Karachi, n.d.,?1949).
Y.B. Mathur, *British Administration of the Punjab (1849–72)* (Delhi, n.d.).
Peter Mayne, *Saints of Sind* (London, 1956).
Thomas R. Metcalf, *The Aftermath of Revolt: India, 1857–1870* (Princeton, 1965).
N. Mukherjee, *The Ryotwari System in Madras, 1792–1827* (Calcutta, 1962).
Priscilla Napier, *I have Sind: Sir Charles Napier in India 1841–1844* (Salisbury, 1990).
W.C. Neale, *Economic Change in Rural India: Land Tenure and Land Reform in Uttar Pradesh, 1800–1955* (Yale University, 1962).
Jawarharlal Nehru, *The Discovery of India* (London, 2nd ed., 1947).
M.H. Panhwar, *Source Material on Sind* (Hyderabad, 1977).
Jethmal Parsram, *Sind and its Sufis* (1924).
C.H. Philips (ed.), *The Evolution of India and Pakistan, 1858–1947: Select Documents* (Oxford, 1962).
M.B. Pithawalla, *An Introduction to Sind* (Karachi, 1951).
——, *A Physical and Economic Geography of Sind* (Hyderabad, 1959).
Thomas Postans, *Personal Observations on Sindh* (Karachi, 1973; 1st ed. London, 1843).
Mushtaqur Rahman, *A Geography of Sind Province Pakistan* (Karachi, 1975).
Jagdish Raj, *The Mutiny and British Land Policy in North India, 1856–1868* (London, 1965).
K. Ramani (ed.), *Sindhi Short Stories* (Karachi, n.d.).
P. Hari Rao, *The Bombay Acts (Civil, Criminal and Revenue (1827–1923)* (Bombay, 1924).
Gur Rewachand, 'The Socio-Cultural Pattern of the Sindhi Hindu Communities settled in Balochi Areas,' *The Sind University Journal of Education*, vol. VIII (Jan. 1963).
Peter Robb (ed.), *Rural India: Land, Power and Society under British Rule* (London, 1983).
John Romer, *The Valley of the Kings* (London, 2nd ed., 1988).
J.R. Roseberry III, *Imperial Rule in the Punjab: The Conquest and Administration of Multan, 1818–1881* (Lahore, 1988).
John Ruedy, *Modern Algeria: The Origins and Development of a Nation* (Indiana University Press, 1992).
Edward W. Said, *Culture and Imperialism* (London, 1993).
H.V. Sathe, *Annotated Edition of the Land Revenue Code* (Poona, 1892).
Annemarie Schimmel, *Pain and Grace: A Study of two Mystical Writers of Eighteenth-Century Muslim India* (Leiden, 1976).
W.C. Sellar & R.J. Yeatman, *1066 and All That* (London, 1962; 1st ed., London, 1930).
M.L. Seth, 'Indian Money-lender in pre-British Times,' *The Research Bulletin (Arts) of the University of the Panjab*, S. no. XV, Economics, I (1955).
The Sind Kossid (Newspaper), 1856–1858.
A.K. Snelgrove, *Geohydrology of the Indus River West Pakistan* (University of Sind, 1967).

H.T. Sorley, *Shah Abdul Latif of Bhit* (Oxford, 1940).
Eric Stokes, *The English Utilitarians and India* (Oxford, 1959; reprinted 1969).
——, *The Peasant and the Raj: Studies in Agrarian Society and Peasant Rebellion in Colonial India* (Cambridge, 1978).
G.M. Sayed, *Struggle for New Sind: A Brief Narrative of the Working of Provincial Autonomy in Sind During a Decade (1937–1947)* (Karachi, 1949).
Ian Talbot, *Punjab and the Raj, 1849–1947* (New Delhi, 1988).
Salman Taseer, *Bhutto: A Political Biography* (London, 1979).
Richard Temple, *Men and Events of my Time in India* (London, 1882).
D.K. Thadani, 'Materials for Sindhi Drama,' *The Sindhian World*, vol. I, no. 1 (1939).
T.S. Thadani, 'The Lohanas,' *The Journal of the Sind Historical Society*, vol. VIII, no. 3 (Jan. 1948).
U.T. Thakur, *Sindhi Culture* (University of Bombay, n.d.).
S.S. Thorburn, *Musalmans and Money-lenders in the Punjab* (Edinburgh & London, 1886).
T.H. Thornton, *Colonel Sir Robert Sandeman: His Life and Work on our Indian Frontier* (Quetta, 1977; 1st ed. London, 1893).
Mortimer Wheeler, *The Indus Civilization* (Cambridge, 3rd ed., 1968).
Elizabeth Whitcombe, *Agrarian Conditions in Northern India, vol. I, The United provinces under British Rule, 1860–1900* (University of California, 1972).
Who Was Who, 1916–1928 (London, 1929).
A. Jeyaratnam Wilson and Dennis Dalton (eds), *The States of South Asia: Problems of National Integration – essays in Honour of W.H. Morris-Jones* (London, 1982).
Stanley Wolpert, *Zulfi Bhutto of Pakistan: His Life and Times* (Oxford, 1993).
M.E. Yapp, *Strategies of British India: Britain, Iran and Afghanistan, 1798–1880* (Oxford, 1980).
Keith Young, *Scinde in the Forties*, ed. by A.F. Scott (London, 1912).

INDEX